THE BOOK OF AWESOME WOMEN

BOUNDARY BREAKERS, FREEDOM FIGHTERS, SHEROES & FEMALE FIRSTS

Becca Anderson

Published by Mango Publishing Group, a division of Mango Media Inc.

Cover Design and Layout Design: Elina Diaz

For permission requests, please contact the publisher at:

Mango Publishing Group
2850 Douglas Road, 3rd Floor
Coral Gables, FL 33134 USA
info@mango.bz

For special orders, quantity sales, course adoptions and corporate sales, please email the publisher at sales@mango.bz. For trade and wholesale sales, please contact Ingram Publisher Services at customer.service@ingramcontent.com or +1.800.509.4887.

The Book of Awesome Women: Boundary Breakers, Freedom Fighters, Sheroes and Female Firsts

Library of Congress Cataloging
ISBN: (paperback) 978-1-63353-583-1, (ebook) 978-1-63353-584-8
Library of Congress Control Number: 2017909207
BISAC category code : HIS058000 HISTORY / Women

Printed in the United States of America

TABLE OF CONTENTS

· FOREWORD ·

The Book of Awesome Women provokes a question I've asked myself dozens of times: Where was this treasure-house of a book when I went to school? From the first grade on, I sat at my desk, listlessly listening to the cliched tales of heroes from history, all of them — or so it seemed — male. Meanwhile, as I grew up in the Pacific Northwest of the fifties, many of the women profiled in this book were busy making history, making changes, making intellectual contributions, and making waves. Did I hear about any of them in school? In the media? On that shiny new world of communications called television? Rarely, if ever.

Would my life have been different if I'd had these daring examples to aspire to, to take courage from, to lean on as my own personal support group from history? Most definitely.

For instance, when my mother and father pushed me toward a particular college, I asked what they saw me doing with my education, and they said, "A nurse, perhaps. Or a teacher." I turned angrily from their narrow vision and their well-meant path of higher education. It was decades before I saw the learning (as valid when enrolled in the university life as well as in more traditional institutions) would set me free, free to become whatever I set my mind to be.

Over the years, as I made my way as a writer and researcher, many of the sheroes in this book became my personal sheroes, too. The lives and deeds of women like Mary Leakey, Karen Silkwood, Margaret Mead, Rachel Carson, and Eleanor Roosevelt moved me deeply and

Billie Jean King

helped me grow. As a thirtysomething college reporter, for instance, I got to write my first news story about Billie Jean King's rout of Bobby Riggs—and in so doing, the sheer audacity of Billie Jean's actions struck home. The Book of Awesome Women brings all of my favorite women, and hundreds more, to luminous life—a brilliant and encyclopedic achievement for one book.

Of late, I've been thinking a lot about just how and why the jigsaw of our whole human history came to have so many female pieces missing. Since 1995, the publication date of *Uppity Women of Ancient Times*, my first book about real-life female achievements of long ago, I have given hundreds of lectures, workshops, and talks to audiences about the frisky, risk-it-all women from our ancient, medieval, and Renaissance past. I point out that many of these trailblazers were famous—or infamous—in their own day. Invariably, someone in the audience asks: "If these women were household words, how and why did they become invisible?"

At this point, I mention a trio of female names and say: "What do these names mean to you?" After having given this pop quiz to several thousand people now (many of them well-read women whose educations far exceed my own), I regret to say that no one has known the answers. No one. Not one person has identified three key women who I selected at random from our own, very recent American history.

This response—or lack of one—leads me to my most telling point. "You see? Even in the late twentieth century, the historical invisibility process often begins immediately—in a woman's own lifetime."

The Book of Awesome Women, is a perfect antidote to that process, a bold and colorful portrait of women who dared to pursue their dreams. In that pursuit, they themselves become raw material, the idea matrix for other women's dreams. They become, in a word, sheroes—a word, and a notion, whose constituency is going to grow ever more clamorous in the brave new second millennium.

—**Vicki Leon,** author of the *Uppity Women in history series*, published by Conari Press.

P.S. Take my "invisible women" quiz yourself and see how well you do. Identify the following twentieth century women: Junko Tabei, Sally Louisa Tompkins, and Gerti Cori.

Answers: Junko Tabei—first woman to climb Mount Everest, on May 16, 1975. This housewife led an all-woman Japanese team to the top. Sally Louisa Tompkins—only woman to be named an officer in the Confederate Army, where she ran the hospital she'd already established (at her own expense) with the lowest mortality rate of any soldier's hospital in the South. Gerti Cori—first female doctor to win a Nobel prize; awarded in physiology and medicine in 1947 and shared with her husband.

. INTRODUCTION .

Women have always been powerful. So much so, in fact, that several millennia of oppression have only made us stronger. And no amount of witch burnings, stiletto heels, and lack of basic human rights can stop the blossoming forth of the boldest, bravest wave of women and girlpower ever, here at the dawn of the new millennium.

Women have always been heroes. But, it is no longer enough to say so. As we shake off the last traces of a major patriarchal hangover, women need a new language, a new dialect, and a freshly forged paradigm to express an untrammeled femininity that has nothing to do with bondage—unless, of course, that's your bag. Women of courage, in addition to taking back their power, must have a name of their own. Any wise woman can tell you that words have power. As Rumpelstiltskin knew, the naming of a person or thing is to have ownership and power over the named. He was quaking in his leathery dwarf boots for fear that the princess he had imprisoned (so she could spin straw into gold for his moldering coffers) would figure out his name. Sure enough, our girl psyched it out with good, old-fashioned women's intuition and his game was up. As sheroes, all women can fully embrace and embody all their fiery fempower and celebrate the unique potency of our gender-tribe. By taking, telling, and proudly touting the title and banner of sheroes, women can identify with the traits of strength, courage, and no-holds-barred individuality, thus sharing and spreading the power around. Taking back power doesn't necessarily mean that power has to be taken away from someone else; there is enough for all. No need to repeat the mistakes of the past.

Power. Share it; it grows!

Packing estrogen, and, not infrequently, a pen and a sword, awesome women come in every imaginable shape, size, and color, and manifest their sheroism in infinite ways. Our sheroic foremothers of the past centuries paved the way for the cybersheroes and screen goddesses of today at a time when women were relegated to the status of second-class citizens, if they were fortunate enough to be citizens at all. Their accomplishments are stunning in light of the fact that there was, for all practical purposes, a tacit caste system with one gender on top. Battling exclusion and seclusion, these incredible women risked it all to create the freedom we enjoy and uphold today. Women warriors, they didn't take no for an answer and went to the head of the class without passing go, oftentimes through a gauntlet of disapproval, bad press, and all other odds against them.

THE SHERO'S JOURNEY

Heroes and their trips have gotten plenty of air time thanks to the erudite scholarship of the late mythographer Joseph Campbell, who popularized the genre. His delineation of the hero's journey begins with restlessness and hearing the call to action; it moves to the middle road of dragon slaying and an underground passage through hell and back where the hero faces death, to the culmination of the visionary quest in self-awareness and the return home.

The heroic archetype was brought to the world's attention when George Lucas extrapolated Campbell's explication of the hero's journey in the *Star Wars* trilogy. It is important to bear in mind that not every would-be hero who sets upon the path to greatness succeeds. In fact, the most promising candidates may fall—look at Lancelot, the flower of France and the finest knight in King Arthur's court, who betrayed his liege lord and lost his honor. Heroism is no guarantee! The question for us to consider here is how a shero's journey differs, if at all, from the hero's journey. Having been obsessed with this very question for the better part of a year, I have concluded that it is, indeed, different.

Interestingly, Campbell himself never tackled the subject, but commented that the question always came up after his lectures. (Can't you just see Sarah Lawrence women giving him the business?) His position was that "if a woman engages in the man's task of achievement, then her mythology will be essentially the same as that of the male hero."

Aside from the fact that achievement in and of itself is not the true hallmark of a human's psychospiritual evolution, women have been achieving great things since women took primitive society from hunting and gathering to agricultural-based communities. For that matter, we might as well go back to the beginning, to Eve, who would've burned her bra if she'd had one, and her predecessors among the first femmes, including the first feminist Lilith, whom Yahweh attempted to hook up with the utterly human Adam. Lilith, being semidivine, would have none of this mundane human-beingness and bailed immediately. But, according to the early Christian Gnostic Gospels, before there was Adam and before there was God even, there was Sophia, the primordial and very female entity embodying the ultimate wisdom associated with the unknowable heart of darkness.

Marion Woodman, doubtless one of the preeminent Jungian analysts of our time, does examine the "heroine's journey," as she calls it, deeply and brilliantly. In her excellent book on the subject, *Leaving My Father's House*, Woodman cuts to the heart of the repression of women's adventurous and powerful energies and advocates a transcendence of the old patriarchal model for women through dumping obsolete control systems and dangerous daddy complexes to illuminate the world with our true spirit and our excellence. "So long as a woman accepts a man's archetypal projection, she is trapped in a male understanding of reality," she notes. The shero's journey, she explains, is an awakening to consciousness, and "staying with the process is what matters." The shero needn't necessarily go underground; she can turn inside to the intuitive and occasionally superconscious wisdom at the core of her being—Sophia, divine feminine wisdom. Woodman urges women to share these stories of transformation and growth to "open the path to freedom" for other women.

The Book of Awesome Women is a collection of the life stories of the harbingers of female transformation. Each of the sheroes in this book, and the legions who are not, have done this work. They have released their full energy and, in so doing, changed the world for us by blazing trails, breaking down barriers, and empowering other women to do the same.

Sister-sheroes, suffragists, amazons, and priestess-healers laid the foundations for the post-modern sheroes of today, who are making new strikes in art and letters, the business world, and in the power and sports arenas. From Madeleine Albright, who declared politics "is not a fraternity anymore!" to the courageous televised outing of lesbian Ellen DeGeneres, women are making enormous strides today that should see us to a fabulously feminized twenty-first century. A delightful irony I've noticed is that the aforementioned *Star Wars* Trilogy contains the perfect parallel journey of hero and shero, although that hasn't seemed to get nearly the air time among all the hype of the incredible international success of this mythical sci-fi series. You will recall that Luke Skywalker has a twin sister, none other than Princess Leia Organa. While Luke was playing with droids and scooting around his planet in jerry-rigged spacecrafts, Princess Leia was masterminding the rebellion against the fascist Darth Vader. Talk about leaving your father's house!

TRIPPING THE LIGHT FEMTASTIC

This book of sheroes is intended to be a call to action as well, and a challenging exhortation to honor bold and brave women by telling their stories. This book is only the tip of the sheroic iceberg, however. If I had my way, it would never end, because I wanted to include every shero who ever lived. My greatest hope is that it will spark something in you, the reader—who are your personal sheroes? Let me know (see the personal note in the back of the book).

Ethnographer Marina Warner, in her compelling examination of women in fairy and folktales, *From the Beast to the Blonde*, concludes that words and the wielding of words is the realm of women: "The story itself becomes the weapon of the weaponless. The struggles of women, for example, are not resolved by combat on the whole (one or two Amazon heroines excepted), as the contests of men may bring heroic epic...women's arts within fairy tales are very marked, and most of them are verbal: riddling, casting spells, conjuring, understanding the tongues of animals, turning words into deeds." Storytelling is a way of weaving the fabric of consciousness, introducing new strands, new awareness. In this way, the shero stories can, on an archetypal level, shift, transform, and create new reality for ourselves, and, most importantly, for young women and girls. Imagine a neo-Amazonian utopia where every adolescent girl has sky high self-esteem—no Ophelias to revive! Estrogen empowered, full-esteem ahead, and absolutely, unabashedly glorious.

This brings me back to the original point of this storytelling adventure for me. In the beginning was the word. Logos. Sophia. In the new beginning was the word—sheroes! The term *women heroes* is no longer sufficient for a post patriarchal populace, and the auditory twinning of heroine to the supremely addictive opiate is certainly a turn-off, and reason enough to embrace the mantle of sheroism. For this, I must thank poet shero Maya Angelou, who used the word in a speech and sparked the muse for me. In closing, I want to thank all the women who set the standards and knocked down the walls of oppression, brick by brick. Often, as I researched the lives of these women, I was moved to tears with the realization of what they went through for their magnificent accomplishments—by, among others, Elizabeth Blackwell, who got into medical school on a joke and had the last laugh, by supermodel superwoman Waris Dirie battling against the scourge of female circumcision, and by every working-class shero who demands her due. I dedicate this book to every shero whose story remains untold and whose unquenchable spirit lives on!

• CHAPTER ONE •

Amazons Among Us

Since the fall of Troy, Amazons have never gone out of style. Now, in the new millennium, they have never been hotter! The global phenomenon of Wonder Woman Xena, Warrior Princess and her Amazon sidekick, Gabrielle, is proof positive that Amazons are, once again, ruling the world. Archetypically, Amazons represent aggressiveness on the part of women. (Say, if you can call upon the muse, why can't you invoke Amazonian courage? And tell me why, for that matter, isn't there a self-help book for empowering women by "embracing your inner Amazon"?)

The myth of the Amazon nation tells of an all-woman country by the river Thermodon with a very advanced gynocentric government and the finest army on earth. Occasionally, they socialized with the men of other nations for the purpose of begetting children. The fate of the male babies in Amazonia was woeful; they were neutered and enslaved. The ancient historian Diodorus Siculus recorded stories of Amazon military campaigns on swift and well-trained horses, sporting bows, arrows, double-headed axes, and a single breast (they would cut off one breast to be better archers in battle and in order to wear their special shields), with which they conquered a wide swath from Asia Minor to Egypt. Greece and Africa weren't the only cultures to celebrate womanly valor. Norse mythology has a sort of afterlife Amazon, the Valkyries, "choosers of the slain" from Old Norse culture.

Handmaidens of Odin, the Valkyries include Gondul, "she-fowlf"; Skuld; death-bringer Skorn; Brunnhilde, "she who calls out"; Hrist, "storm"; and Thrud, "force," who ride through the heavens on charging horses getting ready for Ragnarok, the battle marking the end of the world.

These and all other avenging angels and hell-spawned hags break all stereotypes about women as the gentler gender. Epitomizing the "take no prisoners" attitude, these women warriors punched, kicked, stabbed, shot, and charioteered their way to the top. Gorgons, furies, pirate queens, warrior princesses, martial nuns, maenads, gladiatrices, and guerrillas from antiquity to the twenty-first century represent sheroism at its most visceral and thrilling.

PENTHESILEA: THE REAL THING

The daughter of Orithia, Penthesilea was the ruler, along with her sister Hippolyte, of Amazonia, the Bronze Age Amazon nation in an area of the Black Sea. A fierce warrior, Penthesilea's name means "compelling men to mourn." During Orithia's reign, repeated attacks from Greek war parties eroded the borders of their once widespread empire. The nation of Amazonia itself, however, lived in peace; its women warriors were regarded as the most highly skilled soldiers among all the armies of the world. Even the piratical adventurers of myth, the Argonauts, dropped their plans to invade Amazonia when they saw how peaceful and self-sufficient the country was.

Penthesilea was the greatest Amazon of all times. At first, her excellence with weaponry was primarily for the purpose of hunting. When her sister died, falling on Penthesilea's spear during a hunt, Penthesilea chose to channel her grief and rage into battle. At the request of Queen Hecuba, she liberated the city of Troy, under siege by the Greeks for years. The link between Troy and Amazonia predates Homer and Euripides by centuries, and many scholars believe that Homer adapted his famous story from the Egyptian poetess Phantasia and reoriented it toward the patriarchal tastes of his Greek audience.

Essentially, Penthesilea's Achilles heel was her desire to lead the attack on Troy, the last Goddess worshiping city-state in the Mediterranean Asia Minor. The legends vary, but the consensus among historians is that Achilles took one look at the powerful and pulchritudinous Penthesilea and fell deeply in love. They battled ruthlessly one-on-one, and the Amazon queen proved to be the only soldier Achilles had ever encountered who was his equal. One version depicts the great Penthesilea taking Achilles' and dozens of other Greeks' lives on the battlefield surrounding Troy, only to be confounded when the God Zeus brought Achilles back to life. In this version, she died, but Achilles' grief was so severe that he killed several of his allies who had mutilated her corpse (in one version he rapes her corpse in a wanton necrophilic lust). Other tellings of the tales have Penthesilea brutally killing the Greek and falling in love with him as his dying eyes lock with hers, then setting upon his corpse and devouring him, in a final act of savage love.

Only sections of the ancient poem *Aethiopis* that describe Penthesilea and the liberation of Troy have managed to survive from antiquity. They include a suffragistic speech made by the amazing amazon herself: "Not in strength are we inferior to men; the same our eyes, our limbs the same; one common light we see, one air we breathe; no different is the food we eat. What then denied to us hath heaven on man bestowed? O let us hasten to the glorious war!"

OTHER FIGHTING FEMMES OF THE ANCIENT WORLD

Marpesia, "The Snatcher," was the ruler of the Scythian Amazons along with Lampedo. In frenzies, Maenads were fierce creatures, not to be toyed with, especially after a few nips of ritual new grape wine, Marpesia wrestled and tore off the head of her own son, Pentheus, in one of her ecstasies, mistaking him for a lion. She then paraded around proudly holding his decapitated head up for all to see. Her husband met a similar end in another rite. Agave was a Moon-Goddess and was in charge of some of the revelries that were the precedent for Dionysus' cult. Euripides celebrated the ferocity of Agave and her fellow Maenads, Ino and Aunonoë, in his *Bacchae*, as soldiers report how "we by flight hardly escaped tearing to pieces at their hands" and further describe the shock of witnessing the semi-divine females tearing young bulls limb from limb with their terrible "knifeless fingers." In his version, Pentheus died while trying to spy on the private ritual of the Maenads in transvestite disguise.

Aba was a warrior who ruled the city of Olbe in the nation of Tencer around 550 B.C. She got support from some very high places such as the likes of Cleopatra VII and Marc Anthony! Tencer remained a matriarchy after her rule, passing to her female descendants.

Abra was Artemesia's (Queen of Caria and military advisor to Xerxes) sister and a warrior-queen (circa 334 B.C.) in her own right. The brilliant military strategist Alexander helped her regain her throne from her invasive brother. She led and triumphed in the siege of the capital's acropolis, after which she was able to take the city. Her ferocity was aided by the intense emotions of a cross-gender civil war within her family, "the siege having become a matter of anger and personal enmity," according to Strabo.

Hercules was the fiercest, that is, until he ran up against Admete, aka "The Untamed," who bested him and made him serve the Goddess Hera, the wife of Zeus who detested Hercules. Hera rewarded Admete for her loyalty and excellence by appointing her head priestess of the island refuge Samos; Admete, in turn honored by her Goddess with her evangelical fervor, expanding the territory of Hera's woman cult to the far reaches of the ancient world.

Aëllopus was a Harpy who fought the Argonauts; her name means "Storm-Foot."

Cratesipolis was Queen of Sicyon around 300 B.C. She stood in battles beside her husband, the famous Alexander the Great, and fought on even after he died. She ruled several important Greek cities very successfully and managed a vast army of soldier-mercenaries. She went on to take Corinth for Ptolemy and nearly married him, but the plans fizzled.

Larina was an Italian Amazon who accompanied Camilla in the Aeneid along with fellow comrades-in-arms, Tulia, Acca, and Tarpeia. According to Silver Latinist poet Virgil, "they were like Thracian Amazons when they make the waters of Thermodon tremble and make war with their ornate arms, either around Hippolyte or when warlike Penthesilea returns in her chariot and the female armies exult, with a great ringing cry and the clashing of crescent-shaped shield."

Rhodogune, queen of ancient Parthia in 200 B.C., got word of a revolt when she was taking a bath. Vowing to end the uprising before her hair was dressed, she hopped on her horse and rushed to lead her army to defense. True to her word, she directed the entire, lengthy war without ever bathing or combing her hair. Portraits of Rhodogune always faithfully depict her dishevelment. (Another queen of the ancient world, **Semiramis**, also pulled herself from the bath to the battlefield act when her country needed a brave leader.)

Of the royal lineage of Cleopatra, **Zenobia Septimus** preferred the hunt to the bath and boudoir. She was queen of Syria for a quarter-century beginning in 250 A.D. and was quite a scholar, recording the history of her nation. She was famed for her excellence on safari, specializing in the rarified skill of hunting panthers and lions.

When the Romans came after Syria, Zenobia disgraced the empire's army in battle, causing them to turn tail and run. This inspired Arabia, Armencia, and Periso to ally with her and she was named Mistress of Nations. The Romans licked their wounds and enlisted the help of the barbarians they conquered for a Roman army including Goths, Gauls, Vandals, and Franks who threatened to march against Zenobia's league of nations. When Caesar Aurelius sent messengers requesting her surrender, she replied, "It is only by arms that the submission you require can be achieved. You forget that Cleopatra preferred death to servitude. When you see me in war, you will repent your insolent proposition." And battle they did. Zenobia fought bravely, holding her city Palmyra against the mass of invaders for longer than anyone thought possible. Upon her capture, Zenobia was taken to Rome in chains, jewels, and her own chariot, and she was given her own villa in Rome where her daughters intermarried into prominent families who ruled Rome.

Boudicca's name means "victorious" in the language of the Celts. She is the legendary warrior-queen of the Iceni of Norfolk who led a rebellion against the invading Romans in the year 61 A.D., and sacked the Roman's settlements, including Verulamium and Londinium, which she put to the torch. She took the lives of 70,000 Romans in her battles and was reputed to be "tall of person, of a comely appearance, and appareled in a loose gown of many colors. About her neck she wore a chain of gold, and in her hand she bore a spear. She stood a while surveying her army and, being regarded with a reverential silence, she addressed them an eloquent and impassioned speech." She died in battle at her own hand, taking poison rather than be killed by an enemy of the Celts. Many women fought to defend their land and culture; the Celtic army consisted of more women than men!

EUROPEAN BATTLE AXES AND FREEDOM FIGHTERS

The Germanic princess **Modthryth** referenced in *Beowulf* was an actual female ruler in 520 A.D., "a good folk queen" with soldierly aspirations. According to folktales handed down in Sweden, any man who looked upon her with desire was challenged to fight her and be felled by her sword!

Lathgertha was also a ruler immortalized in *Halfdanar Saga*, which tells her story under the name Hladgerd. She rallied to hero Halfdanar's cause, leading twenty ships in battle to save the day. She is also commemorated in a Saxo Grammaticus tale where he supplied more background about what inspired Lathgertha to take up the battle girdle—she and a group of noblewomen were taken for slaves by invading Norwegians who locked them into a prison brothel. The noblewomen refused to suffer this indignation and turned the tables on their captors, taking their weapons and going into battle. Grammaticus describes her as endowed with "a man's temper in a woman's body. With locks flowing loose under her helm, she fought in the forefront of the battle, the most valiant of warriors. Everyone marveled at her matchless feats."

Aethelburg was an ancient British battle-queen of Ine. According to the writings of Damico, she erected a fortress in Taunton in 722 A.D.

One hundred-fifty years after Aethelburg's rule, **Aethelflaed** took up the sword and swore herself to chastity-belted celibacy after her intensely unpleasant experience of childbirth. She and her husband became friends and fellow warriors. When her husband died in 912 A.D., she kept on fighting to defend her father, Alfred the Great, and his kingdom against invading Danes. She had a brilliant tactical mind, uniting the pre-England kingdoms of Wales and Mercia. She died in battle at Tammoth in the borough of Stratfordshire and her one child, daughter **Aelfwyn**, ascended the throne until her jealous, power-hungry uncle managed a coup.

Good King Wenceslas was actually quite mad. His wife, **Queen Sophia** of Bohemia had to hold the royal stronghold by herself against German's invading emperor Sigismund and a barbarous cyclopean Bohemian named Ziska, who fancied he would overtake and rule Bohemia himself. **Ziska's Army of Women** was a ragtag bunch of Bohemian reformers and patriots, largely women and children, who took down Sophia's professional soldiers with such original tactics as removing their clothes and tossing them on the battlefield to entangle the legs of the warhorses the Bohemian Royal Army rode.

The Knights Templar are quite well known, but their counterparts, the numerous crusading battle nuns known as the **Martial Nuns** are not, having been effectively "whited-out" of history—probably by jealous scribe monks! But there were armed nuns who accompanied fighting monks in the Crusades in the 1400s. But even nuns who stayed home were often armed—they had to defend their convents by themselves in the aggressively territorial Dark Ages. For example, when the anti-Christian Espartero invaded Spain in his famous siege, the nuns of Seville fought back and won. One nun who took up the pen and the sword wrote of her crusade to Jerusalem at the time of Saladin's attack on the holy city, "I wore a helmet or at any rate walked on the ramparts wearing on my head a metal dish which did as well as a helmet. Women though I was I had the appearance of a warrior. I slung stones at the enemy. I concealed my fears. It was hot and there was never a moment's rest. Once a catapulted stone fell near me and I was injured by the fragments."

Careful study of European military history shows a number of women armies, including many women of the cloth. Ultimately, success was too threatening to the men they fought beside and several popes declared such women to be heretics. **Joan of Arc**, of course, was the most famous. She was burned at the stake in 1431 on the letter of a law that was hundreds of years old that forbade women from wearing armor. At the same time, Joan was the national shero of France, having led the battle to free the French from the foreign power of England, at the advice of the voices of saints. Several women were inspired by Joan's example and moved to courage by her murder. The most successful was **Joan, the Maid of Sarmaize**, who attracted a religious following that supported her in Anjou. She claimed to be the Joan of Arc returned and, like her predecessor, dressed in men's clothing and armor. Several of Joan of Arc's friends and family took her in and accepted her. Her actual identity was never known.

Onorata Rodiani was an ahead-of-her time portrait and mural painter who was busy immortalizing the Tyrant of Cremona in oils when an "importunate nobleman" barged into the sitting. Onorata whipped out her dagger and ended the rude noble's life on the spot, but was forced to go underground as a fugitive. She put down the brush and took up the sword as the captain of a band of mercenaries and died in 1472 in an attempt to defend her birthplace of Castelleone.

In 1745, a Scottish woman named **Mary Ralphson** fought at Fontenoy right beside her husband. Known as "Trooper

Mary," she wasn't deterred by having only five fingers and one thumb, living through war to the grand age of 110.

The Amazon of the Vendeans, **Mademoiselle de la Rochefoucalt** fought the Republicans when Louis XVI was murdered. She was only a teenager, but was famed for her speeches on the battlefield, "Follow me! Before the end of the day we either sing our victory on earth, or hymns with the saints in heaven."

Alexandra Dourova was a Russian shero who fought against Napoleon as a colonel in the Fourth Hussars. In World War I, the very same regiment enlisted another fighting woman—**Olga Serguievna Schidlowskaia**.

Nancy Wak

Major **Tamara Aleksandrovna** was in charge of an all-female air force for Russia in World War II. Their phenomenal success is evidenced by their record of flying 125 combats, 4,000 sorties, and shooting down 38 Nazi aircraft. Other amazonian aviatrixes were **Captain Budanova**, **Nancy Wak** of New Zealand who flew for the allies in France and **Ludmilla Pavlichenko** who killed 309 Nazis by herself!

Nina Teitelboim, called "Little Wanda with the Braids," was an anti-Nazi fighter who commanded a special force of Poland's People's Guard which blew up the elite Cafe Club, a hangout for the top-ranking Gestapo. Thus empowered, she was part of a raid on the Nazis, stealing back the enormous stockpiles of cash the Nazis themselves had stolen from the people of Warsaw. After this success, the price on her head was higher than ever, and she was captured and executed.

Florence Matomelo was a soldier in the anti-apartheid resistance movement. In 1965, she was arrested for her role in the African National Congress (Pro Azanian or black South African rebel government) and confined to solitary where she was starved, beaten, interrogated, and deprived of the insulin she needed for her diabetes. She died after five years of this abuse, leaving behind several children. She had led a life of constant courage, defying and protesting the unfair practices of apartheid laws, and she died for her cause, having made invaluable contributions to the changes that finally freed black South Africans from the racist rule set up by colonial whites.

FIERCE ASIATIC FEMALES

In the year 39 A.D., the Vietnamese Trung sisters led a revolt against China. **Phung Thi Chinh** was in the last stages of pregnancy, but fought beside the other women, gave birth in the middle of the rebellion, and kept on fighting with her babe bound to her back with cloth.

Hangaku was a medieval noble's daughter with topnotch archery skills. Born to the Taira shogunate, she fought beside the men to defend the family's castle. She was fully acknowledged for having superior bow and arrow skills in comparison with her father, brothers, and husband, "shooting a hundred arrows and hitting a hundred times." In 1201, a fateful attack on the familiar fortress occurred, during which Hangaku dressed like a boy and stood, unhidden, raining arrows down upon the attackers. Even her flawless archery couldn't save the Tairas that round, and she was felled by an arrow and captured as a prisoner-of-war.

Afra'Bint Ghifar al-Humayriah was a veil-less Arab woman who fought in the legendary tent-pole battles with Khawlah in the seventh century. These resourceful women rebelled against the Greeks who captured them with the only available weapon—the poles of the tents they were imprisoned in!

Hindustan's warrior queen of Gurrah, **Durgautti** led a bold and colorful army of 1,500 elephants and 6,000 horseback soldiers. "Like a bold heroine, mounted within her elephant's howdar, armed with lance and bow and arrow," writes herstorian Eleanor Starling, she bested the invasive Mongol Asaph Khan and his army of 6,000 horses and 12,000 foot soldiers. When he later turned the tables on her, she killed herself with her elephant handler's dagger rather than endure defeat.

Lakshmi Bar, the Rani of Jhansi is one of India's national heroines. Raised in a household of boys, she was fearless and brilliant as a military strategist. When her husband died, she came out of purdah to fight the British, becoming the key figure extraordinaire who trained women for her army with special care. These women came to be known as the "amazons of Jhansi." Lakshmi herself was famous for calmly taunting enemy generals, "Do your worst, I will make you a woman." Her fame spread like wildfire throughout India, making her their national shero when she broke through an encircling ambush of British soldiers during battle and escaped in horseback to a hundred miles away in just twenty-four hours with a ten-year-old boy clinging to her back. She and the boy were the only two survivors of the slaughtered Indian troops. It should also be noted that Lakshmi was in full armor in sweltering 120 degree heat. She died on the battlefield in Gwalior when she was barely thirty; a British general called her the "greatest hero" he'd ever known.

Qui Jin was called a "Heroine Among Women" by Sun Yat-Sen. She was simply amazing! Born in 1874, her hobbies included cross-dressing and riding through the streets of Chinese cities and villages. She founded the first newspaper for women in China, founded a school for girls, and escaped from her arranged marriage to pursue her revolutionary goals of overthrowing the Qing Monarchy. Quite the intellectual, she wrote poetry and took a vow of silence during her imprisonment upon being arrested for plotting the assassination of the Qing governor. Her daughter followed in her mother's pioneering footsteps by becoming China's first aviatrix.

WOMEN WARRIORS OF THE AMERICAS

Coyolxauhqui was an Aztec divinity who fought her own mother, Coatlicue, for defending the warrior-god she had birthed (her brother, I suppose, but enemy nevertheless!) Coyolxauhqui's daunting name means "the one whose face was tattooed with rattlesnakes."

According to herstorian Carolyn Niethammer, **Pohaha** was a brave battle axe with a sense of humor for whom the heat of battle was quite rousing. Of North American Tewa Indian tribal origin, Pohaha's name tells the tale: "po" referred to the wetness between her legs caused by her excitement in battle and "ha ha" was a name given her because of her shrieks of laughter as she warred. Pohaha wanted to make sure her enemies knew they were up against a woman warrior, and would lift her skirt to prove her gender.

Weetamoo, the Squaw of Sachem of Pocasset, lived in the area of what is now Tiverton, Rhode Island, from 1650 for a quarter-century of legendary awesomeness. She commanded an army of 300 women warriors and stunned all who encountered her with her incredible beauty and charisma. She was a good tactician and courageous in battle. When her husband, Wamsutta, was poisoned by the English, Weetamoo went native in a big way and decided to try to eradicate the white invaders from her land. She joined her brother-in-law Metacom and their armies fought side-by-side against the English in King Phillip's War. During the Great Swamp fight of 1675, she drowned in the Tetcut River while being chased by Brits. The Redcoats fished her body out of the flood-swollen river, cut off her head, and put it on display.

Bowdash was an Indian woman who acted as a guide for white men explorers. Born to the Kutenai tribe in Montana, she was a folk shero in her part of the west, celebrated for being a peacemaker, prophet, messenger, and warrior in song and story, passed down orally through generations. Her story is both gory and glorious. According to Kutenai legend, when she was being killed by her enemies by their knives, her wounds magically sealed up.

Elizabeth Custer was the very independent wife of the famous Major General George A. Custer who traveled west after the Civil War. "Libbie" rode with the Seventh Cavalry beside her husband and other notables such as Wild Bill Hickok and Medicine Bill Comstock. She was an extraordinary horsewoman, able to ride forty miles a day easily. Her overprotective (to say the least!) husband instructed his regiment to kill her themselves rather than let her fall into enemy hands. This never happened, because she and her sister missed out on the Battle of Little Big Horn when they left the fort for some horseback adventures of their own. Libbie also traveled to India and rode a horse through the Khyber Pass to Afghanistan. She lived to the ripe old age of ninety-two and was buried in West Point's military cemetery beside George.

Pauline Cushman was a gypsy woman of great beauty who fought in the Civil War and gained the rank of major for her courage in fighting behind enemy lines in Tennessee. Her life was incredibly colorful—after the war, she went out west and gave speeches in full Union uniform. She also acted, amazing audiences, favoring the role and costume of an Amazon. For a time, she settled in Arizona where she ran a hotel and kept the peace with her trusty Colt 45. Upon moving to the Wild West outpost of San Francisco, she took the law into her own hand again and bullwhipped a man in public for libeling her. No doubt, people thought twice before speaking ill of gypsy soldier gal Pauline Cushman after that!

Poker Alice Ivers was one of the special breed of "Wild West Amazons" who ran a casino, smoked cigars, and sported a six-shooter she used with skill. In the 1880s, she ran across a card dealer in Pecos who cheated; she waited and watched until the pot was worth taking, held her gun to his head and then made off with the $5,000 prize, shouting, "I don't mind a cheat, it's a clumsy cheat that I can't stand."

Belle Starr fought for the Yankees as an underground guerilla on the other side of the Mason Dixon Line. Unfortunately for her and a few hundred others, these guerilla groups were outlawed and Belle was on the lam, unable to go home. Forced to a life of crime as an accidental fugitive, Belle showed a flair for stickups and cattle rustlings, and generally supported her bad self as a gun-for-hire. Belle has gotten a bum rap as a colorful criminal; she and the others from the underground were patriots who served their country well in extreme danger only to have the rug (or flag, as it were) pulled out from under them.

Calamity Jane was born in 1852 and remains a household name for her skill as a sharpshooter, muleskinner, midwife, gambler, and horseback scout. Her real name was Martha Jane Canary, and she died a pauper in 1903, even though she herself would give the shirt off her back to the needy or sick. She also wouldn't think twice about shooting the hat off any man who disrespected her!

Woman Chief, the "Absaroka Amazon," was a Gros Ventre girl raised by the Crow tribe who captured her in a hunt shortly after her birth, estimated to have been in 1806. Like Shoshone **Sacajawea**, without whom Lewis and Clark would have made the Donner Party look like a walk in the park, Woman Chief was a highly skilled hunter, guide,

negotiator, and translator, who specialized in buffalo hunting, horse thieving, and close-range battle. Her reputation swelled to mythic proportion when she killed and wounded several men in her first skirmish. Her fellow warriors sang songs in her honor, and she made for hot fireside chat. As a hunter, she was reputed as "capable of killing five buffalo during a hunt and then butchering them and loading them on to packhorses singlehandedly." Her sleight-of-hand style of horse trading won her a place on the Council of Chiefs and the title of Woman Chief. She was murdered by a Gros Ventre warrior in the middle of negotiations for peace she was undertaking between the Crows and her native tribe.

Her courage and glory is celebrated in Zapata's revolutionary song, "Adelita." However, **Adelita** was very much a real person, not just a romantic notion in a popular song. She was a gaucha at the turn of the twentieth century in Zapata's, and later Pancho Villa's army. There were many women soldiers in the peasant armies of the revolution called "soldederas" who started following the army as cooks, water-bearers, and camp followers helping the cause by helping the men. They eventually evolved into their own organization, divided up into ranks of their own design, and they carried pistols, rifles, and knives, becoming "warriors as fierce as the men."

And then there were more modern women warrior-aviatrixes, like the "Night Witches" of World War II, and Eileen Collins, who, far from being a space cadet, was a space commander... and Lotfia ElNadi, who defied Egyptian patriarchal culture to become a pilot in 1933.

LOTFIA ELNADI : FLYING IN THE FACE OF TRADITION

Lotfia ElNadi was the first Middle Eastern woman as well as the first African woman to become an aviator. And as if that is not enough, she was actually the first female pilot in the world. Born in 1907 to a middle class family in Cairo, Egypt, she was expected to complete primary school and then become a housewife. Her mother encouraged her to go to the American College, which had a modernized curriculum and taught languages. ElNadi saw an article about a newly opened local flying school, and decided to find a way to study flying there, despite her father's belief that higher education was a waste of time for a daughter. She tried asking a journalist to help her, but when that didn't work out, she daringly made a direct approach to the director of the EgyptAir airline to see if he would assist her. He recognized the PR potential for EgyptAir of an Egyptian female airplane pilot and agreed to help, and she started aviation school as the only woman in a class of men, telling her father that she was going to a study group to conceal her aviation ambitions. Since ElNadi had no money to pay the tuition, she worked in trade as the school's secretary and telephone operator.

In September of 1933, she earned her pilot's license after only 67 days of study; her achievement made headlines worldwide. At first her father was angry when he found out, but once he saw the positive press she was getting, he agreed to let her fly him on a trip over the pyramids. Three months later, ElNadi flew in the international race between Cairo and Alexandria at velocities averaging over 100 mph; she would have won if not for missing a mark but was disqualified on the technicality. However, she still received a prize of 200 Egyptian pounds and the congratulations of King Fuad for her stab at it. Feminist leader Huda Sha'arawi then raised funds to buy ElNadi a plane of her own. ElNadi served as secretary general for the Egyptian Aviation Club and flew for around five more years until her back was seriously hurt in an accident. For about 10 years after ElNadi achieved her aim of becoming a pilot, other Egyptian women followed suit; however, after that period, no others managed it until Dina-Carole El Sawy became a pilot for EgyptAir decades later. In 1989, ElNadi was invited back to Cairo to participate in the 54th anniversary of civil aviation in Egypt and received the Order of Merit of the Egyptian Organization of Aerospace. In her 80s, she moved for a time to Toronto to live with a nephew and his family, but she returned at last to Cairo to live out her days. She never married and lived to be 95.

"When something is excessive, it turns to its opposite. The excessive pressure forced upon me made me love freedom."

— **Lotfia ElNadi,** *from Take off from the Sand, a biographical documentary.*

WITCHES HUNTING

Nazis dubbed them the "Night Witches" (*"Nachthexen"*) - and they were terrified of these highly skilled Soviet women pilots. This colorful name came about due to the way these fierce female flyers would stop their aircraft engines and silently swoop in before dropping their bombs; the "swooshing" sound as they passed overhead was said to resemble that of a witch's broomstick. The Soviet Union was struggling mightily in 1941 to stop the Nazis' advances. Stalin himself ordered the formation of three all-women air force units. One of the first volunteers was 19-year-old Nadezhda Popova, who would go on to become one of the most celebrated heroes of the Soviet Union; she flew 852 missions against the Germans in wobbly wooden biplanes and was shot down several times. Her unit, the 588th Night Bomber Regiment was equipped with obsolete two-seater Polikarpov PO-2 biplanes made of wood and cloth. As such, they weren't very fast and were extremely unwieldy and hard to maneuver. These pilots had neither radios, guns, nor even parachutes, and they had to navigate using a stopwatch and a paper map. Too exposed to fly during the day, the Night Witches only flew under the cover of darkness. Their mission was to harass German positions and take out troop encampments, storage depots, and supply lines. They were extremely good at their job and were also noteworthy as the first women in the world to fly as military pilots.

"In winter when you'd look out to see your target better, you got frostbite, our feet froze in our boots, but we carried on flying. You had to focus on the target and think how you could hit it. There was no time to give way to emotions."

– Nadezhda Popova

EILEEN COLLINS - ROCKET WOMAN: FIRST U.S. SPACE SHUTTLE COMMANDER

Ever since she was a little girl, Eileen Collins wanted to be a pilot. She attended Corning Community College in New York, and then completed her B.A. in mathematics and economics at Syracuse University in 1978. After Syracuse, she was chosen along with three other women for Air Force pilot training at Oklahoma's Vance Air Base; her class was one of the base's first to include women. After earning her wings in 1979, she stayed on for three years as a T-38 Talon pilot instructor before being transferred to Travis Air Force Base in California, for cross-training in the C-141 Starlifter. She earned a master's degree in operations research at Stanford in 1986, then a second master's in space systems management from Webster University in 1989.

That same year, Collins was accepted at the competitive Air Force Test Pilot School at Edwards Air Force Base in California. In 1989, she became only the second woman to graduate as a test pilot. She rose to the rank of Colonel in the Air Force before being being selected by NASA to be an astronaut in 1990. In 1995, Collins became the first female astronaut to pilot a space shuttle mission, serving as second-in-command of the shuttle Discovery. She piloted a second mission on the space shuttle Atlantis in 1997. After having logged over 400 hours in space, she was chosen by NASA to command the space shuttle Columbia on a mission in 1999, and became the first astronaut ever to pilot any of the shuttles through a 360 degree pitch maneuver, as well as the first American woman ever to command a space shuttle. In 2006, Collins retired from NASA to pursue other interests and spend time with her family. Since her retirement, Collins has received numerous awards and honors, including induction into the National Women's Hall of Fame, and has made appearances as a commentator covering space shuttle flights for CNN.

"My daughter just thinks that all moms fly the Space Shuttle."

– Eileen Collins

• CHAPTER TWO •

Eco Awesome: Saving Mother Earth

Whether fighting to save gorillas in the mists of Africa or chaining themselves to trees to stop the logging of old growth forests, women have been at the forefront of the green revolution around the world. Indeed, the person said to be responsible for the birth of the modern environmental movement was a woman born at the beginning of the twentieth century, Rachel Carson.

Being an eco warrior often means putting your very life in danger. Judi Bari of Earth First nearly died when someone planted a bomb in her car after she got too successful in her campaign to save the redwoods of northern California, and hundreds of peasant women in India have looked down the barrel of a gun in their attempts to preserve the trees that maintain their climate and provide the essentials of life in rural villages.

Perhaps it is only natural that the nurturing power of women be directed back toward the source of all life—Mother Gaia. At the cusp of a new millennium, we face the continual extinction of species, the razing of precious rainforests—the "lungs" of the planet—and the scare of toxic oceans, thinning ozone, and global warming. Although governmental and corporate spin doctors deny the threat of an overheated planet, environmentalists work assiduously to ensure a healthy world for future generations. The dream of a better, healthy world is an issue that certainly affects every human being. The stories of these courageous women should inspire everyone to do what we can—recycle, reuse, reduce, get out of our cars, plant trees, garden, compost, and work together to protect the environment. This is one area in which we all have infinite opportunities to be sheroes and heroes every day, one small act at a time. This movement has grown to become the critical issue of our day. These eco-sheroes and preservationist pioneers are, literally, saving the world!

RACHEL CARSON: "THE NATURAL WORLD… SUPPORTS ALL LIFE"

World famous ecologist and science writer Rachel Carson turned nature writing on its head. Before she came along, notes *Women Public Speakers in the United States*, "the masculine orientation [to the subject] emphasized either the dominant, aggressive encounter of humanity with wild nature or the distancing of nature through scientific observation." By creating a different, more feminine, relationship to nature, one which saw humans as part of the great web of life, separate only in our ability to destroy it; Rachel Carson not only produced the first widely read books on ecology, but laid the foundation for the entire modern environmental movement.

Rachel inherited her love of nature from her mother, Maria, a naturalist at heart, who took Rachel for long walks in woods and meadows. Born in 1907, Rachel was raised on a farm in Pennsylvania where the evidence of industry was never too far away. By the beginning of the twentieth century, Pennsylvania had changed a great deal from the sylvan woodlands named for colonial William Penn. Coal mines and strip mines had devastated some of the finest farmland. Chemical plants, steel mills, and hundreds of factories were belching pure evil into the air. As she grew, Rachel's love of nature took an unexpected turn toward oceanography, a budding science limited by technological issues for divers. The young girl was utterly fascinated by this particular biological science, and though she majored in English and loved to write, she heard the ocean's siren song increasingly. While in college at Pennsylvania College for Women in the middle 1920s, she changed her major to biology, despite the overwhelming advice of her teachers and professors to stay the course in English, a much more acceptable major for a young woman. Her advisors were quite correct in their assertions that women were blocked from science; there were very few teaching positions except at the handful of women's colleges, and even fewer job prospects existed for women.

However, Rachel listened to her heart and graduated with high honors, a fellowship to study at Woods Hole Marine Biological Laboratory for the summer, and a full scholarship to Johns Hopkins in Maryland to study marine zoology. Rachel's first semester in graduate school coincided with the beginning of The Great Depression. Her family lost the farm; her parents and brother came to live with her in her tiny campus apartment. She helped make ends meet with part-time teaching at Johns Hopkins and the University of Maryland, while continuing her studies. In 1935, Rachel's father suffered a heart attack and died quite suddenly. Rachel looked desperately for work to support her mother and brother only to hear the same old discouragements—no one would hire her as a full-time university science professor. Brilliant and hardworking, Rachel was encouraged to teach grade school or, better yet, be a housewife because it was "inappropriate" for women to work in science.

Finally, her unstinting efforts to work in her field were ultimately rewarded by a job writing radio scripts for

Elmer Higgins at the United States Bureau of Fisheries, a perfect job for her because it combined her strength in writing with her scientific knowledge. Then a position opened up at the Bureau for a junior aquatic biologist. The job was to be awarded to the person with the highest score: Rachel aced the test and got the position. Elmer Higgins saw that her writing was excellent, making science accessible to the general public. At his direction, she submitted an essay about the ocean to the *Atlantic Monthly*, which not only published Rachel's piece, but asked her to freelance for them on a continuing basis, resulting in a book deal from a big New York publishing house.

By now, Rachel was the sole support of her mother, brother, and two nieces. She raised the girls, supported her mother, and worked a demanding full-time job, leaving her research and writing to weekends and late nights. But she prevailed nonetheless. Her first book, *Under the Sea Wind*, debuted in 1941 to a bemused and war-preoccupied public. It was a completely original book, enacting a narrative of the seacoast with the flora and fauna as characters, the first indication of Rachel's unique perspective on nature.

Rachel's second book, *The Sea Around Us*, was a nonfiction presentation of the relationship of the ocean to earth and its inhabitants. This time, the public was ready, and she received the National Book Award and made the *New York Times* bestseller list for nearly two years! *The Edge of the Sea* was also very well received, both critically and publicly. Rachel Carson's message of respect and kinship with all life combined with a solid foundation of scientific knowledge found a real audience in postwar America. However, shy and solitary Rachel avoided the spotlight by accepting a grant that allowed her to return to her beloved seacoast, where she could be found up to her ankles in mud or sand, researching.

As her popularity rose and her income from book royalties flooded in, Rachel was able to quit her job and build a coastal cottage for herself and her mother. She also returned the grant money, asking it be redistributed to needy scientists. In 1957, a letter from one of Rachel's readers changed everything for her. The letter came from Olga Owens Huckins, who was reporting the death of birds after airplanes sprayed dichloro-diphenyl-trichloroethane, DDT, a chemical then in heavy use. Rachel Carson was keenly interested in discovering DDT's effects on the natural habitat. Her findings were shocking: if birds and animals weren't killed outright by DDT, its effects were even more insidious—thin eggshells that broke before the hatchlings were fully developed. It was also suspected of being carcinogenic to humans.

Rachel vowed to write a book about the devastating impact of DDT upon nature "or there would be no peace for me," she proclaimed. Shortly after, she was diagnosed with cancer. Despite chemotherapy, surgery, and constant pain, Rachel worked slowly and unstintingly on her new book. In 1962, *Silent Spring* was published. It was like a cannon shot. Chemical companies fought back, denied, and ran for cover against the public outcry. Vicious charges against Rachel were aimed at what many of the captains of the chemical industry viewed as her Achilles heel—her womanhood. "Not a real scientist," they claimed. She was also called unstable, foolish, and sentimental for her love of nature. With calm logic and cool reason, Rachel Carson responded in exacting scientific terms, explaining the connections among DDT, the water supply, and the food chain.

Ultimately, President John F. Kennedy assigned his Science Advisory Committee to the task of examining the pesticide, and Rachel Carson was proven to be absolutely correct. She died two years later, and although her reputation continued to be maligned by the chemical industry, her work was the beginning of a revolution in the responsible use of chemicals and serves as a reminder of the reverence for all life.

"Perhaps if Dr. Rachel Carson had been Dr. Richard Carson the controversy would have been minor...The American technocrat could not stand the pain of having his achievements deflated by the pen of this slight woman."

— Joseph B.C. White, *author*

MARJORY STONEMAN DOUGLAS: PATRON SAINT OF THE EVERGLADES

Although not native to the southernmost state, Marjory Stoneman Douglas took to the Florida Everglades like a "duck to water," becoming since 1927 the great champion of this rare habitat. She was born to lake country in Minnesota in 1890, during one of her father's many failed business ventures, which kept the family moving around the country. On a family vacation to Florida at the age of four, Marjory fell in love with the Floridian light and vowed to return.

Marjory escaped her unstable home life in the world of books. An extremely bright girl, she was admitted to Wellesley College when higher education for women was still quite uncommon. Her mother died shortly after her graduation in 1911. Feeling unmoored, she took an unrewarding job at a department store, and shortly thereafter married a much older man, Kenneth Douglas, who had a habit of writing bad checks.

Leaving for Florida with her father for his latest business pursuit seemed like the perfect way to get away from her petty criminal husband and sad memories. Frank Stoneman's latest ideas, however, seemed to have more merit: founding a newspaper in the scruffy boom town of Miami (the paper went on to become the *Miami Herald*). Marjory eagerly took a job as a cub reporter. Opinionated, forward-thinking, and unafraid to share unpopular views, both Stonemans found their niche in the newspaper trade. One of the causes they were in unswerving agreement on was Governor Napoleon Bonaparte Broward's plan to drain the Everglades to put up more houses. Father and daughter used the paper as their soapbox to cry out against this ghastly idea with all their might.

Roused to action, Marjory educated herself about the facts surrounding the Everglades issue and discovered many of the denizens of Florida's swampy grassland to be in danger of extinction. The more she learned, the more fascinated she became. When decades later she decided to leave the newspaper to write fiction, she often wove the Everglades into her plots. Marjory learned that the Everglades were actually not a swamp, but rather wetlands. In order to be a swamp, the waters must be still, whereas in the Everglades water flows in constant movement. Marjory coined the term "river of grass" and in 1947 wrote a book about this precious ecosystem entitled *The Everglades: River of Grass*.

More than anything else, Marjory's book helped people see the Everglades not as a fetid swamp, but as a national treasure without which Florida might become desert. After the publication of her book, Harry Truman designated a portion of the Florida wetlands as Everglades National Park. The triumph was short-lived, however. The Army Corp of Engineers began tunneling canals all over the Everglades, installing dams and floodgates. As if that weren't enough, they straightened the course of the Kissimmee River, throwing the delicate ecosystem into complete shock.

At the age of seventy-eight, Marjory Stoneman Douglas joined in the fight, stopping bulldozers ready to raze a piece of the Everglades for an immense jetport. Almost blind and armed with little more than a big floppy sun hat and a will of iron, Marjory founded Friends of the Everglades, going on the stump to talk to every Floridian about the devastation to this rare resource and building the organization member by member to thousands of people in thirty-eight states. "One can do so much by reading, learning, and talking to people," she noted. "Students need to learn all they can about animals and the environment. Most of all, they need to share what they have learned."

Marjory Stoneman Douglas and "Marjory's Army" as her group came to be known, stopped the jetport in its tracks, garnered restrictions on farmers' use of land and chemicals, saw to the removal of the Army's "improvements," and enjoyed the addition of thousands of acres to the Everglades National Park, where they could be protected from land grabbing developers. In 1975 and 1976, Marjory was rewarded for her hard work by being named Conservationist of the Year two years in a row. In 1989, she became the Sierra Club's honorary vice president. Protecting the Everglades became Marjory's life work, a job she loved. She never considered retiring and continued living in the same house she'd been in since 1926 and worked every day for Friends of the Everglades until her passing in 1998 at 109 years old. She saved millions of acres.

"Find out what needs to be done and do it!"

— Marjory Stoneman Douglas

Join Marjory's Army!

You can contact Friends of the Everglades and continue her work: *www.everglades.org*

MARJORIE KINNAN RAWLINGS: BARD OF THE BACKWOOD

Marjorie Kinnan Rawlings used to play "Story Lady" in Washington, D.C., as a girl, making up stories to tell the boys from her neighborhood. As an adult, she and her husband moved to Cross Creek, Florida, where she fell in love with the unique people of south Florida and their hearts in the face of hardship, poverty, and starvation, which she immortalized in her memoir *Cross Creek*. Like Marjory Stoneman Douglas, Rawlings helped focus the nation's attention on an area previously disregarded as a "wasteland" through her O'Henry award-winning short stories, like "Gal Young Un" and "The Black Secret," and her novels—*South Moon Under*, *The Sojourner*, and the children's classic, *The Yearling*. *The Yearling* shows Rawlings at the top of her craft, with her beautifully rendered story and sense of place winning a Pulitzer prize award in 1939. *The Yearling* was made into a film that received both critical and popular acclaim; both the novel and the film are regarded as classics for their sensitive portrayal of life in the Florida Everglades.

GERTRUDE BLOM: BEARING WITNESS

Born in 1901, pioneer rainforest activist Gertrude Elizabeth Loertsher's fascination with native peoples began as a child in Switzerland when she read about American Indians and acted out the stories with her friends after school. She didn't feel the same pull toward academia, however, and pursued horticulture and social work rather than a more traditional educational career. She spent a year in England with a Quaker family whose way of life and pacifist philosophy she found imminently appealing. After a failed marriage to a neighbor's son back home in Bern, Trudi, as she liked to be called, traveled to

Germany in the 1930s, where she was shocked by the rise of fascism. The daughter of a Jewish mother and a Protestant minister father, Trudi's own sensibility toward peace and justice was poles apart from the Nazi party. Upon Hitler's election as chancellor in 1933, the Nazis' power was dominant; any actions or talk against it were treated as treason.

Trudi's sympathies were entirely anti-Nazi, and she risked her life many times to get information about Nazi horror stories to the newspapers in her native Switzerland, outsmarting the ruling party of martinets and murderers again and again. Times got harder and getting out of Germany became increasingly difficult; Gertrude finally inveigled passage to France, where she worked for the Resistance, traveling to the United States to aid other European refugees. Upon returning to France, she was put in prison after the Nazi takeover.

Ultimately the Swiss government got her out of France, and she made her way to Mexico to rest and get some distance from political strife. She developed a new interest in photography, making women factory workers her subject. Her photographs were compelling, filled with both a beauty and depth in the faces weathered by difficult lives. Mexico itself filled Trudi with awe; it was both a new home and a muse catapulting her toward discovery. She traveled the vast country in search of the meaning she knew lay in the land. Her first sight of the Mexican jungle was an epiphany: "This jungle filled me with a sense of wonder that has never left me," she noted many years later. The mysterious forest and Lacandon Indians who lived there showed her a way to live in the world that was vastly different from her European background. Trudi learned from these people, studying their traditional ways only to discover their life in the jungle was in jeopardy; Mexican peasants were being relocated to the rainforest state of Chiapas bordering

Guatemala and left to scratch a living from the dirt. Trudi's life was in flux, as well. She met and married Danish archeologist, cartographer, and traveler, Franz Blom, who shared Trudi's fascination with the Mayan culture and Indian peoples. Together, they pursued their love of the rainforest and thirst for knowledge constantly, mapping the land and recording their findings in journals and Trudi's photography, which they published. The husband and wife team came to a deep understanding of the Lacondan rainforest and its people. They perceived the fragility of this environment and sought to preserve it, founding Na Bolom, a research institution and center for visiting scholars, travelers, and anyone caring to learn about the Mayan civilization and its modern descendants.

Trudi also figured a practical way to undo some of the damage Lacandones had suffered. She invited tree experts to assist her in establishing a nursery to replant the rainforest, making the trees free to anyone who would plant them. Trudi worked diligently on the lecture circuit to pay for the seedlings, building the annual crop to 30,000 trees a year before her death in 1993 (her ninety-second year). Na Bolom carries on her work educating and reforesting the Mayan rainforest.

> *"The time has come for us to wake up to what we are doing and take steps to stop this destruction."*
>
> **— Gertrude Blom**

JANE GOODALL: NOT JUST MONKEYING AROUND

Born in 1934, English zoologist Jane Goodall owes her career to the fact that her divorced mother couldn't afford to send her to college. Instead, the amateur naturalist worked in offices and waitressed in order to pay for travel to feed her great curiosity. In 1960, she received an invitation to visit a friend whose family had moved to Kenya. While there, the young woman worked up the nerve to contact Louis and Mary Leakey, who were working there to find evidence of early humans in the Olduvai Gorge in the Great Rift. The Leakeys found her to be an able companion, well suited to work in the field looking for fossil fragments or at Kenya's National Museum of Natural History, reconstructing what they found. Despite the fact that she had no formal scientific training, Dr. Louis Leakey asked Jane to go to Tanzania to conduct a lengthy study of chimpanzees in the wild. He believed that by studying chimpanzees, we stand to learn much about the life of early humans.

Jane, who was much more interested in animals than in Stone Age ancestors, jumped at the change—this would be the first such long-term study of this animal in its natural habitat. When the African government refused to allow her to work alone in the animal refuge, Jane's mother offered to accompany her. Despite her lack of training, Jane was well suited to the task of scientific observation; she kept meticulous notes and went to any length to find chimps, hiking miles into the forest each day. Goodall's work was the stuff of scientific revolution.

She disproved many erroneous beliefs about chimpanzees. For example, she learned that they are omnivores, not vegetarian; make and use tools; have elaborate social structures and a variety of humanlike emotions; and give their young unconditional affection. She has been decried by stuffy male zoologists for giving the chimps names, like Graybeard, instead of numbers in her papers. Jane did it "her way" and outdid all the uptight academics with her commitment, endurance, and plain smarts. In many ways, she received better treatment from her subjects than her peers, especially in the heartwarming moment when a male chimpanzee accepted a nut from Jane's hand, clasping her hand soulfully before discarding the nut. Jane was touched at his attempt to spare her feelings about the unwanted nut.

In 1964, Jane met and married a young photographer who came to her camp to take photos of the chimps, and they had a son. She went on to earn a Ph.D. in ethnology from Cambridge (one of the only people ever to receive one without a B.A.!), and her findings have been published widely. Returning to Africa, she founded the Gombe Stream Research Centre, which is this year celebrating decades of continuous research in Gombe National Park. In recent years, her work has taken a slightly different turn, however, in protecting the chimpanzees she studied and befriended in Africa through the Chimpanzee Guardian Project. She lectures around the world to raise money to try and stop the continued shrinking of their habitat and their decline in numbers from more than 10,000 during the time of her study to less than 3,000 today.

The author of many books and the winner of a multitude of awards, Jane Goodall pursues her interests with singular purpose and passion. In a realm where money and education are usually the deciding factors, she started with nothing but her natural intelligence and an open, curious mind. She went on to achieve the top recognition in her field and to become one of the most beloved figures in science today.

> *"Every individual matters and has a role to play in this life on earth. The chimpanzees teach us that it is not only human but also non-human beings who matter in the scheme of things."*
>
> **— Jane Goodall**

MARY LEAKEY: DIGGING FOR TRUTH

Mary and Louis Leakey worked together in the search for the origins of man. Mary's fabled perspicacity for digging and sifting was matched by her acerbic manner and love of good strong cigars. Of the famous duo, Mary was the one with the lucky spade. In 1948, Mary uncovered the skull and facial bones of the much ballyhooed hominid that came to be known as "the missing link." In her trademark no-nonsense manner, Mary mused, "For some reason that skull caught the imagination." In 1959 in the Olduvai Gorge of northern Tanzania, she discovered some teeth and the palate bone of the oldest ancestor of man up to that point. Upon finding other bones, they were able to determine that the five-foot, barrel-chested, small-brained, and browless hominid Zinjanthropus had walked upright a million years ago. Three years after Louis Leakey's death in 1972, working widow Mary surpassed her own historical findings when she found the tracks of bipedal creatures 3.6 million years old, preserved in volcanic ash, and she later unearthed the jawbones of eleven other humanoids carbon-dated to 3.75 million years old! Mary passed the torch, or rather spade, to her son when she died in December of 1996 at the age of eighty-three. We owe a great deal of our new understanding of human evolution to Mary's nose for old bones! "Her commitment to detail and perfection made my father's career," said son Richard E. Leakey. "He would not have been famous without her. She was much more organized and structured and much more of a technician."

DIAN FOSSEY: GORILLAS AND THE MYTH

Occupational therapist Dian Fossey felt a primal call to go to Africa, where she could study mountain gorillas. Taking out a personal loan, in 1963 she headed to the southern hemisphere, stopping by to say hello to Jane Goodall and the Leakeys, who encouraged her to do a gorilla field study. Traveling to Zaire (otherwise known as the "heart of darkness" to you Conrad fans), she found her research subjects—or rather sniffed out the odoriferous primates. "I was struck by the physical magnificence of the huge jet-black bodies blended against the green palette of the thick forest foliage." Taking the "when in Rome" tack, she won the apes over by mimicking their moves, eventually living among fifty-one gorillas. Indeed, her observations proved that the mountain gorillas were actually peaceful vegetarians in great danger of extinction from poaching and habitat shrinkage.

Dian Fossey defended her gorillas and their turf bravely, earning the enmity of Rwandan tribespeople. She was devastated when her beloved gorilla Digit and two others were slaughtered in what seems to have been a threat to her in 1978. Fossey made a plea to the world to help her save the gorillas, greatly furthered by her book *Gorillas in the Mist* and the eponymous movie featuring Sigourney Weaver in the starring role. After teaching at Cambridge and raising cash for the "Digit fund" to help the mountain gorillas, Dian Fossey (called Nyiramachabelli by the Rwandans: "the old lady who lives in the forest without a man") returned to stay with her gorilla families again, but her reunion was short-lived. She was found murdered on Christmas Eve of 1985 in the gorilla park habitat. Dian Fossey was buried beside Digit. Her murder has never been solved.

PETRA KELLY: GREEN KNIGHT

Environmental activist Petra Karin Kelly was interested in social issues from a very early age. Born in West Germany in 1947, she moved to Columbus, Georgia, with her mother and stepfather, U.S. Army Lieutenant Colonel John E. Kelly, in 1960, where she immediately became involved in the civil rights movement. Learning English quickly, during high school she had called a weekly radio program in current affairs. For college, she attended the school of International Service at American University where she studied world politics and graduated with honors in 1970. In addition to her studies, she was also very active in campus political movements—antiwar, antinuclear, and feminist, as a volunteer for Robert Kennedy's presidential campaign, and later for Senator Hubert H. Humphrey, with whom she maintained a friendship and correspondence. Her focus shifted when her sister Grace died from cancer in 1970. Petra Kelly created a citizen action group centered in Europe to study the connection between cancer and environmental pollution, eventually campaigning full-time for the Green Party she cofounded in 1979 and spearheading the Campaign for a Nuclear-Free Europe. In one year, she estimated she held more than 450 meetings in order to get the Greens elected to the German parliament, becoming the first German woman at the head of a political party.

Petra had an innate understanding of the inner workings of politics, and together with her fellow Green Party members, including her lover, Gert Bastian, was surprisingly successful in getting candidates into the governments not only of Germany, but throughout Europe, despite the Green Party's radically pro-

environment stances. As time went on, Petra's actions became increasingly radical and drew more criticism from conservatives than ever before—she put together a "war crimes tribunal" at Nuremberg on the issue of nuclear weapons, and in 1983, staged a no-nukes demonstration that ended in her arrest, followed by another protest in Moscow. Petra led the Greens into more frays—blockading military bases all over Germany and leading protests in the U.S., Australia, and Great Britain.

Petra was an immensely charismatic leader, capturing the attention of thousands of people, especially young people, around the world. Her pure idealism and willingness to take personal risks captivated the youth of Europe. She received hundreds of letters each week offering support and was in high demand for lectures, articles, and books. Issues pertaining to children were especially close to her heart. She adopted a young Tibetan girl, Nima, and worked to educate the world about Tibetan genocide.

In 1991, Petra and her soulmate, Gert, were discovered dead in a suburb of Bonn by police, summoned by Kelly's worried grandmother. They had both been shot and were in an advanced state of decomposition. Police have never been able to solve the double death, although the police believed it to be a double suicide. Others may have claimed it was a murder plot by anti-Green neo-Nazis who Gert had decried in newspaper articles. Police are basing the double-suicide theory on a powder burn on Gert's hand and the lack of other fingerprints or footprints in the apartment, and they have produced background information on Gert Bastian as a former SS agent who had worked for the Nazis in his youth. Thirty years older than Petra, he had once been a virulent right-winger before doing a 180-degree turnaround to join the Green Party. Close friends recall Gert depressedly saying that the "new" Germany reminded him of the old Germany of his fascist youth.

Although we may never know what really happened to Petra Kelly, we do know that while she lived, she made important inroads to drawing the world's attention to nuclear armaments, environmental destruction, children's rights, and world peace. She lived entirely for the benefit of humankind.

KAREN SILKWOOD: CHAIN REACTION

The story of Karen Silkwood is a mystery wrapped in an enigma. On November 13, 1974, she died in a car crash under suspicious circumstances after she very vocally criticized the safety of the plutonium fuels production plant she worked for in Crescent, Oklahoma. She had been on her way to meet with a *New York Times* reporter to give him evidence that Kerr-McGee was knowingly passing off defective fuel rods as good.

Prior to her death, she was inexplicably exposed to extremely high levels of plutonium. Karen had learned to routinely test herself for exposure, but nothing prepared her for the discoveries made by the Healthy Physics Office upon her request. Although no plutonium was found on any surfaces in the lab she was working in, her apartment was found to have been contaminated. Starting with a measure of 1 disintegrations per minute or dpms as the lowest possible positive result, these measurements were found in her house, according to PBS' online information site: 400,000 dpm on a package of bologna and cheese in the fridge, 25,000 on the stove sides, 6,000 on a package of chicken, and 100,000 on the toilet seat. After her death, an autopsy determined that Karen Silkwood's exposure to plutonium had been very recent and the plant could never come up with an explanation for her exposure. A year after her death, the plant closed.

The speculation surrounding her death has never stopped, but proof of company malfeasance has remained inconclusive. It is known, however, that it was Kerr-McGee who sold rods to the nuclear power plant at Three Mile Island, where defective fuel rods broke down and released radioactivity into the atmosphere.

WANGARI MAATHAI: GREEN GODDESS

Wangari Maathai is a remarkable woman. She set her sights on saving the farmlands, forests, and grasslands of the most politically unstable continent she calls home—Africa. To that end, she has started the Green Belt Movement. "We wanted to emphasize that by cutting trees, removing vegetation, having this soil erosion, we were literally stripping the Earth of its color," she remarks.

Wangari comes from a sacred spot for all of mankind; the rural village she was born in is beside the Great Rift Valley, the birthplace of the first humans who walked upright. Many call Wangari's home the cradle of life. Early on, she was instructed by her mother about the importance and sanctity of land and that which grows upon it, especially trees. In 1960, she left her village and took a scholarship offered to Kenyans by the United States. She found higher education to be very much her bailiwick, receiving a master of science from the University of Pittsburgh and a doctorate from the University of Nairobi, the first woman ever to do so. She then went on to rack up a number of other firsts in her homeland, including becoming the University of Nairobi's first female professor, first department chair, and first woman in the anatomy department.

Even though she enjoyed a happy marriage to a member of Kenya's Parliament, had a thriving career, and was raising three children, she still found time to become involved with women's rights. Her Kikuyu background was different from the district in Nairobi her husband was assigned to. As a Kikuyu woman, Wangari had been free to express her opinions and be actively involved in village affairs. In Nairobi, she was regarded as much too uppity for her own good. Proving them right, Wangari decided to run for Parliament and quit her job at the university to work full-time on her campaign. When she was told she was ineligible to run for Parliament because she was a woman, the university refused to hire her back.

Wangari then turned her prodigious energy to the environment. On World Environment Day in 1977, she and her supporters planted seven trees in a public park and laid the foundation for the Green Belt movement. Put down by many, and even beaten with clubs, she was accused of throwing her education and talent away. This time, she proved everybody wrong. Wangari discovered that only 3 percent of the Kenyan forest was still standing. As a result, Kenyan villagers were suffering malnutrition, erosion of their farmland, and the subsequent loss of water as springs and creeks dried up. She quite accurately foresaw famine and environmental disaster unless trees were again planted to restore the environment to its natural state. Wangari traveled throughout Kenya, teaching village women how to plant trees and how to start them from seeds they collected. Soon children got involved in the Green Belt planting projects, and by 1988, more than 10,000 trees were planted.

Wangari's brilliant strategy is simple. She doesn't try to convert villagers to the program. She waits for word of the good work and practical results to spread and, soon enough, the Green Belters are asked to come to another area. In addition to helping to stem the tide of complete destruction of Kenya's ecosystem, Wangari's Green Belt movement has provided many economic opportunities for Kenya's women.

Over the years, Wangari Maathai has received greater recognition for founding the Green Belt movement than any parliamentary seat would have provided. She has received many awards, become a Nobel Laureate, received a "Woman of the World" award from Diana, Princess of Wales, and the encouragement to continue her invaluable work in the regreening of Africa's precious heartland.

"One person can make the difference."

— Wangari Maathai

TREE-HUGGERS UNITE!

The Chipko movement in India began in 1973 when a group of Indian women protested a government action to log near their village. When the loggers decided on a different spot, the women went there to stop the tree-cutting. In a country where widows are still burned with their dead husbands in some places, this concerted action is truly courageous. A year later, the tree action moved to yet another location. Gaura Devi, a respected elder and widow from the village of Reni, was tipped off by a little girl herding cows that loggers were on the way. Gaura flew into action and got a troop of women. When a logger threatened Devi with a gun, she replied with a fierce calm, "Shoot us. Only then will you be able to cut down the forest." From this point on, the strength of the

Chipko movement increased tremendously and even got requests from men to join. Chipko means "to hug;" these grassroots environmentalists encircle their trees, holding hands to protecting their fellow beings from destruction.

JUDI BARI: SHERO OF THE FOREST MOVEMENT

The day after Judi Bari died, someone wearing an Earth First! t-shirt lowered the Willits Post Office Flag to half-mast. The flag stayed grieving until the postmaster put it back up some time later. The postmaster had to do a lot of raising the flag that week because every day the flag was lowered until the day of her wake, when the city hall flag stayed at half-mast for the day.

Judi was loved because she was an inspiration; she was admired and vilified because she was a great organizer. She knew how to organize all kinds of people—hippie kids to homesteaders—into an alliance that, by 1991, was beginning to include loggers and other timber workers. And for this she was bombed. She has the astute sense when to invoke the neighborhood and when not to. And for this she was bombed. She had the principled courage to stand in the face of macho Earth First!-ers and renounce tree-spiking; and she continued to do this in spite of being crippled and in chronic, unrepairable pain for the last six years of her life.

Here was the shero's journey: to achieve the respect and honor due her work from loggers and other timber workers. Loggers who were tired of slogging right and left to cut baby trees to make a living; millworkers who saw that the company didn't care for them any more than it cared for the forest. She brought them to understand that the company was cutting them out of a job; she was good at pointing out that putting the quarterly report before the health of the forest would destroy it for our children.

And workers were beginning to understand her message; and "Big Timber" couldn't stand that kind of message, so she was bombed. By somebody who is still out there.

A veritable army of people, whose desire to vilify Judi seemed endless, was led by the FBI, which labeled her a terrorist, charged her with bombing herself, and accused her one month before her death of faking cancer to gain sympathy from the public. Why on earth, why? I believe it was because she espoused and lived by a philosophy she called "biocentrism," which holds that humankind as a species is only one of a continuum, an organism, and therefore had little right to exploit the resources of the planet to the resources' destruction. She believed that giant corporations were betraying the public trust by the extraction of resources for obscene profit; naturally, this was appalling to those guardians of corporate America. So, if bombers could not destroy her body, then the FBI would destroy her reputation. If she could not be stopped from forming an alliance with workers, then she could be slowed down by intimidation, threats, isolation, and misinformation. It didn't work; she came back, and never stopped until cancer struck her down six years after the bombing.

That was her sheroism. She challenged all kinds of macho forces on their own ground. When Louisiana-Pacific Security shoved her to the ground and conned the cops into arresting her falsely, she replied a few days later by leading a circle of women through their gate at Albion, surrounded the security officer while chanting the many names of the Great Goddess. "My God, they've cast a spell on me!" he cried, eyes rolling back into his head. When in the process of discovery she obtained Oakland Police Department photos of her bombing, she looked at them over and over until she could harden herself to reliving the trauma, and actively conduct her case against the FBI for harassment, slander, and other equally slimy machinations conducted by their COINTELPRO program.

Judi inspired many of us to embrace Earth First! principles, because she lived and worked by those principles and the principles of nonviolent direct action. She inspired us to learn the principles of forest management from all sides. She saw clearly and led us to see that the trust of honest men, who believed the forest would still be there for their children the way it had been for them, had been betrayed and broken by the giant corporations. She inspired us to work to save the trees of our backyards, stretching through northern California to the Oregon border and beyond: the Cascades, the Siskiyous, the Kalmiopsis Wilderness, Clayoquot Sound, clearcut after clearcut all the way to the Brooks Range.

Six years—the last years of her life—of relentless organizing true to her shero's mission, cleaning up the corporate Augean Stables as if the corporate steeds were eating and eliminating the world. She never gave up, and she never lost her laugh. Great, deep, holding all the world laughter, even through the pain of her last months. She was cut off too soon—way too soon. What the bombing didn't do, breast cancer—the women's neutron bomb—did. Judi made the sheroic decision to die with dignity, surrounded by her children, her family, and her friends. In the months left to her after the 1996 Headwaters Rally, the greatest mass civil disobedience in the history of the U.S. forest movement (1,033 arrests that day; over 200 actions in the months following) she organized, explained, and delegated the mountains of material she had amassed: from the stuff for making banners (her last hangs on the Skunk Train Line proclaiming L-P OUT! and it's coming true) to extensive files on her case against the FBI.

In that time, she also had the opportunity to see how much the hometown folks loved her. There was a benefit tribute a month before she died. Judi was there and took the time to express her joy and thanks by singing,

"I am a warrior of the earth; I came alive in the Ancient Redwoods," clutching all the while a bottle of Headwaters water, and, lastly, toking a bit of medical marijuana and blowing it into the Willits High School Auditorium air. "I've liberated Willits High!" she cried, and as we cheered and cried and howled to see that ephemeral smoke ascend the shaft of the spotlight, we knew we would never be the same for knowing her, having seen the Spirit pass among us once more with her great belly laugh. Viva Judi! Presente Siempre.

"The woman brave enough to sit in the crotch of a tree had hers blown up today."

— Robin Rule, on the bombing of Judi Bari

• CHAPTER THREE •

Awesome Athletes: Leveling the Playing Field

Greek mythology tells us of the first female Olympian, Atalanta of Boetia. Born to Schoeneus, she cared not for weaving, the kitchen, or for wasting her precious time with any man who couldn't hold his own against her athletic prowess. Her father, proud of his fleet-footed Boetian babe, disregarded the norms of ancient Greek society and didn't insist on marrying his daughter off for political or financial gain, and supported her decision to marry the man who could out-run her. Her suitors were, however, given a head start, and Atalanta "armed with weapons pursues her naked suitor. If she catches him, he dies." She was outfoxed by Hippomenes who scattered golden apples as he ran, slowing down the amazonian runner as she stopped to pick them up. Well matched in every way, they were happy together, even going so far as to desecrate a shrine to Aphrodite by making love on the altar! For this, the Goddess turned Atalanta into a lioness, where she ruled yet again with her wild and regal spirit.

In real life, women athletes have been crushing barriers and high jumping their way to fame since the nineteenth century. In 1972, they got a bit of help from the federal government in the form of Title IX. Although President Richard Nixon signed the law stating, "No person in the United States shall, on the basis of sex, be excluded from participation in, be denied the benefits of, or be subjected to discrimination under any education program or activity receiving federal financial assistance," it is still hotly debated as to whether this legislation is enough to give women parity. Since the passage of Title IX, statistics have shown a 7 percent increase in the ratio of women athletes in high school. Although this is a definite improvement, there's still a long way to go to reach the 50 percent mark.

Even without full equality in funding, sports is an arena where women can compete with men openly again now, thanks to such sheroic trailblazers as tennis star Billie Jean King, who went up against Bobby Riggs in the heavily hyped match of 1973. Riggs, with preening braggadocio and banty-rooster crowing, declared that he would exhaust King because men were "stronger" and "better tennis players." Telecast from Houston's Astrodome, the world watched while Billie Jean King beat the shorts off the chauvinist Riggs and leveled the playing fields (and courts!) for every woman and girl on that herstoric day. Like King and today's stars, Venus and Serena Williams, the sheroes portrayed here have bucked the odds with passion, pure guts, and sheer ability to make it to the top of their games.

SUZANNE LENGLEN - SHE RULED THE COURT

Before Venus and Serena or even Chris Evert, there was Suzanne Lenglen, a flamboyant, brandy-loving Parisian trendsetter named "La Divine" by the French press, who in her brief life transformed women's tennis. Suzanne was born in Paris in 1899; as a child, she was frail and suffered from many health problems including chronic asthma. Her father decided it would benefit her health if she built her strength up by competing in tennis. Her first try at the game was in 1910, on the family's tennis court on their property. The 11-year-old liked the game, and her father continued to train her, with training methods including an exercise where it is said he would lay a handkerchief in different parts of the court and have Suzanne hit the ball towards it. Only four years later, at age 14, Lenglen made it to the final of the 1914 French Championships; she lost to reigning champion Marguerite Broquedis, but later that spring won the World Hard Court Championships at Saint-Cloud on her 15th birthday, making her the youngest person in tennis history to this day to win a major championship.

At the end of 1914, most major tennis competitions in Europe were abruptly halted by the onset of World War I. Lenglen's promising career was on hold for the next five years. The French championships were not held again until 1920, but Wimbledon resumed in 1919. Lenglen made her debut there, taking on seven-time champion Dorothea Douglass Chambers in the final. The historic match was played before 8,000 onlookers, including King George V and Queen-Consort Mary of Teck. Lenglen won the match; however, it was not only her playing that drew notice. The media squawked about her dress, which revealed her forearms and ended above the calf; at the time, others competed in body-covering ensembles. The staid British were also shocked by a French woman daring to casually sip brandy between sets.

Lenglen dominated women's tennis singles at the 1920 Summer Olympics in Belgium. On her way to winning a gold medal, she lost only four games, three of them in the final against Dorothy Holman of England. She won another gold medal in the mixed doubles before being eliminated in a women's doubles semifinal, and a bronze after their opponents withdrew. From 1919 to 1925, Lenglen won the Wimbledon singles championship in every year except 1924, when health problems due to jaundice forced her to withdraw after winning the quarterfinal. No other French woman won the Wimbledon ladies singles title again until Amélie Mauresmo in 2006. From 1920 to 1926, Lenglen won the French Championships singles title six times and the doubles title five times, as well as three World Hard Court Championships in 1921–1923. Astoundingly, she only lost seven matches in her entire career.

Lenglen sailed to New York City in 1921 to play the first of several exhibition matches against the Norwegian-born US champion, Molla Bjurstedt Mallory, to raise reconstruction funds for the parts of France that had been devastated by World War I. She was sick the entire storm-ridden voyage, which was delayed, arriving only one day before the tournament. When she arrived, Lenglen was told they had announced her as a participant in the US Championships. Due to immense public pressure, she agreed to play even though she was quite ill with what was later diagnosed as whooping cough; she was only given a day to recover as a concession. When another player defaulted, Lenglen ended up facing Mallory in the second round as her first opponent. She lost the first set, and just as the second set began, she began to cough and burst into tears, unable to go on. Spectators taunted her as she left the court, and the U.S. press was harsh. Under doctor's orders, she cancelled her exhibition match and returned home in a despondent state. But at the Wimbledon singles final the following year, she defeated Mallory in only 26 minutes, winning 6–2, 6–0, in what was said to be the shortest ladies' major tournament match on record. The two faced off again later in 1922 at a tournament in Nice where Lenglen completely dominated the court; Mallory failed to win even one game.

In a 1926 tournament at the Carlton Club in Cannes, Lenglen played her only game against Helen Wills. Public attention for their match in the tournament final was immense, with scalper ticket prices hitting stratospheric levels. Roofs and windows of nearby buildings were

crowded with onlookers. The memorable match saw Lenglen scraping by with a 6–3, 8–6 victory after nearly losing it on several occasions. It is said that her father had forbidden her to play Wills, and since Lenglen had almost never defied him, she was so stressed out that she was unable to sleep the whole previous night. Later in 1926, Lenglen seemed to be on course for a seventh Wimbledon singles title; but she withdrew from the tournament after learning that due to a mixup about the starting time, she had kept Queen Mary waiting in the royal box for a preliminary match to begin, which was seen as an affront to the English monarchy by the aristocracy.

Suzanne Lenglen was the first major female tennis star ever to go pro. Sports promoter C.C. Pyle paid her $50,000 to tour the U.S. playing a series of matches against Mary K. Brown, who at 35 was considered past her best years for tennis, though she had made it to the French final that year, only to lose to Lenglen, having only scored one point. This was the first time ever that a women's match was the headliner event of the tour, even though male players were part of the tour as well. When it ended in early 1927, Lenglen had won every one of her 38 matches; but she was exhausted, and her doctor advised a lengthy respite from the sport. She decided to retire from competition and set up a tennis school with help and funding from her lover, Jean Tillier. The school gradually grew and gained recognition; Lenglen also wrote several tennis texts in those years. Many criticized her for leaving amateur tennis competition, but she fired back, "Under these absurd and antiquated amateur rulings, only a wealthy person can compete, and the fact of the matter is that only wealthy people do compete. Is that fair? Does it advance the sport? Does it make tennis more popular – or does it tend to suppress and hinder an enormous amount of tennis talent lying dormant in the bodies of young men and women whose names are not in the social register?"

In 1938, Lenglen was suddenly diagnosed with leukemia and died only a few weeks later at age 39 near Paris. But her talent, verve, and style had changed women's tennis forever; before the arc of her brilliant career, very few tennis fans were interested in women's matches. The trophy for the Women's Singles competition at the French Open is now the "Coupe Suzanne-Lenglen." She was also inducted into the International Tennis Hall of Fame in 1978, and many hold her to be one of the best tennis players ever.

"I just throw dignity against the wall and think only of the game."

- Susanne Lenglen

BABE DIDRIKSON ZAHARIAS: THE GREATEST

Babe (real name Mildred) Didrikson always strived to be the best at any activity she undertook. Insecure, she figured sports was a great way to build up herself and her self-esteem. She got that right! She excelled at every sport she tried: running, jumping, javelin throwing, swimming, basketball, and baseball to name just a few. In her prime, she was so famous that she was known around the world by her first name.

Babe had a supportive home environment for the sporting life; her mother, Hannah Marie Olson, was a figure skater. Babe's family was loving, but they had a tough time making a living in the hardscrabble Texas town from whence they hailed. As a youngster in the twenties, Babe worked after school packing figs and sewing potato sacks at nearby factories, but somehow she still found time to play. No matter what the game, Babe was always better than the boys.

In high school, Babe tried out for basketball, baseball, golf, tennis, and volleyball; her superior athletic skills created a lot of jealousy among her peers. A Dallas insurance company offered her a place on their basketball team; Babe worked at the firm, finished high school, and played on the team. In her very first game, she smoked the court and outscored the other team all by herself. Fortunately for her, Employers Casualty also had track, diving, and swim teams. Track held a particular lure for Babe; she set records almost immediately in the shot put, high jump, long jump, and javelin throw. In 1932, Babe represented the Lone Star State as a one-woman team, and out of eight competitions she took awards for six. In 1932, Los Angeles was the site of the Summer Olympics; Babe drew the eyes of the world when she set records for the 80-meter hurdles and the javelin throw. She would have won the high jump too, but the judges declared her technique of throwing herself headfirst over the bar as unacceptable. There is no doubt she would have taken home even more gold except for the newly instated rule setting a limit of three events per athlete.

For Babe, making a living was more important than the accolades of the world. Unfortunately the options for women in professional sports were extremely limited in the 1930s. She made the decision to become a professional golfer; although she had little experience, she took the Texas Women's Amateur Championship three years later. In typical Babe Didrikson style, she went on to win seventeen tournaments in a row and also took part in matches against men, including a memorable match against the "crying Greek from Cripple Creek," George Zaharias, whom she married in 1938. Babe quickly saw the need for equality in women's golf and helped found the Ladies Professional Golf Association. Babe died at forty-three, after making a stunning comeback: winning the U.S. Open by twelve strokes less than a year after major surgery for intestinal cancer. She is thought by many to have been the greatest female athlete of all time.

"It's not enough to swing at the ball. You've got to loosen your girdle and really let the ball have it."

— Babe Didrikson Zaharias

HALET ÇAMBEL: HER SWORD WAS MIGHTIER

How many people can say they dissed Hitler? Halet Çambel, an Olympic fencer, was the first Muslim woman ever to compete in the Olympics as well as an archaeologist. She was born in 1916 in Berlin, Germany, the daughter of a former Grand Vizier to the Ottoman sultan. When her family moved back to Istanbul, Turkey, in the mid-1920s, Halet was "shocked by the black-shrouded women who came and visited us at home." Having survived bouts with typhoid and hepatitis as a child, she decided to focus on exercise to build her strength and health. In an interview, she said, "There were other activities like folk dancing and other dances at school, but I chose fencing." Halet eventually rose to the level of representing Turkey in the women's individual foil event at the 1936 Summer Olympics. The 20-year-old had grave reservations about attending the Nazi-run Games, and she and her fellow Turkish athletes drew the line at a social introduction to the Führer; she later said, "Our assigned German official asked us to meet Hitler. We actually would not have come to Germany at all if it were down to us, as we did not approve of Hitler's regime," she recalled late in life. "We firmly rejected her offer."

Upon returning home after the Games, Halet met communist poet and journalist Nail Çakırhan and fell in love. Her family didn't approve of his Marxist ideas, so they were married in secret; their marriage endured for 70 years until his death in 2008. She studied archaeology

in Paris at the Sorbonne in the 1930s before earning a doctorate at Istanbul University in 1944, then became a lecturer in 1947; that same year, she worked as part of a team excavating the 8th century Hittite fortress city of Karatepe in Turkey, which was to become her scholarly life's work. She spent half of each year there for the next 50 years, working with others to achieve a deeper understanding of Hittite hieroglyphic writing and other aspects of their culture. In 1960, Halet became a professor of Prehistoric Archaeology at Istanbul University and founded its Institute of Prehistory, achieving emeritus status in 1984. She lived to be 97.

ALICE COACHMAN: RUNNING FOR HER LIFE

Boy, could Alice Coachman run and jump! Because of World War II, however, national competitions were as far as an athlete could aspire in the forties, and the young African American athlete held the national titles for the high jump for twelve consecutive years. Her chance to achieve international recognition finally came in the 1948 Olympics; Alice was thought to be past her prime, but she decided to go for it anyway. Her teammates lost every race; finally it was Alice's turn for the high jump. She took the gold, defeating an opponent who towered above her in height, to become at age twenty-four, the first black woman to win Olympic gold and the first American woman to go for the gold in track and field.

Alice was warmly welcomed back to America with an invitation to the White House, a victory motorcade through her home state of Georgia, and a contract to endorse Coca Cola. Not surprisingly, the racist and sexist America of the forties didn't fully embrace Alice as it should have. She was, however, lionized in the black community as a favorite daughter and truly was the trailblazer for every black woman athlete to come after her.

ALTHEA GIBSON: NEVER GIVE UP

From the ghetto to the tennis court, Althea Gibson's story is pure sheroism. At a time when tennis was not only dominated by whites but by upper-class whites at that, she managed to serve and volley her way to the top.

Born in 1927 to a Southern sharecropper family, Althea struggled as a girl with a restless energy that took years for her to channel into positive accomplishments. The family's move to Harlem didn't help. She was bored by school and skipped a lot; teachers and truant officers predicted the worst for Althea, believing that she was a walking attitude problem whose future lay as far as the nearest reform school.

Although things looked dire for Althea, she had a thing or two to show the naysayers. Like many sheroes, Althea had to bottom out before she could get to the top. She dropped out of school and drifted from job to job until, at only fourteen, she found herself a ward of New York City's Welfare Department. This turned out to be the best thing that could have happened to Althea—a wise welfare worker not only helped her find steady work, but also enrolled her into New York's police sports program. Althea fell in love with paddle ball, and upon graduating to real tennis, amazed everyone with her natural ability. The New York Cosmopolitan Club, an interracial sports and social organization, sponsored the teen and arranged for her to have a tennis coach, Fred Johnson. Althea's transformation from "bad girl" to tennis sensation was immediate; she won the New York State Open Championship one year later. She captured the attention of two wealthy patrons who agreed to sponsor her if she finished high school. She did in 1949—and went on to accept a tennis scholarship to Florida Agricultural and Mechanical University.

Althea's battles weren't over yet, though. She aced nine straight Negro national championships and chafed at the exclusion from tournaments closed to nonwhite players. Fighting hard to compete with white players, Althea handled herself well, despite being exposed to racism at its most heinous. Her dignified struggle to overcome segregation in tennis won her many supporters of all colors. Finally, one of her biggest fans and admirers, the editor of *American Lawn and Tennis* magazine, wrote an article decrying the "color barrier" in tennis. The walls came down. By 1958, Althea Gibson won the singles and doubles at Wimbledon and twice took the U.S. national championships at the U.S. Open as well.

Then, citing money woes, she retired; she just couldn't make a living at women's tennis. Like Babe Zaharias, she took up golf, becoming the first black woman to qualify for the LPGA. But she never excelled in golf as she had in tennis, and in the seventies and eighties she returned to the game she truly loved, serving as a mentor and coach to an up and coming generation of African American women tennis players.

Through sheer excellence and a willingness to work on behalf of her race, Althea Gibson made a huge difference in the sports world for which we are all indebted.

MARTINA NAVRATILOVA: ALWAYS HERSELF

One of the all-time tennis greats, Martina Navratilova was a Czechoslovakian native who defected to the United States so she could manage her own career, rather than having the Czech government tell her what to do and where to go. During the eighties, she was the top-ranked women's tennis player in the world with a career record of seventy-five straight wins. She approached her career and training as serious business, a pure athlete in the truest sense. One of the first openly gay celebrities, Martina has been linked amorously with Rita Mae Brown, who penned a novel about their affair and was sued in a "galimony" suit by another lover, Judy Nelson, who went on to share a bed with Rita. Opines Martina, "I never thought there was anything strange about being gay."

THE ALL-AMERICAN GIRLS BASEBALL LEAGUE: BACKWARD AND IN HIGH HEELS

For the briefest time in the 1940s, women had a "league of their own." And while it was not intended to be serious sports so much as a marketing package, the All-Girls Baseball League stormed the field and made it their own. The league was the brainchild of chewing gum magnate Phillip K. Wrigley, whose empire had afforded him the purchase of the Chicago Cubs. He came up with the concept of putting a bunch of sexy girls out on the field in short skirts and full makeup to entertain a baseball-starved population whose national pastime was put on hold as baseball players turned fighting men.

He was right—the gals did draw crowds, enough to field teams in several mid-sized Midwestern cities. (At the height of its popularity, the league was drawing a million paying customers per 120 game season.) A savvy businessman catering to what he believed were the tastes of baseball fans, Wrigley had strict guidelines for his "girls"—impeccable appearance and maintenance, no short hair, no pants on or off the playing field. Pulchritude and "charm" were absolute requirements for players. Arthur Meyerhoff, chairman of the league, aptly characterized it as: "Baseball, traditionally a men's game, played by feminine type girls with masculine skill." For Meyerhoff, "feminine type" was serious business and he kept a hawkeye on his teams for the slightest sign of lesbianism. He also sent his sandlot and cornfield trained players to charm school to keep them on their girlish toes. Although the rules seemed stringent, the players were eager to join these new teams called the Daisies, the Lassies, the Peaches, and the Belles because it was their only chance to play baseball professionally. Pepper Pair put it best in the book she and the other AAGBL players are profiled in, "You have to understand that we'd rather play ball than eat, and where else could we go and get paid $100 a week to play ball?" After the war, men returned home and major league baseball was revived. However the All-Girls league hung on, even spawning the rival National Girl's Baseball League. With more opportunity for everyone, teams suddenly had to pay more money to their best players in order to hang on to them, and both leagues attracted players from all around the U.S. and Canada.

Penny Marshall's wonderful film, *A League of Their Own*, did a credible job portraying the hardship and hilarity of professional women athletes trying to abide by the rules and display feminine "charm" while playing topnotch baseball. Ironically, the television boom of the fifties eroded the audience for the AAGBL as well as many other semi-pro sports. The death blow to the women's baseball leagues came, however, with the creation of the boys-only Little League. Girls no longer had a way to develop their skills in their youth and were back to sandlots and cornfields, and the AAGBL died in 1954.

"The fans thought we were the best thing that ever came down the pike."

— player **Mary Pratt**

JOAN JOYCE: PERFECT PITCH

Joan Joyce should be a household name. In the words of a tournament umpire who watched her pitch a game, she was "one of the three best softball pitchers in the country, and two of them are men." Joan ended up in softball when she was blocked from playing baseball in the fifties. She recalled in an interview in *Sports Illustrated*, "I started playing softball at eight because my father played it and because it was the only sport open to me at the time." By her teens, she was astounding players, coaches, and parents alike with a fast ball clocked at 116 miles per hour. At eighteen, she joined the Stamford, Connecticut, all-girl team, the Raybestos Brakettes, and pitched the team to three consecutive national championships. Soon, the Brakettes were the force to be reckoned with in amateur softball, winning a dozen championships in eighteen seasons. Joyce's record was an unbelievable 105 no-hitters and thirty-three perfect games.

Joyce's reputation as an "unhittable" pitcher led to a challenge in 1962 between Joyce and Ted Williams, then a batting champion with a .400 average per season. A roaringly appreciative crowd watched her fan thirty pitches past the bemused Williams. He managed only a few late fouls and one limp hit to the infield. On that day, Joan Joyce showed she was not only just as good, but better than any man!

WILMA RUDOLPH: LA GAZELLE

Runner Wilma Rudolph's life is the story of a great spirit and heart overcoming obstacles that would have stopped anyone else in their tracks, literally! Born in Bethlehem, Tennessee, in 1955, Wilma contracted polio at the age of four and was left with a useless leg.

Wilma's family was in dire straits with a total of eighteen children from her father's two marriages. Both parents worked constantly to feed the burgeoning brood, her father as a porter and her mother as a house cleaner, and it was more important to feed Wilma and her siblings than it was to get the medical attention Wilma needed to recover the use of her leg. Two years later circumstances eased a bit, and at the age of six, Wilma started riding the back of the bus with her mother to Nashville twice a week for physical therapy. Although doctors predicted she would never walk without braces, Wilma kept up her rehabilitation program for five years and not only did the braces come off, but "by the time I was twelve," she told the *Chicago Tribune*, "I was challenging every boy in the neighborhood at running, jumping, everything."

Her exceptional ability didn't go unnoticed. A coach with Tennessee State University saw how she was winning every race she entered in high school and offered to train her for the Olympics, which Wilma hadn't even heard of. Nevertheless, she qualified for the Olympics at sixteen and took home a bronze medal in the 1956 Summer Games for the 100-meter relay. Still in high school, she decided to work toward a gold medal for the 1960 games.

Well, she did that and more. The three gold medals she won in the 1960 Olympics in Rome—in the 100-meter dash, the 200-meter dash, and the 4 X 100 relay—turned her into a superstar overnight. Wilma was the first American woman ever to win triple gold in a single Olympics. People were stumbling over the top of each other to find the superlatives to describe her. The French named Wilma "La Gazelle," and in America she was known as "The Fastest Woman on Earth." Wilma was everybody's darling after that, with invitations to the JFK White House and numerous guest appearances on television. The flip side of all the glory was, however, that Wilma received hardly any financial reward for her public appearances and had to work odd jobs to get through college.

One year later, Wilma again set the world on fire by breaking the record for the 100-meter dash: 11.2 seconds. Unpredictably, Wilma sat out the '64 Olympic Games and stayed in school, graduating with a degree in education and returning to the very school she had attended as a youngster to teach second grade. In 1967, she worked for the Job Corps and Operation Champion, a program that endeavored to bring star athletes into American ghettos as positive role models for young kids. Wilma herself loved to talk to kids about sports and was a powerful symbol with her inspiring story.

That Wilma touched the lives of children is best evidenced in a letter writing campaign taken up by a class of fourth graders in Jessup, Maryland, who requested the *World Book Encyclopedia* correct their error in excluding the world-class athlete. The publisher complied immediately! Wilma has also been honored with induction into both the Olympic Hall of Fame and the National Track and Field Hall of Fame. A film version of her autobiography *Wilma* starring Cicely Tyson was produced to tremendous acclaim. Her death from terminal brain cancer took place shortly after she received an honor as one of "The Great Ones" at the premiere National Sports Awards in 1993.

"I have spent a lifetime trying to share what it has meant to be a woman first in the world of sports so that other young women will have a chance to reach their dreams."

— Wilma Rudolph

EVELYN ASHFORD: THE POWER OF PERSISTENCE

"(Wilma Rudolph) inspired me to pursue my dream of being a runner, to stick with it," says runner Evelyn Ashford, whose incredible athletic staying power in a sport with a high burnout rate was notable. She participated in Olympic games for nearly twenty years, returning to pick up a gold medal in 1992 as a thirty-five-year-old mother of one. Evelyn was always gifted at sports, but never took herself seriously until a male coach noticed her speed and issued a challenge for her to race his male track team. When she beat the "best guy" on the field, Evelyn suddenly got the attention and positive support that spurred her on.

By 1975, she had earned a full scholarship to UCLA. One year later, she was a member of the Olympic team, but had to wait for the next games four years later to make her mark. In 1980, in protest of the Soviet Union's invasion of Afghanistan, President Carter made the choice to boycott the Summer Olympic games. Along with her peers, Evelyn Ashford's chances to win were dashed. But her persistence paid off in spades; she came back after the terrible disappointment and won a gold medal for the 100 meter sprint and another gold medal for the 400 meter relay in the 1984 Summer Olympic Games held in Los Angeles. Renowned as the perfect model of a good sport, on and off the field, she takes enormous joy in running with fellow champions Alice Brown, Sheila Echols, and Florence Griffith-Joyner, and promoting track and field as a sport. There's no doubt that Wilma Rudolph would be proud of Evelyn Ashford's accomplishments.

JACKIE JOYNER-KERSEE: QUEEN OF THE FIELD

Arguably the greatest cross category track and field star of all time, Jackie Joyner-Kersee has a string of firsts to her credit and keeps racking them up at an astonishing rate: she's the first U.S. woman to win gold for the long jump, the first woman ever to exceed 7,000 points for the heptathlon, and the first athlete, man or woman, to win multiple gold medals in both single and multiple events in track and field. Since her debut in the 1984 Los Angeles Summer Events, Jackie has been at the top of her game.

Along with her athletic prowess, Jackie's charisma and style made her an overnight sensation. In addition, she has a policy of giving back as good as she gets to the community she's from. She has a strong desire to nurture athleticism and scholarship in urban settings where access to a place to run and play is the first of many challenges ghetto kids face. Her foundation, the Jackie Joyner-Kersee Youth Center Foundation, is currently developing a recreational and educational facility for kids in East St. Louis where area kids will have access to a computer lab, library, ball fields, basketball courts, and of course, indoor and outdoor tracks.

Like several other outstanding athletes, Jackie comes from poverty, an alum of the poorest part of East St. Louis. Fortunately, Jackie received encouragement from her family to participate in sports. She discovered track and field at the Mayor Brown Community Center, and her Olympic dreams started when she saw the 1976 Olympics on television. Jackie quickly emerged as a veritable "sporting savant" and started breaking national records at fourteen, excelling at basketball and volleyball while maintaining a super grade point average. Soon she was courted by many tantalizing college scholarships, ultimately deciding to attend UCLA, where Bob Kersee would be her coach.

Bob Kersee, whom she married in 1986, convinced both Jackie and the powers-that-be at UCLA that Jackie's career lay in multitrack events. Looking back, it's hard to imagine Jackie anywhere but in the event where she is the best in the world. Jackie's forte is the seven-event heptathlon, a previously overlooked event in which athletes earn points by running a 200-meter dash, compete in both high and long jumps, throw both the javelin and shot put, run the 100-meter hurdles, and complete an 800-meter run, all in two days. These herculean challenges alone call for super-sheroism, and Jackie has not only made the heptathlon her own, but through her prowess made the event a track and field favorite.

She is one of the few African American athletes to get prestigious product endorsement contracts and is very aware of her opportunity to provide a positive role model, telling *Women's Sports & Fitness*, "I feel that as an African American woman the only thing I can do is continue to better myself, continue to perform well, continue to make sure that I'm a good commodity. If doors aren't opened for me, then maybe it will happen for someone else."

"I understand the position I am in, but I also know that tomorrow there's going to be someone else. So I try to keep things in perspective."

— Jackie Joyner-Kersee

FLORENCE GRIFFITH-JOYNER: GOING WITH THE FLO JO

Jackie Joyner-Kersee's brother, Al Joyner, was an Olympic athlete too. When he met the flamboyant Florence Griffith in 1984, the runner who made her mark on the track world as much for her long fingernails and colorful attire as for being "the world's fastest woman," she was working days as a customer service rep for a bank and moonlighting as a beautician at night. The former world-class runner had lost the gold to Valerie Brisco in 1980 and had given up. At Al's urging, she began training again. They also started dating seriously and got married soon after. This time, Florence had the will to win and stormed the 1988 Seoul Olympics to take home three gold medals. Off the track, "Flo Jo," as the press dubbed her, has devoted herself to working with children, hoping to educate the youth of America to "reach beyond their dreams," eat right, play sports, and stay away from drugs. After her record-setting gold medal races in Seoul, *Ms.* enthused, "Florence Griffith-Joyner has joined the immortals, rising to their status on the force of her amazing athletic achievement, aided by the singular nature of her personality and approach."

"Looking good is almost as important as running well. It's part of feeling good about myself."

— Florence Griffith-Joyner

ARLENE BLUM: "A WOMAN'S PLACE IS ON TOP"

Arlene Blum has made a success by doing what she's not "supposed" to do. Born in Chicago in 1945 and raised by her mother's parents, Arlene overcame "arithmaphobia" to go to the top of her class in mathematics and science, where she developed a taste for competing academically with boys. She decided to study chemistry at Portland's Reed College, ultimately earning a doctorate in chemistry from U.C. Berkeley. In an interview with *Ms.* in 1987, she indicated that this spirit of competition still propelled her, "I know that...girls weren't supposed to be chemists. And it's always sort of nice to do things you're not supposed to do." Reed's location near Oregon's mountain peaks was auspicious for the young scientist. She fell in love with mountain climbing and even worked it into her academic regimen by analyzing volcanic gas from the top of Mount Hood.

More exotic ranges beckoned, and Arlene soon trekked

to Mexican and Andean peaks. An eye-opening event happened when she submitted an application to be a part of a team destined for Afghanistan and was turned down for being a woman. After a second ejection for an Alaskan expedition, Arlene Blum took the "bull by the horns" and put together her own all-woman team of six climbers, all of whom made the peak of Alaska's Mount Denali (formerly known as Mount McKinley) in 1970. This was just the beginning for the barrier-breaking shero, who in 1978 took another all-woman team to Annapurna, one of the highest mountains in the world. At the time, only four teams had ever made it to the top of Annapurna, a treacherous mountain known for fierce storms and dangerous avalanches. In addition to the danger, such treks are always extremely expensive. Ever plucky, Blum and her team of Sherpas and sheroes paid their way to the top of Annapurna, the world's tenth highest peak, by selling t-shirts and gaining corporate sponsorship. The t-shirts became real conversation starters with the winning slogan, "a Woman's Place is on top...Annapurna!"

Amazing Arlene has gone on to walk the entire Great Himalayan mountain range, crest Everest, and organize many expeditions and explorations. She has also excelled at her other profession, chemistry, and helped identify a carcinogenic flame-retardant in children's clothing. Arlene's daughter Annlise joins her mother on climbs now, part of the generation of women for whom Arlene cleared the path. Arlene Blum showed the world that, when it comes to excluding women from sports, there "ain't no mountain high enough" to keep a good woman down!

"People say I've organized all-women's expeditions to show what we can do; but it wasn't like that. It was more a rebellion against being told I couldn't do something, or...that women couldn't do something."

— **Arlene Blum**

OTHER GALS WHO CLIMBED TO THE TOP

Fifty years earlier, Arlene Blum would not have been allowed in certain areas in the Great Himalayan range. It was an entirely different kind of explorer who helped open those gates. In 1924, spiritual seeker **Alexandra David-Neel** was the first Western woman to visit Tibet's "Forbidden City," Lhasa, in its mountain perch. Dressed as a beggar and traveling so light that they didn't even have blankets, the fifty-five-year-old Alexandra and a young monk, made the perilous climb up 18,000 feet to the holy city. Her travelogue is one of the most treasured resources in Asian studies, published as *My Journey to Lhasa.*

Opera singer turned scholar, the intrepid Frenchwoman also has the honor of being the first Western woman to have an audience with the Dalai Lama in his Indian exile. Alexandra never did anything halfway, and she found the study of Buddhism so appealing that she moved into an ascetic's snowy cave and undertook the studies and spiritual practice of a Buddhist nun. She became so adept that she reportedly was able to control her body temperature through meditation, and there are legends of levitation and other psychic phenomen. Pooh-poohing "the supernatural," her explanation for these matters is simple and practical: she learned from the Tibetans that it is all a matter of management of natural energies. One of the world's earliest scholars in Eastern Studies and Oriental mysticism, Alexandra David-Neel's unique combination of daring and curiosity made her one of the most fascinating women in any part of the world.

Then there's **Lynn Hill**. Although many of our sportsheroes have made strides for women simply by being the best, others, like Lynn Hill, have done so with

great intention. Lynn Hill is a world class climber whose stated mission is to create equality for women climbers in an admittedly steep arena. In what was previously a totally male-dominated sport requiring strength women "aren't supposed" to have, Lynn Hill rocketed to the top, demanded to be allowed to climb as well as any man. As she says, "If extreme athletics improves you as a person, why can't that be feminine?"

And don't forget **Annie Smith Peck**. She was a classical scholar born in 1850 with a yen for heights. Wearing a suit of animal skins explorer Robert Edwin Peary had brought back from his exploration of the Arctic Circle, she climbed the Andean apex of Mount Huascaran, and went on to become the foremost female mountain climber of her day. She was fifty-eight years old at the time. She wrote about her exploits and became quite a popular travel writer. One of her most sheroic exploits involved climbing the formidable Mount Coropuna in Peru and hanging a banner at the summit reading, "Votes for Women!" She didn't stop climbing until a year before her death at age eighty-five.

MYRIAM BEDARD: CANADIAN BI-ATHLETE

Well on her way to a successful career as a figure skater, Myriam Bedard hung up her figure skates as a young teenager to become a pioneer in one of the Olympic's newest sanctioned sports competitions for women: the much less glamorous and far more rigorous biathlon. It has an interesting history: for ancient Scandinavians, skiing and stalking prey were necessary for survival in their wintry climes. Infantry soldiers in World War II came to the same conclusion for completely different reasons, leading to the formation of military ski patrols in Norway, Finland, Sweden, and other parts of Scandinavia. The biathlon is a refinement of these origins but wasn't reorganized as an Olympic sport for men until 1960.

Women biathletes had to wait thirty-two more years to compete on the Olympic games. The young Myriam was ready.

She had been training for several years in a suburb outside Quebec City and quickly discovered the prohibition on firearms in Canada's public bus system. Resourcefully, she figured out how to tear her gun down so it could be transported in an innocent-looking violin case. Highly driven, Myriam started winning races at fifteen, even though the only ski boots she had were so big she had to stuff paper in the toes. Nevertheless, at the Lillehammer Olympics, she won the bronze medal for the 15-kilometer race.

Myriam's career has been cloaked in both mystery and controversy. Upon winning her Olympic prize, she stirred debate with her absolute refusal to sign Biathlon Canada's contractual agreement to cycle a portion of other earnings back to the organization, accompanied by a "gag order" to prevent media appearances by national biathletes. Her stubbornness, or independence, depending on the point of view, concluded in her suspension from Canada's team. A truce was won in time for her to rejoin the team and lead them to an exciting win in the 1993 world championships in Bulgaria. Bedard did Canada proud in Bulgaria, shooting past the Russian skier who had bested her in '92.

Her critics love to harp on her solitary ways and her secrecy with her private coach, whose name she refuses to reveal. When she performed with less than stellar speed at the 1993 winter trials, the naysayers came out in droves to predict gloom, doom, and disaster for Canada. Resolute in her own judgment and that of her "mystery coach," Myriam had simply decided to reserve her strength for the 1994 Olympic games in Lillehammer. Although her starting position for the 15-kilometer race was third from last, with the fierce concentration that has become her trademark, Bedard swept to the front and took the gold, following that victory with a second

win on the 7.5-kilometer race. A fascinating footnote to the Lillehammer triumphs is that she realized after her second race that she had on mismatched skis!
The reticent Myriam Bedard has become a much sought-after speaker in Canada and a national hero to Canada's youth, who cherish that she is one of the nation's all-time greatest Olympic champions. Bedard tries to balance all this with motherhood (she married a fellow biathlete in 1994) and her love of a quiet life. She walked her own path every step of the way and carved out a destiny in what is arguably the toughest of all Olympic sports.

"I like it when I strike sparks in people...after all, that's why I'm here!"

— Myriam Bedard

BONNIE BLAIR: SPEED RACER

Bonnie Blair has skated her way into the hearts of America. She comes from an entire family of skaters; Bonnie is the "baby" of the family, born in 1964. She was skating with ease by the age of two and was a competitor by four! When Bonnie was seven, her family moved from her birthplace of Cornwall, New York, to the Midwestern town of Champaign, Illinois. She won the state speed skating championship for her age group that same year.

In Illinois, Bonnie was fortunate to hook up with a great coach, Cathy Priestner, an Olympic champion herself. Cathy directed her toward Olympic-style speed skating and away from the pack racing that had been her strength. Age sixteen was certainly sweet for Bonnie when she skated 500 meters in 46.7 seconds at her debut as a potential Olympian. This gave her a taste of what it could be like to be the fastest woman on skates. However, Bonnie had some bumpy ice ahead—she didn't make the cut in the actual trials later. Another stumbling block that nearly felled her was money problems; the grueling expense of travel expenses and coaching was more than the Blairs could handle. But Bonnie's hometown rose to the occasion, and the local police force ran a ten-year campaign to raise funds to pay for their Olympic hopeful through sales of bumper stickers and t-shirts. Their generous spirit paid for Bonnie's training with the U.S. men's speed skaters in the Big Sky country of Butte, Montana.

Bonnie first came into global view in the Sarajevo games in 1984. She finished quite honorably, ranking eighth in the 500-meter speed skating race, but Bonnie knew she could do better. For the next Olympics, she focused even harder and increased the difficulty of her regimen—weight-training, running, biking, and roller-skating, all over and above the intense skating. Pushing herself was key for Bonnie. She started breaking world records in 1986 and took the U.S. championship every year from 1985 to 1990. In a power sport, Bonnie actually measured in as much smaller and lighter than many of her rivals from around the world.

After adopting her new style of training, 1988 was the first Olympics Bonnie participated in. She took a gold medal in the 500-meter race and set a world record of 39.10 seconds, beating out a German skater in the first place who had just set a world record. Bonnie didn't stop with that and took home the bronze for the 1,000-meter sprint. Bonnie became the best speed skater in the world in Calgary that day and kept her title at the 1992 games in Albertville, France, with two more gold medals. Bonnie also started winning hearts with her friendly, open manner and lack of pretension.

Odds were somewhat against veteran Bonnie in Lillehammer in 1994, but she did what no other woman has done and took two more gold medals. The emotional highlight of the games that year was not the other drama queen figure skaters—Harding and Kerrigan—but Bonnie Blair. Half the world cried with her as she took her gold and cried while the national anthem played during what was to be Bonnie's last Olympics. Bonnie Blair: the first woman to earn gold medals in three straight Olympic games and the first American woman to win five gold medals in the history of the Olympics.

"...I'm in this because I love what I'm doing."

—Bonnie Blair

SUSAN BUTCHER: THE LAST GREAT RACE ON EARTH

New Englander Susan Butcher had an unusual upbringing in the fifties, her parents Charles and Agnes Butcher felt girls should be treated the same as boys. With this atmosphere, their two daughters were exposed to carpentry, mechanics, shipbuilding, and anything else they cared to learn. Susan really enjoyed boat-building and restoration, and she applied to a special training school at sixteen but was turned down for being female. She also loved any activity where she could be outdoors. Every chance she got, she was outside with her beloved dog, Cabee. Her love of animals was such that her family thought she might aspire to veterinary science because she was "more comfortable with animals than she was with people." But Susan threw everyone a curve when she chose her life's work.

Moving to mountainous Boulder, Colorado, seventeen-year-old Susan opted against college to take up "mushing"—dogsled racing. Later, she moved to Fairbanks to attend the University of Alaska in order to participate in a special project helping forestall the extinction of musk oxen. Susan was definitely in the perfect setting to practice mushing; she got three dogs, moved to a remote Wrangell Mountain log cabin outside Fairbanks, and lived pioneer style, hunting for food and sledding her way around the snowy countryside. In 1977, her work with the endangered musk oxen took her to Unalakleet, the home of the "Last Great Race on Earth." Here, she met Joe Reddington, Sr., the founder of this race, more commonly known as the Iditarod Trail Sled Dog Race. Reddington immediately became a fan of Susan's who saw her talent with dogs and how hard she worked at mushing. He declared that one day Susan Butcher would be an Iditarod champion. His prescience was soon proven.

In the 1978 race, Butcher placed nineteenth as a first-timer. She then met a young lawyer and sled racer named David Monson. Although the relationship started out in a dispute over Susan's rather large, past-due debt for dog food to the company Monson represented, they fell in love, got married, and settled in Eureka, a hundred miles south of the Arctic Circle. They founded the Trail Breaker Kennels, and built 120 houses for racing dogs and four one-room cabins for human visitors and fellow racers. Friends say that she has a uniquely close bond with her dogs, treating them as she does people and finding the unique qualities that make each dog different. Susan just says the dogs are her "best friends."

She has continued to race every year since getting married, winning many times. Despite blizzards and eighty mile-per-hour winds, moose attacks, and a bad sled wreck, Susan has set records for speed in the Iditarod and made headlines around the world as the woman who could outrace any man in the most extreme climate on earth.

"Alaska—Where Men are Men and Women Win the Iditarod"

—slogan on more than one million t-shirts

sold since Susan Butcher first won "The Last Great Race"

OF COCKPITS, COCKS AND BULLS, AND OTHER "LADYLIKE" PURSUITS

Adalynn (Jonnie) Jonckowski: This card-carrying member of the cowgirl hall of fame has an unusual idea of a good time—hopping on the back of an angry bull and hanging on as long as possible. Called the "Belle of Billings" (Montana), she has repeatedly proved to be the world's best bull rider. Adalynn's winning attitude is evidenced here, "Any time you have the freedom to do what you want to do and exercise that freedom, you're a champ."

While Jonnie Jonckowski clings to the backs of angry Brahma bulls, **Julie Krone** has her own wild rides. Petite and determined, Julie Krone was the first female jockey to win Triple Crown, a race at the Belmont Stakes. She had shown that women can ride the winning race and has $54 million worth of purses to show for it. (Jockeys keep 10 percent of the take, quite a motivator!) Even though Julie says that "times have changed" for women, she will still occasionally be heckled with yells of "Go home, have babies, and do the dishes," when she *loses*. The wealthy winner's final comment: "In a lot of people's minds, a girl jockey is cute and delicate. With me, what you get is reckless and aggressive."

Shirley Muldowney, born Belgium Roque, took on one of the last bastions of machismo—drag racing—and came up a winner. She fell in love with cars at the age of fourteen in Schenectady, New York, racing illegally "when the police weren't looking." At fifteen, she married mechanic Jack Muldowney, and they became a hot-rodding couple. Shirley put up with enormous hostility from race fans and outright hatred from fellow drivers.

In 1965, she became the first woman to operate a top-gas dragster and went on to win seventeen National Hot Rod Association titles, second only to Don Garliz. Queen of the cockpit, Shirley Muldowney became an internationally famous superstar with a critically acclaimed film about her life and achievements, "Heart Like a Wheel."

Hockey is certainly no sport for lightweights. For many, taking shots from a bunch of big men with sticks might seem like a risky business, but to French Canadian **Manon Rheume**, it's the sport she loved. She is goalie for the Atlanta Knights and, as such, is the first woman to play professional hockey in the men's leagues. At five feet six and 135 pounds, Manon is slight compared to many of her team members and opponents, but she has proven her ability to stop a puck. The world is finally taking note of women's ability to play this sport overall; in the year 1998, women's ice hockey became a full medal sport at the Winter Olympics, no small thanks to Manon and others like her.

Then there's **Angela Hernandez**, surely to be admired for fighting for her right to bullfight in the birthplace of macho—Spain! In the polyester-laden year 1973, she demanded to be allowed to compete in the male-only zone of the bullring. This caused quite a commotion; how dare she question the 1908 law forbidding women to participate in the sport of horseback bullfighting. Twenty-year-old Angela took her case all the way to the courts, where the Madrid labor court ruled in her favor, allowing her to fight, but only on foot. But threatened males found another way to thwart her—the Ministry of the Interior wouldn't issue her a license. Would-be torero Angela refused to go quietly into the Seville sunset, loudly contesting her plight, "These damned men. What do they think they are doing? Women fly planes, fight wars, and go on safaris; what's so different about fighting bulls?"

JUDI SHEPPARD MISSET: SHE MADE THE CONNECTION

Not every shero's interest in physical fitness and sports results in Olympic glory. For most of us, just taking care of our bodies and ourselves is a herculean challenge in the wildly paced workday world. One unsung shero who offers solutions for this issue is Iowa's Judi Sheppard Misset, the founder and CEO of Jazzercise, Inc., who took her own passions for jazz music and dance and created a creative and healthy way for the not-necessarily-athletic to achieve health, fitness, and fun. A pioneer for this innovative program, Judi has devoted the last thirty years to developing a program that includes comprehensive nutrition and children's fitness awareness as well as options for the elderly and for inner-city families who have no access to playgrounds, gyms, and sports outside the streets. Judi has offered the benefit of accessible, easy, and joy-filled exercise that builds community at the same time. Obviously, in addition to "inventing" Jazzercise, Judi has also founded a very profitable empire along the way. A shero to the bone, Judi gives millions of dollars to myriad philanthropic causes. Apparently the Misset clan is a matriarchy, as evidenced by her daughter Shanna Misset's role as Vice President and latest spokesperson for Jazzercise. Brilliant and beautiful, Shanna is poised to lead

her mother's company into the new millennium!

• CHAPTER FOUR •

She Blinded Them With Science: Breaking New Ground

Parade magazine, one of the most widely read publications in the world, features a favorite columnist, Marilyn Vos Savant. Aside from drop-dead wit, tons of common sense, and apparent omniscience, Marilyn's distinction is that she has the highest I.Q. in the world. So you could certainly say the smartest person in the world is a woman.

Women dispelled the notion that men are smarter some time ago, thanks to the tireless efforts of shero scholars, thinkers, and scientists who dealt with the issue head on. As hard as it is to imagine, it wasn't all that long ago that women and minorities were shunted aside, blocked from opportunities, political office, and employment because of the age-old smear campaign that started with Eve (the Marilyn Vos Savant of her time, who quite obviously had more curiosity and chutzpah than Adam), indicting women on the charge that emotionalism lessened their intelligence and decision making abilities.

The ground-breaking women profiled in this section changed that for us by taking former Congresswoman Pat Schroeder's comment, "I have a brain and a uterus, and I use both" very seriously. In the fields of science, medicine, astronomy, genetics, physics, anthropology, and psychology, women have made their mark. From computer pioneer and mathematician "Amazing Grace" Murray Hopper who helped engineer the first commercial computer and COBOL computer language in 1955 to today's digerati diva Ester Dyson, women are forging ahead with sagacity, savvy, and inventive, original thinking. These brainy brilliants discovered galaxies, created theories, won Nobel Prizes in science, and in general were as at home (if not more so) in the lab or the field or the classroom as in the kitchen. They are an inspiration to us all.

CAROLINE HERSCHEL: SUPER STAR

Caroline Herschel's childhood in Hanover, Germany, didn't exactly prepare her to become one of the top two astronomers of her day! Born in 1750, her education didn't extend beyond violin lessons, playing, and learning to do household chores. Indeed, though she longed for an education and her father wished her to be trained as her brothers were in French, mathematics, and music, her mother had other plans for her, insisting that Caroline become her domestic slave. At ten, she got typhus, which stunted her growth—she never grew taller than four foot three inches, which prompted her father to proclaim that she must prepare for a life as an old maid. When she was in her early twenties, her elder brother, William, moved to Bath, England, and took Caroline along to keep house for him. An accomplished musician, William took pity on Caroline and gave her voice lessons. Soon she was the most famous soprano in the area.

William also had an avocation, which he supported with his musician's wages—he was an amateur astronomer, and Caroline ended up helping him around the observatory. Together, they scoured the heavens and later built telescopes to resell so they could build the equivalent of the Hubble of their day. Caroline became an expert in grinding and polishing the mirror they used to search the skies. William frequently traveled on business, and Caroline would fill in for him while he was gone. Soon visitors recognized her contributions, and King George III decreed that she should have a pension of fifty pounds. It was the first time a woman was recognized for her scientific contribution.

Then William discovered the planet Uranus, originally called Georgium Sidus, and soon he got the top gig as the Royal Astronomer. Meanwhile, Caroline was exploring on her own and went on to discover fourteen nebulae and eight comets. She also published a catalogue of 2,500 star clusters and nebula, as well as several other seminal astronomical references for which she received medals from England, Denmark, and Prussia. To discover the nebula, she had to teach herself mathematics; because she learned so late in life, she never was able to memorize the multiplication tables. She had to carry them around in her pocket.

One of the most famous women of her day, in 1828, when she was seventy-seven, the Astronomical Society awarded her its gold medal for her contributions to the celestial science. At eighty-five, she was elected with Mary Somerville as an honorary member of the Royal Astronomical Society, the first women to receive such an accolade.

"(I am) minding the heavens."

— Caroline Herschel

ADA LOVELACE - A SINGULAR MIND

Lord Byron remains a famed leader of the Romantic

movement, with his brilliant rhapsodic poetry, prose, and flamingly vivid personality and excesses; what is far less well-known is that his daughter was one of the great geniuses of all time and is considered the world's first computer programmer. Augusta Ada Byron was born in 1815; her father abandoned the family when she was one month old, and she never knew him. She was educated by private tutors, and her mother pushed her to focus on logic, math, and science, both because these were interests of her mother's and because her mother thought it might prevent Ada from manifesting the insanity she thought ran in Lord Byron's family. Ada was also forced to lie still for extended periods of time because her mother believed it would help her develop self-control.

In 1833, at age 17, Ada met Charles Babbage, a mathematician, mechanical engineer, philosopher, and inventor, who is credited with inventing the first mechanical computer; it was the beginning of a long friendship and working relationship. When she saw his prototype of the "difference engine", as he called it, she was captivated, and made a study of its blueprints as well as industrial steam machines to understand its function. Two years later, she married the Earl of Lovelace and was then known as Ada King-Noel, Countess of Lovelace. In 1841, she resumed her studies of mathematics and was given high-level research tasks by Professor Augustus de Morgan of the University of London. She also advanced her studies with the long-distance guidance of Mary Somerville.

In 1842-43, she translated an article in French by Italian engineer Luigi Menabrea on Babbage's new "analytical engine"; Babbage read her translation and asked her why she had not written such an article herself, since he considered her well able to do so, and urged her to articulate her own ideas on the subject. She responded by adding an extensive "Notes" section to the translated article, which were three times as long as the original article. These "Notes" included the first-ever algorithm – a mathematical computer program; also, within this text she broke new ground with her insight that an "analytical engine" could go beyond mere mathematical calculation and serve other purposes. They were published in an English science journal; Ada's authorship was identified only by her initials, "AAL" – in all likelihood this was because women were not seen as credible scientists at the time. Unfortunately, after this brilliant conceptual work, she became increasingly unwell and died of cancer at age 36 in 1852. Ada's contributions to computer science were not acknowledged until the 1950s; since then, she has received many posthumous honors for her work. In 1980, the U.S. Department of Defense named a newly developed computer language "Ada" after her. Ada died of uterine cancer in London in 1852.

"The intellectual, the moral, the religious seem to me all naturally bound up and interlinked together in one great and harmonious whole."

— Ada Lovelace

SOFYA KOVALEVSKY: IT PAYS TO BE CALCULATING

Russian child prodigy Sofya Kovalevsky wasn't allowed to study her favorite subject, mathematics, because of her gender. Her parents even threatened not to allow her to be educated at all if she was caught studying math. Wily and willful, Sofya found a way: working out equations on the back of old wallpaper in an unused room in her house, thus keeping her passion for numbers safely secret. She faced similar barricades when she was older and was denied admission to a university. Around 1870, Sofya married to get away from her stifling mother and an equally repressive Mother Russia and escaped to Germany, where she attended the University at Heidelberg. Soon she was calculating rings around other students and acquired a reputation as a top-notch mathematician in the elite realm of partial differential equations. By thirty-three, she received a professorial post at Stockholm's select university and was awarded the Prix Bordin from the French Academy of Sciences. A true Renaissance woman, Sofya also wrote a few novels and plays before her creativity was halted by an early death at a mere forty-one.

ELIZABETH BLACKWELL: MEDICINE WOMAN

After she was born in England, Elizabeth Blackwell's family moved to the United States in 1831, settling in Cincinatti when their sugar refinery in New York burned down in 1835. They were progressives, and Elizabeth's father, Samuel, had chosen to refine sugar from beets because it could be done without slave labor. However, the malaria-ridden Ohio River Valley soon took Samuel Blackwell's life, and the children all had to work to support the family. Musically talented Elizabeth taught music classes and assisted her siblings in running a boardinghouse in the family home. Elizabeth had a chance to teach in Kentucky but couldn't tolerate the idea of living in a slave state.

Befriended by Harriet Beecher Stowe, Elizabeth became very active in the anti-slavery movement and also exported her literary leanings, joining the Semi-Colon Club at Stowe's urgings. Elizabeth needed more intellectual stimulation than even the writing club offered, however, and spurned the attention of Cincinnati's young men in order to keep her mind clear for higher pursuits. When her father was alive, she had become accustomed to the excellent schooling and private tutors Samuel provided for his brood. Children were "thinking creatures," the elder Blackwells proclaimed. Further, they made sure that

the girls were taught all the same subjects as the boys, quite a rare notion for the time.
When her friend Mary Donaldson died of what was probably uterine cancer, Elizabeth Blackwell knew she wanted to become a doctor. Mary had told Elizabeth that she believed her illness would not have been fatal if her doctor had been a woman; a woman would have taken her seriously instead of her being dismissed as suffering from "woman troubles" and emotionalism. Elizabeth knew in her heart that Mary was right. Her long road to becoming a physician was more difficult than she could ever know, but her unswerving dedication to reaching her goal is a testament to Elizabeth Blackwell's character.

Elizabeth Blackwell was turned down by no less than twenty-eight medical schools in her attempt to study medicine! Even her ultimate triumph at the age of twenty-six in finally enrolling at Geneva College in New York was handled insultingly. Pressured by Joseph Warrington, a noted doctor from Philadelphia who admired Elizabeth's fierce combination of smarts and pure pluck, the board at Geneva decided to give Blackwell a chance. Wimpily, they left the vote up to the all-male student body, who as a joke voted unanimously to let her in. Blackwell had the last laugh, however, when she outperformed the lot of jokers and graduated at the top of the class. Far from taking away from her achievement, their mockery made her victory all the sweeter. But she faced more obstacles upon graduation.

Elizabeth first worked in a syphilis ward for women where she was greeted with rancor and resentment by all the male physicians. The only job she could get was in Paris at La Maternite hospital interning in midwifery. Then Elizabeth's hopes of becoming a surgeon were dashed when she lost her left eye to disease. She also interned a year in London, meeting Florence Nightingale and forming a friendship that lasted their lifetime. Blackwell fared no better in the United States when she tried to find work in her profession, finally going into private practice in New York City where she was deluged with obscene letters and accosted on the street as a harlot and an abortionist. Her initial interest in women's health was evidenced by her opening of the New York Dispensary for Poor Women and Children, where the unfortunate could receive medical attention. There, Elizabeth welcomed two more women doctors—Emily Blackwell, her sister, and Marie Zakrewska, both of whom had entered medical school with her help.

Blackwell's pioneering works are considerable: She authored a book titled *The Laws of Life*, lectured on the importance of women in medicine, organized a Civil War nursing outfit, and founded a health-inspection program run by the first African American female physician, Dr. Rebecca Cole. When she moved back to England in 1869, she added sex education and birth control to her lectures, argued against the use of animal testing, cofounded the British National Health Society, was a professor of gynecology at the brand new School of Medicine for Women, and wrote several more books and tracts, including her autobiography, *Pioneer Work in Opening the Medical Profession to Women*. Elizabeth died of a stroke at the age of eighty-nine, sixty-three years after she broke down the walls barring women from medicine.

> *"I am watching, my doubts will not be subdued. (I will) commit heresy with intelligence...if my convictions compel me to do it."*
>
> — **Elizabeth Blackwell**

WOMEN SCIENCE NOBEL PRIZE WINNERS

Physics 1903: Marie Curie, with others, "in recognition of the extraordinary services they have rendered by their

joint researches on the radiation phenomena discovered by Professor Henri Becquerel."
Chemistry 1911: Marie Curie, "in recognition of her services to the advancement of chemistry by the discovery of the elements radium and polonium, by the isolation of radium and the study of the nature and compounds of this remarkable element."

Chemistry 1935: Irene Joliot-Curie, with her husband, "in recognition of their synthesis of new radioactive elements."

Physiology or Medicine 1947: Gerty Theresa Cori, with her husband, "for their discovery of the course of the catalytic conversion of glycogen."

Chemistry 1964: Dorothy Crowfoot Hodgkin, "for her determinations by X-ray techniques of the structures of important biochemical substances."

Physiology or Medicine 1977: Rosalyn Yalow, with others, "for the development of radioimmunoassays of peptide hormones."

Physiology or Medicine 1983: Barbara McClintock, "for her discovery of mobile genetic elements."

Physiology or Medicine 1986: Rita Levi-Montalcini, with a male colleague, "for their discoveries of growth factors."

Physiology or Medicine 1988: Gertrude B. Elion, with others, "for their discoveries of important principles for drug treatment."

Physiology or Medicine 1995: Christiane Nusslein-Volhard, with others, "for their discoveries concerning the genetic control of early embryonic development."

Physiology or Medicine 2004 : Linda B. Buck. Buck and Axel were able to clone olfactory receptors and analyze rat DNA to "determine how the sense of smell works in all mammals." For this, the pair shared the Nobel.

Physiology or Medicine 2008: Françoise Barré-Sinoussi Barré-Sinoussi shared the Nobel for Physiology or Medicine with Luc Mantagnier, her mentor, and Harold zur Hausen, who discovered HPV and developed the cervical cancer vaccine. Barré-Sinoussi continues to work with developing countries to address the spread of and improve the treatment for HIV/AIDS.

Chemistry 2009: Ada E. Yonath For her work on protein biosynthesis and peptide bond formation, Yonath earned the Nobel Prize for Chemistry in 2009. Today, she is the director of the Helen and Milton A. Kimmelman Center for Biomolecular Structure and Assembly of the Weizmann Institute of Science.

Physiology or Medicine 2000: Elizabeth Blackburn and Carol W. Both women research telomeres, the end caps of chromosomes created by repeating stacks of "extra" DNA bases. When DNA replicates, these telomeres are shortened and the chromosomes deteriorate—the cause of aging and chromosome fusion, which leads to cancer. Blackburn and Greider set out to find the enzyme that protects the telomere and did.

Physiology of Medicine 2014: May-Britt Moser Moser was honored for the "discovery of cells that constitute a positioning system in the brain."

FLORENCE NIGHTINGALE: THE LADY WITH THE LAMP

Before Flo got in the game, nurses had little or no medical training and sported a reputation as prostitutes and

drunks. The Lady with the Lamp changed all that. Born in 1820 in Great Britain, Florence was a society girl more accustomed to salons and a silver spoon than trenches and scalpels. Well-traveled and afforded a classical education, Florence heard the call of God to a higher purpose soon after her coming-out ball at seventeen. Her family was shocked at her decision to pursue nursing—it was entirely too disreputable. Despite her parents' objection, she visited hospitals whenever she could. On a family trip to Germany, her parents finally gave in to Florence's pleas and allowed her to enroll in nurse's training at the Institute of Protestant Deaconesses in 1851. Upon graduation, Florence set about reforming the nursing profession with many important innovations and practical improvements at the London hospital for "Sick Gentlewomen" where she worked.

Florence was called to serve her country during the Crimean War when many wounded British soldiers lay dying in despicable conditions in Turkey. Instead of being greeted with gratitude, however, Florence and her brigade of trained nurses were treated with scorn and were regarded as a threat by the army doctors.

Undeterred, Florence flew into action, organizing a field hospital that treated 12,000 soldiers and saved countless lives. Florence earned her reputation as an angel of mercy the hard way, working twenty hours at a time and falling ill to many of the scourges that swept through the camp, including a terrible fever that weakened her joints and left her bald and emaciated. Florence Nightingale emerged as Britain's "national hero" of the war and came home to pomp and circumstance, becoming the first woman to receive the British Order of Merit in 1907. Florence had no time for honors and glory, however, preferring to continue her campaign for reform in medicine and public health until her death.

> *"Never again would the picture of a nurse be a tipsy, promiscuous harridan...In the midst of the muddle and the filth, the agony and the disease, she had brought about a revolution."*
>
> — **Cecil Woodham-Smith**, *historian*

MARIE CURIE: RADIANT MIND

The scientist Albert Einstein most admired was Marie Curie; he once enthused, "(she) is, of all celebrated beings, the only one whom fame has not corrupted." During her lifetime, Marie Curie (nee Marya Sklodowska) was the most famous scientist in the world, progenitor of the atomic age. Born in Warsaw in 1867, she rose from humble beginnings in Russian-ruled Poland as a governess to become the first person ever to earn two Nobel Prizes—in medicine and physics.

From childhood, Marya Sklodowska was known for her prodigious memory. When she was sixteen, her father, a teacher of physics and math, lost his savings, and she had to begin working, first as a teacher and later as a governess. In addition, she secretly took part in the "free university" movement where she read in Polish to women workers, which was strictly forbidden by the Russian powers that be. She helped finance her sister Bronia's education in France, with the provision that Bronia would then help her.

Marie's fortunes rose when she moved to Paris in 1891 and began studying at the Sorbonne, one of the few schools to admit female service students. Three years later, she had earned two degrees in physics and mathematics and

met the man she was to marry, Pierre Curie, who ran the laboratories at the Municipal School of Physics and Chemistry, where he also taught classes. Pierre welcomed his bride to pursue her studies and research independently at his lab. The list of firsts of Marie Curie goes on and on. She was the first to determine that *radioactivity*, a term she coined, begins inside the atom, the first woman to ever win a Nobel Prize in Physics, the first woman lecturer and first woman professor in the venerable Sorbonne's 600-year history, the first mother-Nobel Laureate of a daughter-Nobel Laureate.

Marie and Pierre Curies' discoveries revolutionized science and were the founding of modern physics. Unfortunately, the Curies both suffered from symptoms now known to have been the result of exposure to radiation. But at the time, Marie was on a roll. She identified two new radioactive elements in 1898, radium and polonium, which she named for her homeland. By 1900, Marie developed a hypothesis that moving particles made up the alpha rays emitted from uranium.

The dissertation Marie wrote based on her research was deemed to be the greatest contribution to science ever made by a doctoral student. Sadly, Marie suddenly lost her husband and lab partner, Pierre, to a fatal hit-and-run by a wagon. She carried on, raising her two children, teaching, and publishing her definitive treatise on radioactivity. Despite her accomplishments, Marie came under severe fire for an affair with scientist, Paul Longevin, who was married at the time. The press lambasted her, claiming that being a woman scientist and Polish, at that, certainly explained her indecency. Marie fought back, stating "nothing in my acts...obliges me to feel diminished."

In 1911, she was nominated to the Academy of Sciences and lost by two votes; it was claimed that she was unrecognized because she was a woman. However, said the Academy, the real reason was that she was only forty-three and had plenty of time to wait for another vacancy; the man they selected was old and would not have another chance for the honor. During World War I, she devoted herself to the development of x-ray technology, with the help of her daughter Irene. As her fame grew, she lectured around the world, receiving over 125 awards. Later she developed the Curie Foundation in Paris and, in 1932, helped found the Radium Institute in Warsaw, of which Bronia was the director. She died in 1934 of leukemia, caused by the research that had made her so well-known.

"Nothing in life is to be feared. It is only to be understood."

— **Marie Curie**

IRENE JOLIOT-CURIE: ALL IN THE FAMILY

For Irene Joliot-Curie, it was like mother, like daughter. During World War I, the duo started a mobile x-ray service that treated over a million patients. In 1918, Irene joined the Radium Institute in Paris, and together with her husband, Frederic Joliot-Curie, identified artificial radiation, sharing a Nobel Prize in 1935.

MARGARET SANGER: WOMAN REBEL

Unimaginably, there were laws against the use of contraceptives until the year 1965. But Margaret Sanger worked most of her life—from 1879 to 1966—to fight for women's rights to control their bodies, a battle still going on in the wake of *Roe v. Wade*. Margaret's passion for the topic was born of personal experience: She believed her mother's death at forty-nine was due to the physical

hardship of eighteen pregnancies (out of which eleven children lived).
After her mother's death, Margaret disobeyed her father's wish to stay and run the household for him, instead going to nursing school. She also fell in love with a young architect, William Sanger, during this time, and they were married in 1902. She conceived during their first year of marriage and had a hard time with the pregnancy. After the birth of a son, Margaret was told she would be an invalid for the remainder of her life and admitted to a sanitarium. Margaret, showing the willfulness of an independent mind, quickly bailed out of the sanitarium and took care of herself. This proved to be exactly the right thing to do, as her health again blossomed and she produced two more children.

Full-time housewifery and motherhood bored her, however, and she soon took a job as a nurse and midwife in New York's lower east side. Margaret's activism was stirred by the pitiful sights she saw of young, impoverished mothers "destined to be thrown on the scrap heap before they were thirty-five" dealing with unwanted pregnancies, and she resolved to do something about it.

She saw clearly the connection between reproductive rights for women and women's economic and social equality, convinced that birth control was the key not only to freedom for women but to a better world. Despite censorship laws, she started writing eye-opening articles on birth control and women's sexuality. A trip to Europe to check out the birth control scene there gave Margaret an evangelical fervor to change the state of things back home in America despite enormous opposition. Founding the American Birth Control League, Margaret also began publishing *Woman Rebel*, which nearly landed her in jail when a court ordered her to shut the magazine down after the U.S. Post Office refused to deliver it for using the phrase "birth control." Unstoppable, she circumvented the post office by handing out a circular, *Family Limitation*, telling women everything they needed to know about birth control; by 1917, she had given away 160,000 copies.

In 1916, she started the first birth control clinic in the country in Brooklyn with the help of her sister and a Yiddish-speaking friend. The clinic was an immediate hit with the women of the boroughs, and 500 women visited in less than two weeks before a police raid landed Margaret in jail. All was not lost, however; the judgment handed down from the court stated that doctors could discuss birth control in the context of prevention of venereal diseases. This gave Sanger the opening she needed and her efforts began to bear fruit. During World War I, the U.S. military distributed condoms to the soldiers, along with Sanger's pamphlet. "What Every Girl Should Know." She continued to lecture and founded various birth control clinics. In 1953, she founded the International Planned Parenthood Federation; there are now more than 300 doctor-staffed Planned Parenthood clinics in the country. She was also instrumental in gaining financial support for the initial research into the birth control pill.

Margaret Sanger is truly the mother of reproductive rights. She fought on behalf of the cause for more than fifty years and was jailed nine times. Her battle for voluntary motherhood was an incredibly important step in women's liberation; as historian Ellen Chesler remarked, "Every woman in the world today who takes her sexual and reproductive autonomy for granted should venerate Margaret Sanger."

"No gods! No masters!"

— the slogan of **Margaret Sanger** *Woman Rebel*

FAYE WATTLETON: FOOTSTEPS TO FOLLOW

Faye Wattleton was working as a student nurse at Harlem Hospital when one particular case drew her attention to the importance of safe and legal abortion. It was "a really beautiful seventeen-year-old girl" she recalls. "She and her mother had decided to induce an abortion by inserting a Lysol douche into her uterus. It killed her." That's when Faye became a reproductive rights activist, holding various positions in public health administration and the Planned Parenthood Federation of America (PPFA), before being elected in 1978 to the PPFA presidency. Ironically, Faye was giving birth when she won!

She carries the triple honors of being the first woman, the first African American, and the youngest person ever to head up PPFA. Over the years, she has worked valiantly to fight the barriers constantly being put in the way—President Reagan's "squeal rule" to notify parents of distribution of birth control or information, the "gag rule" preventing abortion counseling, and the Supreme Court's challenge to *Roe v. Wade*. She resigned the presidency in 1992. Pointing to her contributions, Arthur J. Kopp of People for the American Way noted, "her remarkable ability to communicate difficult issues have made her a giant in the ongoing battle to preserve Americans' fundamental liberties."

MARGARET MEAD: COMING OF AGE IN AMERICA

Margaret Mead still stirs controversy in some circles for her pioneering work in social anthropology. Like Rachel Carson, she wrote a scientific study that crossed over into the general population and became a bestseller. For this, she received derision from the academic community. But

that didn't bother the free spirit, who was one of the first women to earn a PhD in anthropology.
Margaret was fortunate to be born in 1901 into a family of academics who disregarded convention and put learning and involvement in the world ahead of society's rules. The firstborn of five children, Margaret's parents were Edward Mead, a professor at Wharton School who taught finance and economics, and Emily Fogg Mead, a teacher, sociologist, and ardent feminist and suffragist. Margaret was homeschooled by her very able grandmother, a former teacher and school principal.

Margaret didn't fall too far from the tree when she started The Minority, an antifraternity at DePauw University, where she was attending. Bored, she transferred to Barnard College where the academic standards were more in accordance with her needs. Originally an English major, Margaret attended a class in her senior year given by anthropologist Franz Boas, a virulent opponent of the school of racial determinism. She also met Ruth Benedict, then Boas' assistant, who encouraged Margaret to join Columbia under Boas' instruction. Margaret agreed and went on to graduate school after marriage to a seminary student, Luther Cressman. Soon after, true to her heritage as a free-thinking Mead, Margaret went against her mentor Boas' urgings to do field work with America's Native peoples, a pet project of his; instead she followed the beat of her own different and, as it turns out, tribal drums, setting off for Polynesia to explore the island culture. She reasoned that they were better subjects because they had been less exposed and, therefore less assimilated than Native Americans. She was absolutely right, writing up her field studies after living with and working alongside the Samoans for three years. The date was 1926. Divorcing Luther, she married Reo Fortune, and a mere three years later, published *Coming of Age in Samoa*, a ground-breaking work that shocked some circles for its frank and completely objective report of, among other

things, sexual rituals and practices among the Samoans. Nearly overnight, Margaret was a superstar, fairly rare for anthropologists and even rarer for twenty-six-year-old female anthropologists!

After a stint in the American Museum of Natural History, Margaret got the jones for another field study, so she and Reo headed to New Guinea. Her resulting book, *Growing Up in New Guinea*, was another huge hit in both academic and popular circles. While in New Guinea, Margaret met and fell in love with fellow anthropologist Gregory Bateson; after her second divorce, she and Gregory married and she gave birth to her daughter, Mary Catherine Bateson. They worked together in New Guinea, but ultimately Gregory claimed that she was stifling his creativity and they divorced in 1943.

Margaret Mead spent the rest of her life working full-tilt in the field of anthropology, publishing forty-four books and over one thousand articles and monographs, and working as a curator at the American Museum of Natural History between trips to the field. She also sought to support and finance the work of young anthropologists. At the core of all her work was an analysis of childhood development (she was the first anthropologist ever to study childrearing practices) and gender roles, overturning many time-worn assumptions about personality and place in society for both sexes. Over and over, her studies demonstrated that there is nothing natural or universal about particular "masculine" or "feminine" roles; rather they are culturally determined. Detractors damn her fieldwork as being "impressionistic," but Margaret Mead's success in a male-dominated scientific field was a wonderful contradiction to the typical role for an American woman of her day and age. With forty-four books, she became a household name, made anthropology available for the masses, and blazed a trail for shero scholars of future generations.

"I have spent most of my life studying the lives of other peoples, faraway peoples, so that Americans might better understand themselves."

— **Margaret Mead**

OLGA SKOROKHODOVA: TRUE VISIONARY

Olga Ivanovna Skorokhodova was a Soviet scientist, writer, teacher, and therapist. Born to poor Ukrainian peasant parents circa 1911, she was a sickly child who proved to have great strength of spirit and a powerful mind. Olga lost her sight and hearing at age five after a bout with meningitis. When her mother died in 1922, Olga was sent to a school for the blind in Odessa. Three years later, Olga arrived at the School-Clinic for Deafblind Children in Kharkiv; though at that point she was almost completely mute, under the care of Professor Ivan Sokolyansky she was able to recover the ability to speak. She began to keep self-observation notes. In 1947, she published a book titled *How I Perceive the World*; it drew public interest to how she was able to recover speech and won the K.D. Ushynsky literary prize. She expanded upon this original work with 1954's *How I Perceive and Represent the World* and 1972's *How I Perceive, Imagine and Understand the World*. Olga became a research fellow at the USSR Institute for the Handicapped for the Academy of Educational Sciences in 1948, later rising to be a senior research fellow, and worked there for the rest of her life. She authored a number of scientific works concerning the development of education and teaching of deaf/blind children.

"I must say I owe all of my knowledge and literary speech to reading, above all fiction."

— **Olga Skorokhodova**

KAREN HORNEY: FACING THE FATHER COMPLEX

Freud frequently tarried overlong on theories of hysteria and other so-called female neuroses. The first critic to respond to these theories was Karen Horney who challenged his bias against women, stressing the social rather than the biological factors in feminine psychology. She also argued that neurosis is not inevitable, but arises from childhood situations that are preventable. She met with much opposition for her sensitivity toward the plight of the patient, and her peers were appalled at her cheek in daring to criticize the "Big Daddy" of psychoanalysis.

But she was no stranger to making her own way. Born in Germany in 1885, Karen Danielson surprised her blustery and abusive Norse sea-captain father by insisting on not only seeking higher education, but studying medicine, whether he liked it or not. At university, Karen met a law student, Oscar Horney, and they married in 1909. While earning her medical degree from the rigorous University of Berlin—her thesis was on traumatic psychoses—she had three daughters in four years.

Undergoing psychoanalytic training from 1914 to 1918, she first opened a private practice while a faculty member at the Berlin Institute, where she applied a special affinity for trauma victims while working with shell-shocked veterans of World War I. Beginning around this time, Karen sought to overturn Freud's theory of penis envy, a tired theory at best, reasoning that it is not the penis women envy, but the privilege modern society accords men in contrast to the suppression of women. Horney posited an alternate theory: the castration complex in young girls is brought on by their inability to follow their father's path, when doors open for men are slammed shut for women. Her theory was fairly well received and established her as a force to be reckoned with.

Karen's independent streak didn't end with her neo-Freudian theorizing; she divorced her husband in 1926 and emigrating to Chicago, cofounding the Chicago Institute for Psychoanalysis. The New York Psychoanalytic Institute was next on her plate where she taught, did clinical research, and began a career as an author, publishing *The Neurotic Personality of Our Time* to high praise and *Our Inner Conflict*, a book about denial of pain that sounds like it would do fine in the popular self-help world we live in today. Karen Horney refused to agree with the accepted psychoanalytic gospel of the day and continued to emphasize the effect of environment upon the psyche. "There is no such thing as a normal psychology that holds for all people," she proclaimed.

Perhaps Horney's optimism was the biggest division between her and the rest of the psychoanalytic pack. She believed people could help themselves. She had a severe parting of the ways with her peers when she suggested that patients need not live a life of pain, a Freudian notion, and that people can work out of their neuroses. She was booted out of the New York Psychoanalysis Society and Institute in 1941 upon the publication of her book, *New Ways in Psychoanalysis*, which laid out a series of refutations and refinements of Freud's doctrine. Undaunted, she founded her own institute, taking several other free-thinkers with her.

Karen Horney was way ahead of her time. Had she lived fifty more years, she would be safely ensconced in a comfy chair across from Oprah Winfrey, where her self-help positivity would be fully embraced. Psychoanalytic pioneer and humanist, Karen Horney shows us that even the most sacred of cows need to be led off to pasture, especially if they're wrong! Here's to the shero who deep-sixed penis envy!

"Life itself still remains a very effective therapist."

— Karen Horney

ANNA FREUD: A MIND OF HER OWN

Pop culture may relegate Anna Freud to minor league status because of her associations with two icons, papa Sigmund Freud and patient Marilyn Monroe. But she should be remembered for her own ground-breaking work in child analysis and developmental psychology, collected in her eight-volume *Writings*. Although she didn't overturn her father's theories, she cultivated her own, concluding that an individual's psychology developed uniquely from an influence of a number of what she called "developmental lines." This multicausal approach to therapy was very different from the order of the day, attracting many patients to her clinic, including the famous blonde bombshell actress, the divine MM.

HANNAH ARENDT: A LIFE OF THE MIND

German-born Hannah Arendt was a political theorist and philosopher who climbed out of the ivory tower to take direct action against the spread of Fascism. A student of theology and Greek and the protege/lover of German existentialist philosopher Karl Heidegger, the brilliant student was granted a Ph.D. from the University of Heidelberg at the ripe old age of twenty-two. After a brief arrest by the Gestapo (she was Jewish), she fled to Paris where she worked for a Zionist resistance organization that sent Jewish orphans to Palestine in the hopes of creating a new united Arab-Jewish nation.

By 1940, she had fled to New York where she lived among other immigrants and worked for the Council on

Jewish Relations, as an editor for Shocken Books, and served at the head of the Jewish Cultural Reconstruction, which, post-war, collected Jewish writings that had been dispersed by the Nazis. With her first book, *The Origins of Totalitarianism*, she pointed out the common elements in Nazi and Stalinist philosophies as well as discussing the roots of anti-Semitism and racism through all of Europe. Her subsequent books include *On Revolution, The Human Condition,* and *Thinking and Writing*, as well as discussion of the trial of a Nazi war criminal, *Eichmann in Jerusalem: A Report on the Banality of Evil*, and countless articles and commentaries on such far-reaching subjects as Watergate, Vietnam, and her famous attack on Bertolt Brecht for his "Hymn to Stalin." The first woman to become a full professor at Princeton, she also taught at various other institutions and translated and edited the works of Franz Kafka.

A serious thinker, she became a very public and controversial figure with her beliefs that revolution and war were the central forces of the twentieth century; that there was little organized resistance on the part of the Jews in Europe; and that the Nazis were not monsters but pragmatic rational people accepting evil commands in a banal manner.

Arendt's contributions to the intellectual community are beyond calculating. She made an insular forties America and post-war world look deeply at all the possible causes of the Holocaust. According to his article in *Makers of Nineteenth Century Culture,* Bernard Crick credits Hannah Arendt with "rescue(ing) American intellectuals from an excessive parochiality."

"Human beings...[are] put into concentration camps by their foes and into internment camps by their friends."

— Hannah Arendt

BARBARA MCCLINTOCK: GENE GENIE

When geneticist Barbara McClintock presented her findings about morphing genes in 1951 after a ten-year scientific study, the result was what is commonly known as a "roof job." Her peers just didn't get it; it went right over their heads. A pack of rabid Darwinists, her colleagues preferred to keep to the accepted notions of the day, that genetic change was random in the evolution of a species. Undeterred, Barbara went back to the drawing board and the sixty-hour-a-week lab schedule she set for herself. She preferred the relative peace of her lab to people, preferred corn to fruit flies (the research subject du jour) and she preferred to not publish her work, figuring it would be too much for her uptight colleagues to handle. As it turns out, Barbara McClintock was right an awful lot of the time.

Even as a young child, Barbara McClintock was content in her own company, pursuing her own interests. An avid reader, she was also quite a tomboy, preferring cards and engines to dolls and pots and pans, having no truck with other little girls and the sugar and spice routine. She quickly found her thing—science—and pursued it with a single-minded relentlessness that served her well through the years. Despite the displeasure of her parents, Barbara chose agricultural science as her field of study at Cornell. She performed brilliantly and was asked to stay on for the graduate program in genetics, where she earned a PhD.

She then began to teach and do research, so far ahead of the pack that she became one of only a handful of scientists in the world to first realize chromosomes were the foundation of heredity and to work from this vantage point and understanding. Indeed, she was the scientist to *discover* the nucleolar organizer within the structure of the chromosome that was the indicator of order during cell division. It would be thirty years after her discovery before science was able to explain her finding in terms of molecular biology. Despite this remarkable beginning to her career and an outstanding record as a genetic researcher, Barbara was never given a promotion while at Cornell. She left for Cold Harbor Laboratory, where her work so impressed everyone that she was elected to the national Academy of Sciences in 1944 and went on to become president of the Genetics Society of America. The first woman to do so!

Not one to rest on her laurels, Barbara McClintock continued with her groundbreaking work, racking up all kinds of awards, prizes, and firsts. She became the first woman to receive an unshared Nobel Prize in physiology and medicine, and has been called the most important geneticist of the late twentieth century. She worked at Cold Harbor until her death in 1983 in the lab where she discovered what everyone wasn't ready to see.

It might seem unfair to reward a person for having so much fun over the years."

— Barbara McClintock

MARY JACKSON: A PIONEER BOTH IN RESEARCH AND ENDING DISCRIMINATION AT NASA

Mary Jackson, born in 1921, was an African-American mathematician who rose to the position of NASA's first black female engineer. She had earned double-major bachelor's degrees in mathematics and physical science in 1942, but worked as a schoolteacher, bookkeeper, and clerk for nearly the next decade before being recruited in 1951 to the gender and color-segregated "human computer" department by NACA, NASA's predecessor as an aerospace agency. A couple of years later, she took another NASA position with an engineer working on the

Supersonic Pressure Tunnel; she was encouraged to do graduate-level physics and math studies so she could be promoted to an engineering position. These UVA night courses were given at an all-white high school; she had to petition the city of Hampton, Virginia, her home town, for special permission to attend classes with white students. But nevertheless she persisted, and in 1958 became an aerospace engineer at what was now renamed NASA, researching airflow around aircraft.

While her contributions to aerodynamic studies were significant, after many years Jackson took an in-depth look at the inequalities built into the agency and saw that she could have the greatest impact in a formal human resources role. In 1979, she took on a new role as an affirmative action program manager and federal women's program manager at NASA, taking a cut in pay to do so. In that position, she was able to make changes that empowered women and people of color, and helped managers to see the capabilities of their black and female employees. Even at the point that NASA administrators were finally forced to acknowledge black women's work at the agency, the public generally had no idea about the contributions of the black women of NASA. Mary Jackson, together with two other veterans of the "human computer" segregation of women of color at the agency, inspired Margot Lee Shetterly's book, *Hidden Figures: The American Dream and the Untold Story of the Black Female Mathematicians Who Helped Win the Space Race*, which was recently adapted into an acclaimed motion picture.

Dorothy Vaughan

katherine Johnson

KATHRYN PEDDREW: A "HUMAN COMPUTER"

Kathryn Peddrew was an African-American woman who made mathematical and research contributions to the early development of U.S. space flight, despite racial and gender discrimination. Born in 1922, she graduated from college with a chemistry degree and had hoped to join a research team led by one of her college professors studying quinine-caused deafness in New Guinea, but was denied the opportunity because the team had made no arrangements to house women separately from men. (At the time, coed housing would have been considered a scandal.) Instead, Kathryn decided to apply for a position in the aeronautical agency's chemistry research division. She was hired by NACA, which would later become NASA, in 1943. But when administrators learned she was black, they changed their minds about placing her in the chemistry job and transferred her to the computing division instead, which had a segregated section for the black female "human computers" – even though she had a degree in chemistry. Over the course of her career at NACA/NASA, Kathryn worked in both aeronautics and aerospace, and studied balance in the Instrument Research Division. She spent her entire career there, retiring in 1986.

CHRISTINE DARDEN: WHEN YOU HEAR A SONIC BOOM, THINK OF HER

Racial and gender discrimination in hiring practices at NASA hadn't improved much by the time Christine Darden applied for a position in the late 1960s. Darden, despite her master's degree in applied mathematics, which qualified her for a position as an engineer, was instead assigned to the segregated female "human computer" pool, the same as numbers of other black female scientists. She approached her supervisor, asking why men with the same education as she had wider opportunities, and gained a transfer to an engineering job in 1973, becoming one of a tiny number of female aerospace engineers at NASA Langley. In this role, she worked on the science of sonic boom minimization, writing computer test programs as well as more than 50 research articles in the field of high lift wing design. In 1983, Darden earned a doctorate, and by 1989 she was appointed to the first of a number of management and leadership roles at NASA, including that of technical leader of the Sonic Boom Team within the High Speed Research Program, as well as director of the Program Management Office of the Aerospace Performing Center in 1999. She worked at NASA until retirement in 2007.

"I was able to stand on the shoulders of those women who came before me, and women who came after me were able to stand on mine."

— Christine Darden

ANNIE EASLEY: GIRLS WHO CODE

Annie Easley was an African-American computer scientist and mathematician as well as an actual rocket scientist. After joining NASA in 1955, she became a leading member of the team that wrote the computer code used for the Centaur rocket stage. Easley's program was the basis for future programs that have been used in military, weather, and communications satellites. After taking college courses first one and then two or three at a time, she had to take three months of unpaid leave in 1977 to finish her degree; NASA normally paid for work-related education, but every time she applied for aid, she was turned down. But once she finished her bachelor's degree, personnel decided she had to take yet more specialized training to be considered a "professional," despite this discrimination. Easley continued as a NASA research scientist until 1989, making contributions in many areas, including hazards to the ozone layer, solar energy and wind power, and electric vehicles. She also worked concurrently as NASA's Equal Employment Opportunity officer, a position where she could address discrimination problems in the agency and work for more fair and diverse employee recruitment.

SHIRLEY JACKSON: BLACK BRAINIAC

Shirley Jackson is a highly-regarded physicist and the first black woman to earn a PhD from MIT. Her doctoral research project was in theoretical particles. Shirley has gone on to not only receive numerous awards and the highest praise for her work in elementary particles, but also for her advocacy of women and minorities in the science field. In 1995, Vice President Al Gore celebrated her contributions and her drive to be the best at her swearing in as chairman of America's Nuclear Regulatory Commission. Gore told the audience that a four-year-old Shirley Ann Jackson informed her mother that one day she was going to be called "Shirley the Great." Shirley made good on her promise as she pushed down barriers of segregation and bigotry to become one of the top scientists in the nation.

"I had to work alone...at some level you have to decide you will persist in what you're doing and that you won't let people beat you down."

— Shirley Jackson

SALLY RIDE: PIONEERING THE EXTRATERRESTRIAL FRONTIER

Sally Ride was a physicist and the first American female astronaut. Born in 1951, she grew up in Los Angeles, the daughter of a political science professor. Besides her interest in the physical sciences, she was also a nationally ranked tennis player. She went to Swarthmore College for a couple years, then transferred to Stanford University as a junior. At Stanford, she first earned double major bachelor's degrees in physics and English and then went on to obtain a PhD in physics there in 1978, with a focus on astrophysics and free electron lasers. That same year, Sally was accepted into NASA's astronaut training program - a coup, since a thousand others had applied. After completing their rigorous program, Sally became the first U.S. woman astronaut as part of the crew of the space shuttle Challenger in 1983; only two women made it into space before her, both members of the Russian space program. As part of the Challenger crew of five, she deployed satellites and did pharmaceutical experiments.

The next year, Sally flew another shuttle mission and logged a total of 343 hours in space; she did eight months of special training for a third shuttle mission, but when the Challenger tragically exploded in a disastrous launch malfunction in January of 1986, the mission was canceled. She headed a subcommittee on the presidential commission that investigated the shuttle explosion; many years later, after her death, it was revealed by General Donald Kutyna that she had discreetly given him key engineering information that led to identifying the cause of the explosion. She continued with NASA at their headquarters in Washington, D.C., after which she led NASA's first strategic planning initiative and founded its new Office of Exploration. Sally left NASA in 1987 to work at Stanford's Center for International Security and Arms Control. In 1989, she became a physics professor at UC San Diego as well as director of the university's California Space Institute.

In 2001, Sally started Sally Ride Science, a company that created educational programs and products whose aim was to inspire girls to stay with their interests in science and math, serving as the company's president and CEO. She received the NASA Space Flight Medal as well as the NCAA's Theodore Roosevelt Award and later inducted into the National Women's Hall of Fame and the Astronaut Hall of Fame. Before passing away from pancreatic cancer, Sally Ride left her mark on Earth as well as in space. After her passing, it was revealed that she had been partners with another woman, a school psychology professor, for 27 years; Tam O'Shaughnessy now carries on Sally's legacy as the CEO and chair of the board of Sally Ride Science.

"When you're getting ready to launch into space, you're sitting on a big explosion waiting to happen. You have to reach a level of comfort with that risk."

— **Sally Ride**

MAE JEMISON: FIRST AFRICAN-AMERICAN WOMAN IN SPACE (BUT NOT THE LAST)

How many Americans are multilingual, let alone fluent in Swahili, Japanese, and Russian? Mae Jemison is an engineer and physician as well as a U.S. astronaut - an exceptional achiever by any measure. She was born in 1956 in Decatur, Alabama; her family soon moved to Chicago, for a chance at better schools and jobs. As a child, she remembers assuming that she would one day escape terrestrial confines: "I thought by now we'd be going into space like you were going to work." Though her teachers were not especially supportive of her interest in science, her parents encouraged her; she was also attracted to the art of the dance and studied ballet, jazz, modern, and African dance. She graduated early and started at Stanford University at age 16 on a National Achievement Scholarship, graduating in 1977 with a degree in chemical engineering; she also fulfilled the requirements for a B.A. in African and Afro-American studies. Being a black female engineering major was no easy thing; as she recalls, "Some professors would just pretend I wasn't there. I would ask a question and a professor would act as if it was just so dumb, the dumbest question he had ever heard. Then, when a white guy would ask the question, the professor would say, 'That's a very astute observation.'"

In 1981, Jemison earned an MD from Cornell Medical College. During her years at Cornell, she spent some of her time providing primary medical care in Cuba, Kenya, and a Cambodian refugee camp in Thailand; she also kept up her studies of dance at the Alvin Ailey School. She interned at Los Angeles County-USC Medical Center and then worked as a general practitioner. She joined the Peace Corps in 1983 and spent the next two years as the medical officer responsible for corps volunteers' health in Sierra Leone and Liberia, as well as assisting with CDC vaccine research.

After completing her hitch with the Peace Corps in 1985, Jemison felt that since fellow Stanford alumna Sally Ride had succeeded in her quest to go to space, the time was ripe to follow her longtime dream, and she applied to join NASA's astronaut training program. The Challenger disaster of early 1986 delayed the selection process, but when she reapplied a year later, Jemison made the cut, becoming the first African-American woman ever to do so. She was one of only 15 chosen out of 2,000 who tried. When she joined the seven-astronaut crew of the space shuttle Endeavour for an eight-day mission in the fall of 1992, she became the first African-American woman in space, logging a total of over 190 hours in space. She conducted medical and other experiments while aloft.

After leaving the astronaut corps in spring of 1993, she was named to a teaching fellowship at Dartmouth, and taught there from 1995 to 2002; she is a Professor-at-Large at Cornell, and continues to advocate for science education and for getting minority students interested in science. She has also founded two companies, the Jemison Group and BioSentient Corp to research, develop and market various advanced technologies, as well as the Dorothy Jemison Foundation for Excellence, named for her mother, who was a teacher. "The Earth We Share" science camps are among the foundation's initiatives, as well as the "100 Year Starship" project. Jemison has received many awards as well as honorary doctorates from institutions including Princeton, RPI, and DePaul University. Various public schools and a Chicago science and space museum have also been named for her. She has appeared in several TV shows, including an episode of Star Trek: The Next Generation, by the invitation of LeVar Burton.

"When I'm asked about the relevance to Black people of what I do, I take that as an affront. It presupposes that Black people have never been involved in exploring the heavens, but this is not so. Ancient African empires – Mali, Songhai, Egypt – had scientists and astronomers. The fact is that space and its resources belong to all of us, not to any one group."

— **Mae Jemison**

EILEEN COLLINS: ROCKET WOMAN: FIRST U.S. SPACE SHUTTLE COMMANDER

Ever since she was a little girl, Eileen Collins wanted to be a pilot. She attended Corning Community College in New York, and then completed her B.A. in mathematics and economics at Syracuse University in 1978. After Syracuse, she was chosen along with three other women for Air Force pilot training at Oklahoma's Vance Air Base; her class was one of the base's first to include women. After earning her wings in 1979, she stayed on for three years as a T-38 Talon pilot instructor before being transferred to Travis Air Force Base in California, for cross-training in the C-141 Starlifter. She earned a master's degree in operations research at Stanford in 1986, then a second master's in space systems management from Webster University in 1989.

That same year, Collins was accepted at the competitive Air Force Test Pilot School at Edwards Air Force Base in California. In 1989, she became only the second woman to graduate as a test pilot; she was selected by NASA to be an astronaut in 1990. In 1995, Collins became the first female astronaut to pilot a space shuttle mission, serving as second-in-command of the shuttle Discovery. She piloted a second mission on the space shuttle Atlantis in 1997. After having logged over 400 hours in space, she was chosen by NASA to command the space shuttle Columbia on a mission in 1999, and became the first astronaut ever to pilot any of the shuttles through a 360 degree pitch maneuver, as well as the first American woman ever to command a space shuttle. In 2006, Collins retired from NASA to pursue other interests and spend time with her family. Since her retirement, Collins has received numerous awards and honors, including induction into the National Women's Hall of Fame, and has made appearances as a commentator covering space shuttle flights for CNN.

"My daughter just thinks that all moms fly the Space Shuttle."

— Eileen Collins

ELLEN OCHOA: FIRST HISPANIC WOMAN IN SPACE

Ellen Ochoa is a woman whose intelligence and hard work literally took her into the stratosphere - and beyond. Born in 1958, she grew up in Southern California and graduated Phi Beta Kappa in physics from San Diego State in 1980. She earned a master of science degree at Stanford only a year later and went on to earn a Ph.D in electrical engineering in 1985. She continued her research career at Sandia National Laboratories and the NASA Ames Research Center, where she was the lead scientist of a research group working on optical systems to process information

in ways that would enable automated space exploration. Ochoa holds a patent on an optical system that detects defects in a repeating pattern. She is also a co-inventor on three other patents, for an optical object recognition method, an optical inspection system, and for a way to remove noise in images. She supervised 35 scientists and engineers working on R & D for computational systems for aerospace missions as Chief of the Intelligent Systems Technology Branch at Ames.

In 1990, NASA selected Ochoa to become an astronaut, and in mid-1991 she completed her training. She became the first Hispanic woman ever to go into space in 1993 when she was on the crew for a nine-day shuttle mission studying the ozone layer on the shuttle Discovery. She has since served on three further space flights and has logged almost a thousand hours in space. Ochoa became the Deputy Director of the Johnson Space Center in 2007 and is involved in management and direction of the Astronaut Office and Aircraft Operations. She is retired from spacecraft operations, but still breaking new ground: in 2013, she became the second female and first Hispanic director of NASA's Johnson Space Center. Ochoa has received awards including NASA's Exceptional Service Award in 1997, Outstanding Leadership Medal in 1995, and several Space Flight Medals. And she has had three elementary and middle schools named after her. You can't keep a good woman earthbound!

KALPANA CHAWLA: THE FIRST AND ONLY INDIAN WOMAN IN SPACE

Kalpana Chawla was born in 1962 in Kamal, Punjab, India. Perhaps it was foresight that made her parents name her "Kalpana", meaning "idea" or "imagination", because while other girls her age liked playing with dolls, Kalpana preferred to draw airplanes and had an inquisitive mind. After getting a bachelor's degree in aeronautical engineering from Punjab Engineering College, she moved to the United States in 1982 where she earned a master's in aerospace engineering at the University of Texas at Arlington in two years. Undeterred by the Challenger space shuttle disaster in 1986, Kalpana went on to earn a second master's and then a doctorate in aerospace engineering from the University of Colorado at Boulder in 1988. Later that year, she started work as a NASA scientist, researching power-lift computational fluid dynamics. She joined Overset Methods, Inc. in 1993 as a research scientist as well as vice president. She was also rated as a flight instructor and held commercial pilot licenses for airplanes, gliders, and seaplanes.

When she succeeded in being naturalized as a U.S. citizen in 1991, Kalpana had applied for the NASA Astronaut Corps; she was accepted and began training in 1995, and was soon scheduled for her first space shuttle mission, joining the six-astronaut crew of the space shuttle Columbia. The two-week mission in late 1997 circled the Earth 252 times, and she was in charge of deploying a Spartan satellite using a robot arm; Kalpana had become the first Indian-born woman and the second Indian person ever to fly in space. After the mission, she did technical work for NASA relating to the space station. She was chosen for a second mission in 2000, but technical problems with the shuttle engine prevented it from going forward. At last she returned to space in 2003 aboard Columbia, but after a 16 day mission involving more than 80 experiments by the seven-astronaut crew, the shuttle, which had sustained heat shielding damage to a wing upon launch, did not survive re-entry to Earth's atmosphere, and the entire crew was lost. Kalpana was posthumously awarded Congress' Space Medal of Honor; scholarships were established in her name, and an asteroid was named after her.

"When you look at the stars and the galaxy, you feel that you are not just from any particular piece of land, but from the solar system."

– **Kalpana Chawla**, *at her first launch*

MARISSA MAYER: GOOGLE HER

Marissa Mayer is a proud "cheesehead," a native of the state of Wisconsin. Growing up, she liked math and science as well as baking and design. Though she had planned to become a doctor, while attending Stanford University, Marissa developed a love for computers. She went on to earn a Bachelor and Masters of Science in symbolic systems and computer science with a focus in artificial intelligence. She interned at SRI International and the UBS research lab, which helped her land 14 job offers. Finally, she decided to accept a job with Google, a company that at the time was not yet an internet search giant. Marissa became their 20th employee and its first female engineer. Working at Google, Marissa helped develop Google Maps, Google Earth, Street View, Google News, and Gmail. After helping build Google, she left in 2012 to become president and CEO of Yahoo, which at the time was struggling. Marissa became one of only 20 women running a Fortune 500 company.

"I think it's very comforting for people to put me in a box."Oh, she's a fluffy girlie-girl who likes clothes and cupcakes. Oh, but wait, she is spending her weekends doing hardware electronics."

— **Marissa Mayer**

• CHAPTER FIVE •

Still She Rises: Awesome Women of Color

The story of the civil rights movement is emblazoned with the names of many male heroes, including W.E.B. Du Bois, Martin Luther King Jr., Medgar Evers, and Malcolm X. But every step of the way, these and countless other men were accompanied by sisters, equally fearless: Sojourner Truth, Harriet Tubman, Rosa Parks, Fannie Lou Hamer, and Coretta Scott King, just to name a few.

These powerful and courageous women—and many others unnamed and unrecognized—put their bodies on the line for civil rights in the United States. They freed slaves, marched, sang, and protested until their voices were heard and laws were changed. Each fought the double demons of racism and sexism and emerged victorious. Often they faced not only emotional but physical violence; undeterred, they pressed on despite the cost. They are truly an inspiration for all who struggle against limitations of all sorts—legal, social, and psychological.

Language is one of the tools of oppression. It is, therefore, wonderfully appropriate that the word sheroes emerged from within the idiom of African American women, who bore the brunt of the severest subjugation. Johnetta B. Cole and Dr. Maya Angelou were the visionary pioneers who, to the best of my knowledge, began using the word "sheroes" in their speeches. Slowly and surely, the word, the mantle, if you will, of shero is beginning to crop up here and there in the common parlance. Recently, television's supreme shero Oprah adopted the word into her personal vocabulary. I can only imagine, it will spread like wildfire from here, in the truest sense of word power.

This sisterhood is an especially amazing group—overcoming obstacles unimaginable to others. Sojourner Truth's firebrand speeches give me goosebumps as I reread them over 100 years after she first espoused her glorious independent spirit. Marian Anderson, regarded as the greatest soprano of all time, was denied the stage at a concert in Washington, D.C., based on her race until polishero Eleanor Roosevelt took up the charge and helped unleash Anderson's gift to the nation. Sheroes of color obviously have to fight the twin battles of sexism and racism. Picture young Melba Beals walking the gauntlet of white-hot hatred on that day of desegregation in Little Rock. Think of Fannie Lou Hamer being beaten within an inch of her life for daring to eat in a cafeteria with white people in Mississippi. Remember Harriet Tubman booming a gospel song in code to "carry her people" home to freedom on the underground railroad.

Women of color, starting with the Amazons of North Africa and continuing today at the cusp of the twenty-first century had to fight harder, longer and better. When you look into the very heart of sheroism, I urge you to read beyond these pages and research the lives of these great women who, unbowed and unbroken, showed the true meaning of courage.

SOJOURNER TRUTH: "AIN'T I A WOMAN?"

Sojourner Truth's name alone suggests sheroism. It fits her perfectly—she was a fire-breathing preacher, suffragist, and vigilant abolitionist. Unschooled and born to slavery, she didn't allow these disadvantages to prevent her from becoming one of the most charismatic and powerful orators of the nineteenth century. In fact, like many African Americans of the day, hardship seemed to make her only stronger, like a blade forged by fire.

She hailed from Dutch country in upstate New York and grew up speaking Dutch. Christened Isabella, she was sold away from her parents as a child and was traded many times, until finally landing with John Dumont for whom she worked for sixteen years. At fourteen, she was given to an older slave to be his wife and bore five children. In 1826, one year before she was to be legally freed, Isabella ran away from Dumont and hid with a pacifist Quaker family.

Upon hearing that one of her sons had been sold into lifetime slavery in Alabama, Isabella sued over this illegal sale of her son and, remarkably, won the case. Isabella moved to New York in the 1830s and worked as a maid for a religious community, the Magdalenes, whose mission was the conversion of prostitutes to Christianity.

By 1843, the extremely religious Isabella heard a calling to become a traveling preacher. She renamed herself Sojourner Truth and hit the road where her talent for talking amazed all who heard her at revivals, camp meetings, churches, and on the side of the road, if the occasion arose. She kept her sermons to the simple themes of brotherly love and tolerance. In Massachusetts, Truth encountered liberals who enlightened her on the topics of feminism and abolition. Her autobiography, as told to the antislavery forerunner William Lloyd Garrison, provided a powerful weapon for the cause of abolition when published. Her story, *The Narrative of Sojourner Truth*, was one of the first stories of a woman slave to be widely known and was retold many times, including the charmingly entitled version, "Sojourner Truth, the Libyan Sibyl" by Harriet Beecher Stowe, which was published by the *Atlantic Monthly*.

Sojourner then put her religious fervor into the message of abolition, a holy mission into which she threw all her formidable will and energy. Her call to end the slavery of human beings in this country was powerful. There is a beloved story showing her quick tongue and even quicker mind and spirit: when the great Frederick Douglas openly doubted there could be an end to slavery without the spilling of blood. In a flash, Sojourner replied, "Frederick, is God dead?"

By the middle of the nineteenth century, Sojourner was preaching the twin messages of abolition and women's suffrage. She was unwavering in her convictions and made the eloquent point that "if colored men get their rights and not colored women, colored men will be masters over the women, and it will be just as bad as before." She threw herself into the Civil War efforts helping runaway slaves and black soldiers. President Lincoln was so impressed with the legend of Sojourner Truth that he invited her to the White House to talk.

Sojourner Truth worked, preached, and fought right up to her dying day in 1883. She lived long enough to see one of her fondest hopes—the abolition of slavery—be realized and, along with the estimable Harriet Tubman, is one of

the two most respected African American women of the nineteenth century. Was she a woman? Yes, indeed. And a shero for all time!

"I have ploughed, and planted, and gathered into barns, and no man could head me! And ain't I a woman?"

— Sojourner Truth

KATY FERGUSON: EARTH ANGEL

Born a slave in 1779, Catherine Ferguson accompanied her mistress to church on Sundays until she was freed at sixteen by a white woman benefactor who paid $200 for Katy's emancipation. Two years later, Katy married; by the time she was twenty, her husband and two infant children were dead. Katy, a fantastic baker, made wedding cakes and other delicacies to support herself. On the way to market to sell her baked goods, she would see dozens of poor children and orphans who pulled at the strings of her heart. The indomitable Katy started teaching these waifs church classes in her home on what is now Warren Street in Manhattan, until a Dr. Mason lent her church basement to her in 1814. This is believed to be the origins of what we now call "Sunday school." Katy's classes were so popular that droves of poor black and white children came to learn. Soon, many young, unwed mothers started showing up, too. Katy took them home, cared for them, and taught them self-reliance. Katy died of cholera in 1854, but her work carried on in the Ferguson Home for Unwed Mothers, where kindness, good works, and good learning are the helping hands to a better life.

"Where Katy lived, the whole aspect of the neighborhood changed."

—from an article on her work

HARRIET TUBMAN: HARRIET THE SPY (NOT KIDDING)

In her day, Harriet was lovingly referred to as Moses, for leading her people home to freedom. An escaped slave herself, she pulled off feat after amazing feat and gave freedom to many who would otherwise have never known it. Harriet Tubman was a conductor on the Underground Railroad, perhaps the best that ever was. She is best known for this activity, but she was also a feminist, a nurse, and, for a time, a spy. Her keenest interest was social reform, both for her gender and her people.

Born around 1821 on a plantation in Maryland, Harriet struggled with grand mal seizures after a blow to the head as a child, but the damage from a severely fractured skull didn't stop her from the most dangerous work she could have possibly undertaken: taking groups of slaves to freedom in the north. During her slow recovery from being hit in the head with a two-pound weight by an overseer, she began praying and contemplating the enslavement of blacks, resolving to do what she could, with faith in a higher power. She married John Tubman, a free man, in 1844, and lived in fear that she would be sold into the Deep South. When she heard rumors that she was about to be sold, she plotted her escape, begging John to come with her. He not only refused, but threatened to turn her in.

Harriet escaped to freedom by herself, but immediately plotted to return for her family members, using the Underground Railroad. She ultimately rescued all her family members except John; he had taken a new wife and remained behind. She led more than two hundred slaves to safety and freedom, encouraging her "passengers" with gospel songs sung in a deep, strong voice. She also developed a code to signal danger using biblical quotations and certain songs. Harriet Tubman always outfoxed the whites who questioned her about the groups of blacks traveling with her. She lived in constant threat of hanging, with a $40,000 price on her head, and many close calls. One of the most dramatic incidents shows Harriet's resourcefulness and resolve when she bought tickets heading south to evade whites demanding to know what a group of blacks were doing traveling together. She always carried a gun to dissuade any frightened fugitives from turning tail. "You'll be free or die," she told them—and she never lost a passenger.

Harriet also started connecting with abolitionists in the North, developing a strong admiration for John Brown (she conspired with him in his raid at Harper's Ferry) and Susan B. Anthony. During the Civil War, she nursed black soldiers, worked as a spy for the Union, and even led a raid that freed 750 slaves. After the war, she lived in Auburn, New York, in a house that had been a way station for the Underground Railroad, teaching blacks how to cope with newfound freedom; gathering food, clothing, and money for poor blacks; and founding a home for elderly and indigent blacks. Harriet's last years were spent in abject poverty despite all she had given to others, but she died at the age of ninety-three having accomplished the task she set herself as a girl. She was the great emancipator, offering her people hope, freedom, and new beginnings. Reformer and writer Thomas Wentworth Higginson named her "the greatest heroine of the age."

"When I found I had crossed that line, I looked to my hands to see if I was the same person. There was such a glory over everything."

— Harriet Tubman

IDA B. WELLS: JOURNALIST FOR JUSTICE

Ida Bell Wells-Barnett was an African American journalist and advocate of women's rights, including suffrage. Though she was born a slave in 1862 in Holly Springs, Mississippi, six months later the Emancipation Proclamation freed all slaves. Even though they were legally free citizens, her family faced racial prejudice and discrimination while living in Mississippi. Her father helped start Shaw University, and Ida received schooling there, but when she was 16, her parents and one of her siblings died of yellow fever. This meant that as the eldest, Ida had to stop going to school and start taking care of her eight sisters and brothers. Since the family direly needed money, Ida ingeniously convinced a county school official that she was 18 and managed to obtain a job as a teacher. In 1882, she moved to her aunt's in Nashville with several siblings and at last continued her education at Fisk University.

A direct experience of prejudice in 1884 electrifyingly catalyzed Wells' sense of the need to advocate for justice. While traveling from Memphis to Nashville, she bought a first-class train ticket, but was outraged when the crew told her to move to the car for African Americans. Refusing, Wells was forced off the train bodily; rather than giving in and giving up, she sued the railroad in circuit court and gained a judgment forcing them to pay her $500. Sadly, the state Supreme Court later overturned the decision; but this experience motivated her to write about Southern racial politics and prejudice. Various black publications published her articles, written under the nom-de-plume "Iola". Wells later became an owner of two papers, the *Memphis Free Speech and Headlight and Free Speech.*

Besides her journalistic and publishing work, she also as a teacher at one of Memphis' black-only public schools. She became a vocal critic of the condition of these segregated schools. This advocacy caused her to be fired from her job in 1891. The next year, three African American store owners clashed with the white owner of a store nearby who felt they were competing too successfully for local business; when the white store owner attacked their store with several allies, the black store owners ended up shooting several white men while defending their store. The three black men were taken to jail, but never had their day in court - a lynch mob dragged them out and murdered all three men. Moved to action by this horrible tragedy, she started writing about the lynchings of a friend and others, and went on to do in-depth investigative reporting of lynching in America, risking her life to do so.

While away in New York, Wells was told that her office had been trashed by a mob, and that if she ever came back to Memphis she would be killed. She remained in the North and published an in-depth article on lynching for the *New York Age*, a paper owned by a former slave; she then toured abroad, lecturing on the issue in the hope of enlisting the support of pro-reform whites. When she found out that black exhibitors were banned at the 1893 World's Columbian Exposition, she published a pamphlet with the support and backing of famed freed slave and abolitionist Frederick Douglass, as well as "A Red Record," a personal report on lynchings in America.

In 1896, Wells founded the National Association of Colored Women; and in 1898, she took her anti-lynching campaign to the White House and led a protest in Washington D.C. to urge President McKinley to act. She was a founding member of the NAACP (National Association for the Advancement of Colored People), but later cut ties with the organization, feeling that it wasn't sufficiently focused on taking action. Wells also worked on behalf of all women and was a part of the National Equal Rights League; she continuously fought for women's suffrage. She even ran for the state senate in 1930, but the next year her health failed, and she died of kidney disease at the age of 68. Well's life is a testament to courage in the face of danger.

> *"I felt that one had better die fighting against injustice than to die like a dog or rat in a trap. I had already determined to sell my life as dearly as possible if attacked. I felt if I could take one lyncher with me, this would even up the score a little bit."*
>
> **— Ida B. Wells**

MARY MCLEOD BETHUNE: A DOLLAR AND A DREAM

In 1904 Mary McLeod Bethune started a school on $1.50 and dreams on the grounds of a former dump. "I haunted the city dump retrieving discarded linen and kitchenware, cracked dishes, broken chairs, pieces of old lumber," she remembered later. The humble beginning has now blossomed into Bethune Cookman College in Daytona, Florida.

She wasn't daunted by the idea of all the hard work it would take to make her dreams come true; she was used to picking 250 pounds of cotton a day and pulling the plow when the family mule died. The fifteenth of seventeen children born to former slaves, Mary was brought up as a strict Methodist to believe in the sweat of the brow and faith in God. At the age of twelve, she was given a scholarship by the Quakers to be educated at an integrated school in North Carolina, later going on to Moody Bible College. From these experiences, she had a profound respect for education, particularly for its value in helping her people rise from poverty.

Mary's school succeeded through her combination of penny-pinching abilities and excellent fundraising skills (she even got J.D. Rockefeller to contribute). She trained the students to pick elderberries to make into ink, used burned wood for chalk, and bartered free tuition for food for her students. Soon she added an infirmary on the site when she realized blacks couldn't get medical treatment within 200 miles of that part of the Atlantic Coast; eventually that grew into a training hospital for doctors and nurses. By 1922, the school boasted 300 students, and Mary stayed on as president of the college until 1942.

She had a strong commitment to African Americans, particularly women. While running the school, she led the campaign to register black women voters, despite threats from the KKK. Her civil rights activism and humanitarianism brought her into contact with many people, including Eleanor Roosevelt, with whom she became good friends. Bethune ended up serving people in many leadership roles, including as the founder and president of the National Council of Negro Women, the leading member of the "Black Cabinet" who were advisors to FDR on African American needs and interests, and the Director of the Office of Minority Affairs of the National Youth Administration. When she was seventy-seven, concerned over the inability of blacks to get life insurance, she started the Central Life Insurance Company, becoming the only woman president of a national life insurance company in the entire United States.

For these and other accomplishments, Mary McLeod Bethune was regarded as the most influential black woman in America until her death in 1955. Mary's rise from poverty to national leadership is sheer sheroism.

"I leave you. I leave you hope...I leave you racial dignity."

— Mary McLeod Bethune

NANNIE HELEN BURROUGHS: THE PRACTICAL PROPHET

NAACP pioneer William Picken described Nannie Burroughs this way: "No other person in America has so large a hold on the loyalty and esteem of the colored masses as Nannie H. Burroughs. She is regarded all over the broad land as combination of brains, courage, and incorruptibleness." Born in the Gilded Age in 1879, Nannie Burroughs was fortunate to be born into a family of ex-slaves who were able to establish a comfortable existence in Virginia, affording young Nannie a good education. Nannie applied for a job as a domestic science teacher and wasn't hired because she was "too dark." Later, she was turned down for a job as a government clerk because she was a black woman.

Nannie began dreaming of a way to prepare black women for careers that freed them from the traps of gender and bias. Nannie worked for the national Baptist Alliance for fifty years, starting as a bookkeeper and secretary. In her spare time, she organized the Women's Industrial Club, providing practical clerical courses for women. Through the school she founded in 1909, the National Training School for Women and Girls, she educated thousand of black American women as well as Haitians, Puerto Ricans, and South Africans to send them into the world with the tools for successful careers. Her program emphasized what she called the three Bs: the Bible, the Bath, and the Broom, representing "clean lives, clean bodies, and clean homes."

An advocate of racial self-help, Nannie worked all her life to provide a solid foundation for poor black women so they could work and gain independence and equality. She practiced what she preached. At one point, she wrote to John D. Rockefeller for a donation to her cause. He sent her one dollar with a note asking what a business-

woman like her would do with the money. She purchased a dollar's worth of peanuts and sent them to him with a note asking him to autograph each one and return them to her. She would then sell each one for a dollar.

She founded the Harriet Beecher literary society as a vehicle for literary expression and was also active in the antilynching campaigns. She gave Sojourner Truth a run for her money with dramatic speech-making and stirring lectures such as her headline-making speech in 1932: "Chloroform your Uncle Toms! What must the Negro do to be saved? The Negro must unload the leeches and parasitic leaders who are absolutely eating the life out of the struggling, frightened mass of people."

One of her students once said that Nannie considered "everybody God's nugget." Nannie Burroughs' pragmatic "grab your own bootstraps" approach to racial equality offered that chance to everyone who came into her purview.

"The training of Negro women is absolutely necessary, not only for their own salvation and the salvation of the race, but because of the hour in which we live demands it. If we lose sight of the demands of the hour we blight our hope of progress. The subject of domestic science has crowded itself upon us, and unless we receive it, master it and be wise, the next ten years will so revolutionize things that we will find our women without the wherewithal to support themselves."

— **Nannie Helen Burroughs**

ESLANDA GOODE ROBESON: "AFRICANS ARE PEOPLE"

Eslanda Goode Robeson was the wife of the famous singer and civil rights activist Paul Robeson. However, she was an important shero in her own right, distinguishing herself both in political activism and as an anthropologist.

The daughter of a freed slave, Essie, born in 1896, was passionately interested in Africa and the conditions that made the mother continent vulnerable. Her mother, Eslanda Cardoza Goode, was of mixed race, born among South Carolina's free blacks to an octoroon mother and a wealthy Spanish Jew, Isaac Nunez Cardoza. Essie's uncle Francis Louis Cardoza was named as "the most highly educated Negro in America" by Henry Ward Beecher. When Essie was six, her father died of alcohol abuse and the family moved to New York City just in time for the birth of the Harlem Renaissance. Essie was well educated herself, attending Teachers College at Columbia University and one year of medical school, ultimately receiving her degree in chemistry from Columbia. Her other interests included a strong proclivity for politics and the desire to fight for racial equality. Essie was on her way to becoming a model for the new equality when she became the first black person to work in the pathology and surgery departments of Columbia Presbyterian, where she ran the lab. In the twenties, she met and married Paul Robeson; after hearing him sing at a party, Essie became convinced he had a future in show business. She talked him into performing and soon his career was launched. By the mid-twenties, Paul was the toast of Europe and America; Essie quit her job to travel with Paul and manage his career. However, over and over the duo suffered the sickening hypocrisy of a white society that lauded Paul as the toast of stage and screen while not allowing Essie and him to eat in the same restaurants as the white music patrons. To avoid the pain, Essie began to stay home and focus upon their shared dream of a modern black family—emancipated, educated, and enlightened.

In the thirties, the ever intellectually restless Essie developed an intense interest in anthropology and in Africa. Studying at London University and the London

School of Economics, she became even more radicalized: "I soon became fed up with white students and teachers 'interpreting' the Negro mind and character to me," she wrote later. "Especially when I felt, as I did very often, that their interpretation was wrong."

She decided to make her own conclusions. She traveled to Africa several times, exploring widely, up the Congo and into the heartland by any means available. Her exploration led her to emphasize the importance of racial pride in overcoming racism, and she banded with other black people to found the Council of African Affairs. She was always extremely outspoken about the plight of her people as a result of slavery and colonialism and never backed down from a debate. She drew fire when she suggested the Soviet Union had created a better foundation for equality than the United States. In the forties, during World War II, she was especially vocal, perceiving that the war against Fascism was an opportunity for a more racially united and equal opportunity America. Her book, *African Journey*, was published in 1945; that same year, as a representative of the Council on African Affairs, Essie participated in the conference that founded the United Nations.

In the fifties, the activity and views of the Robesons were brought to the attention of Senator Joseph McCarthy who called her before the House Un-American Activities Committee. McCarthy was no match for the brilliance and verbal dexterity of Essie, who turned the tables on him, drilling him with questions about the black civil rights issue. But McCarthy got his revenge, revoking both their passports, reducing Paul's income from international concert tours to almost nil.

This only spurred Essie on to greater activism—ultimately her passport was reinstated and she traveled to Germany to receive the Peace Medal and the Clara Zetkin Medal, a governmental award for women who have fought for world peace. She continued to write articles and give speeches on behalf of equality and justice until she died in 1965. No matter what the personal cost, Essie fought to free her people from the invisible bonds that still held them back. Her work was invaluable in the civil rights movement; her call for absolute racial equality rang clear and true: "No man can be free until all men are free."

"I believe there will never be peace in the world until people have achieved what they fought and died for."

— Eslanda Goode Robeson

ROSA PARKS: THE FIRST LADY OF CIVIL RIGHTS

Rosa Parks gave a human face to the civil rights movement. She showed how the issues addressed in all of the speeches affected a woman's life in the course of an ordinary day. The woman was Rosa Louise McCauley Parks; the day became an extraordinary day that rocked the nation and changed history.

Born in 1913, Rosa grew up in Pine Level, Alabama, with her schoolteacher mother, Leona. She helped her mother take care of her sickly grandparents and run the household, because Rosa's father had gone to work up north and effectively disappeared from their lives. Later, she moved in with her aunt Fanny and enrolled in the Montgomery Industrial School for Girls, a private school, where she was exposed to the liberal ideals of teachers raised in the north. Rosa took her teachers' lessons to heart, as well as the stories her elderly grandparents told about the evils of slavery, sparking a sense of justice that would only grow.

Rosa vacillated between following in the footsteps of her mother and becoming a teacher and pursuing her own dream of training to be a nurse. Then in 1932, she met and married Raymond Parks, who had struggled up from an impoverished background where he wasn't allowed to attend school because of his color. To augment her husband's income from barbering, Rosa dabbled in many lines of work, including maid, seamstress, and secretary.

Her involvement in civil rights grew. She was the first woman to start attending the Montgomery chapter of the NAACP and also worked in the effort to register blacks to vote. Rosa often walked home from work to avoid the "back of the bus" issue until December 1, 1955, when she was returning home from a long day of sewing at a Montgomery department store. The buses from downtown were always fairly crowded and had a section designated for blacks behind the ten rows of seats in the front for white folks. Rosa was sitting in the first row of the "blacks only" section when the white section filled up, leaving a white man without a seat. The tacit understanding was that, in such a scenario, the black person was supposed to stand and let the white person have the seat. The white bus driver called for the four black people in the front row of the black section to get up and let the white man have the row. Rosa refused and the driver called the police.

Her solitary action started a firestorm of controversy, including a bus boycott and protest march led by Martin Luther King, Jr. and Coretta Scott King. A fascinating footnote to the incident is that Rosa had been evicted by the very same bus driver twelve years before. Though there had been several incidents on Montgomery buses, Rosa stuck to her guns and became the pivotal legal case for the burgeoning civil rights movement's attack on segregated seating. Upon going to trial and being found guilty, she refused to pay her fine and appealed the decision. Her actions cost Rosa and her husband dearly; they both lost their jobs and were the recipients of threats to their lives. Undaunted, Rosa worked with the carpooling efforts that enabled blacks to continue their 381-day boycott of the bus system.

The sacrifices of the black community were not in vain, because the U.S. District Court ruled segregated seating to be unconstitutional. However, due to the controversy, Rosa, the shero who started the battle by keeping her seat, couldn't get a job anywhere in Montgomery. Rosa, Raymond, and Rosa's mother moved to Detroit and started a new life there, Rosa working as a seamstress and for the Southern Christian Leadership Conference. She ultimately found a career in U.S. Representative John Coyner's office.

Rosa Parks' courage in that split second moment when she made her decision is at the very crux of the victorious struggle for African Americans. Rosa worked diligently for the good of her community, traveling and speaking on behalf of the NAACP. She loved to talk to young people about the movement, for the work has truly only begun. Rosa Parks has become a symbol of fearlessness and fortitude. In 1980, Rosa was honored by *Ebony* magazine as "the living black woman who had done the most to advance the cause of civil rights."

"You didn't have to wait for a lynching. You died a little each time you found yourself face to face with this kind of discrimination."

— **Rosa Parks**

FANNIE LOU HAMER: BRAVERY UNBOUND

Fannie Lou Hamer grew up a sharecropper's daughter in Montgomery, Mississippi, where she was exposed to the worst face of racial injustice. Forced to quit school in the sixth grade to work in the cotton fields to help support her family, she got involved in the effort to register blacks

to vote in 1962. At the time, a literacy test was required in order to secure the right to vote, and Fannie helped teach people so they could pass the test. One day, Fannie was on a bus with a group of fellow African American youths who were challenging the "whites only" policy at the bus terminal diner. When they were attacked by state troopers called in to deal with the "insurrection," Fannie was hurt badly and jailed with everyone else from the bus. Her sufferings had only begun, though. Hamer was incarcerated in a cell with two black men who were ordered to beat her with a metal-spiked leather billy club. Fannie was permanently blinded in one eye by this beating and suffered kidney damage, but she emerged with even more inner resolve to put an end to racial injustice. Fannie worked without cessation for many related causes: Head Start for black schools, jobs for poor blacks, and against the Vietnam War because she felt black soldiers were being sent to protect rights they themselves didn't have at home. Fannie Hamer risked her life over and over to improve the lot of her people until her death in 1977, never receiving the attention that was her due. A true unsung shero, her essential belief was, "We serve God by serving our fellow (human beings)."

CORETTA SCOTT KING: UNSHAKEABLE FAITH

Like the Robesons, the Kings had a marriage based on love—for each other and for racial equality. After the assassination of Martin Luther King, Jr. Coretta gained recognition in her own right as a pillar of the civil rights movement. A talented musician, Coretta was born in

Alabama in 1927 and was educated at Antioch, where she got a degree in music and elementary education and was exposed to whites in a very different environment than the South, learning a great deal about techniques to foster interracial communication. In 1953, she married Martin Luther King, Jr. while they were both college students, and they pursued a life together, her music—she got a higher degree at the New England Conservatory of Music—and his theological degree. From a long line of ministers, Martin felt a call to become a pastor, a decision that found the young couple moving to Montgomery, Alabama, after their education. They had their first of four children in their first year at the Dexter Avenue Baptist Church and became deeply involved in the actions of the civil rights movement. Martin Luther King, Jr. led the bus boycott after Rosa Parks' historic bus ride. As the footage shows, Coretta was right beside Martin at every protest, fighting for the rights of all African Americans. She also participated in fundraising for the movement by giving more than thirty concerts in Europe and the United States to raise money for Martin's organization, the Southern Christian Leadership Conference (SCLC).

The Kings traveled extensively in their work—to Ghana, to India, to Nigeria, and in 1964, to Norway to receive Dr. King's Nobel Peace Prize. Four years later, the world watched in horror as Martin was gunned down in Memphis, Tennessee, during a garbage workers strike. Coretta didn't shrink from the work at hand and led a protest in Memphis four days later with her children at her side. Her quiet dignity captured the nation; that year she was voted Woman of the Year and Most Admired Woman by college students.

From that fateful day, Coretta stepped forward and took up the mantle of leadership in the civil rights movement, which she shared with the young Jesse Jackson. Coretta amazed everyone with her stamina and heart as she made speech after speech and led march after march. She has received innumerable awards for her tireless efforts in her lifetime. She founded the Martin Luther King, Jr. Center for Nonviolent Change and has also led the attention of the nation into new directions, organizing antiwar protests, antinuclear and antiapartheid lobbies, and employment for African Americans. More than 100 colleges have given her honorary doctorates. Coretta Scott King has never hesitated to give herself to the struggle for freedom and justice, viewing it as both "a privilege" and "a blessing."

YOLANDA KING AND ATTALLAH SHABAZZ: PASSING ON THE TORCH

The daughters of two very different civil rights warriors, Martin Luther King, Jr. and Malcolm X, have recently paired up to represent the next generation of activism. Although Yolanda King and Attallah (Arabic for gift of god) Shabazz were raised in different faiths and from different philosophical points of view, the commonalities override the dissimilarities. Both lost their fathers to assassins as children under the public eye, and both desired to escape the attention and live their own lives. Yolanda and Attallah grew into two creative spirits for whom the arts provide release, solace, and strength. They were wary of each other upon meeting in New York City where they were both trying to start acting careers. It wasn't long, however, before a bond was forged and they started working on a play together, "Stepping into Tomorrow," a musical dramedy with a powerful message of empowerment for youth. The play began a career of collaboration and activism in which both Yolanda and Attallah travel extensively lecturing on civil rights, the importance of the arts, and the legacy of their fathers. In Yolanda King's words, "I see these responsibilities not as a burden, but as an extension of who I am."

DAISY BATES: FIGHTING THE SYSTEM AND WINNING!

The image of an eight-year-old black girl in her perfectly starched blouse and skirt walking through a gauntlet of hatred to go to school was etched in the minds of every American in the sixties. Everyone was touched by the grace and dignity shown by the young girl who was spat at and heckled, as cameras shoved in her face recorded it for all posterity. Activists for integration won a huge victory that day and with an even greater strength and resolve went on to flatten every segregation wall that presented itself.

Daisy Bates was one of the civil rights warriors who were first called into action in the fight for desegregation. Born in 1920, Daisy was adopted into a loving family in Little Rock, Arkansas, and never knew what happened to her birth mother until the taunts of schoolchildren made the eight-year-old question her adoptive mother. On that day, she found out that her mother had been raped and murdered by three white men who then dumped her body in a pond. Her father left town to escape having the crime pinned on him.

When Daisy was twenty-one, she married L.C. Bates, a black man who had been educated as a journalist. Together, they took over a Little Rock newspaper, the *Arkansas State Press*, and turned it into a platform for "the people," reporting crimes committed against blacks that the white paper ignored. Daisy worked as a reporter, covering with complete honesty, for example, the cold-blooded murder of a black soldier by military police. The white business community was outraged over the *State Press'* coverage: They feared the army would leave their town and withdraw all advertising. However, the Bates' brave courage in the face of brutality to blacks curtailed these crimes, and Little Rock became a more liberated town despite itself.

Then the movement toward desegregation heated up, with Daisy Bates right in the thick of things. The Supreme Court had declared segregation of schools unconstitutional in May of 1954, giving Southern schools the chance to describe how and when they would make the required changes. The local school board had responded by saying that they would take on the notion of integration "gradually." Little Rock's black community was up in arms about the foot dragging and after butting their heads in the many stony-faced meetings, they opted to take matters into their own hands. The state and local NAACP decided that they would try to enroll the students into the segregated schools and build up cases of denied admission in order to create a true challenge to the policy of gradualism. Daisy Bates, as president of the NAACP in Little Rock, worked with the *State Press* and other papers to publicize this flouting of the Supreme Court's ruling. Finally, in 1957, they decided to integrate the high school, come hell or high water. The children who would put their bodies on the line would become famous overnight as "Daisy's children" and suffer personal agony for the cause of racial injustice.

When nine children were selected to attend the "whites only" Central High School, Daisy acted as their escort and protector. Answering a poll screened by school officials, the group of young heroes and sheroes consisted of: Carlotta Walls, Thelma Mothershed, Melba Patillo, Ernest Green, Terrence Roberts, Gloria Ray, Minnijean Brown, Jefferson Thomas, and Elizabeth Eckford. When Little Rock school superintendent Virgil Blossom decreed that no adults could accompany the black students, Daisy called all of their homes and told them there would be a change of plans.

Elizabeth Eckford's family had no telephone, so she showed up on opening day—to be faced by an angry white mob who also attacked the reporters and photographers. The mob siege lasted seventeen days until 1,000 paratroopers showed up in response to orders from the White House to carry through the order of legal integration of the school.

However, the students were on their own once inside, prey to taunts, shoving, and threats of violence. Daisy Bates continued to protect and advise the children throughout the ordeal, accompanying them to every meeting with a school official when racial incidents happened. The struggle at Little Rock was only the first in a round of actions that ultimately led to full legal desegregation. Though difficult, the victory was entirely to Daisy and her "children" who showed the nation that you could stand up to hatred and ignorance with honesty and dignity. You can fight a losing battle and win.

OPRAH WINFREY: THE QUEEN OF THE TALK SHOW

Although most people think of The Oprah Winfrey Show when they think of Oprah, besides ruling the media world as a television and talk show host, her curriculum vitae also includes being an actress, producer, magazine publisher, entrepreneur, CEO, and philanthropist. None of this was handed to her – she was born to a teenaged mother on a farm in Mississippi in 1954, and her unmarried parents soon separated and left her there in her grandmother's care. She was exceptionally bright; her grandmother taught her to read at the tender age of two and a half, and she was skipped through kindergarten and second grade. At age six, Oprah was sent to live with her mother and three half-siblings in a very rough Milwaukee ghetto. She has said that she was molested as a child starting at age nine and in her early teens by men her family trusted.

At twelve, she was again uprooted and sent to live with her father, a barber, in Nashville. This was however a relatively positive time for the young Oprah, who started being called on to make speeches at churches and social gatherings. After being paid $500 for a speech on one occasion, she knew she wanted to be "paid to talk". She was further bounced back and forth between both her parents' homes, compounding the trauma of the abuse she had suffered. Her mother worked long and variable hours and was not around much of the time. At 14, Oprah became pregnant with a son; he did not survive early infancy. After some years of acting out including running away once, she was sent to her father to stay, this time; she credits her father with saving her with his strictness and devotion, his rules, guidance, structure, and books. It was mandatory that she write a book report every week, and she went without dinner unless she learned five new vocabulary words every day.

Things completely turned around for Oprah. She did well in school and then managed to land a job in radio while still in high school. After winning an oratory contest, she was able to study communication on a scholarship at Tennessee State University, a historically black college. She was a co-anchor of the local evening news at age 19, and before long her emotional verve when ad-libbing took her into the world of Baltimore's daytime talk shows. After seven years on *Baltimore Is Talking*, she had better local ratings than those of famed national talk show host Phil Donahue. She then took a local Chicago talk show from third place to first, and then she was on her way with the launch of her own production company. In 1985, a year after taking on *A.M. Chicago*, producer Quincy Jones spotted Oprah on air and decided to cast her in a film he was planning based on Alice Walker's novel *The Color Purple*. Her acting in this extremely well-received film had a meteoric effect on the popularity of her talk show, which was by now *The Oprah Winfrey Show*, and the show gained wide syndication. She had taken a local show and changed its focus from traditional women's concerns and tabloid fodder to issues including cancer, charity work, substance abuse, self-improvement, geopolitics, literature, and spirituality.

Oprah launched *O: The Oprah Magazine* in 2000; it continues to be popular. She has spearheaded other publications as well, from four years of *O At Home* magazine to co-authoring five books. She is currently soon to release a memoir, *The Life You Want*. In 2008, Oprah created a new channel called OWN: Oprah Winfrey Network and put her self-branded talk show to bed. She has earned the sobriquet of "Queen of All Media" and is accounted as the richest African-American and the most pre-eminent black philanthropist in American history. She is at present North America's first and only black multi-billionaire and is considered to be one the most influential women in the world, despite the many setbacks and hardships she endured in early life. She has been awarded honorary doctorates from Duke and Harvard universities, and in 2013, Oprah received the Presidential Medal of Freedom from President Barack Obama.

MICHELLE OBAMA: FEARLESS FLOTUS

Michelle Obama not only served as the 44th First Lady of the United States of America, but is also an American lawyer, writer, and the founder of *Let's Move!*, an initiative towards the prevention of child obesity, as well as an advocate of civil rights for women and LGBT people.

Michelle Robinson was born in Chicago in 19
she graduated from Princeton, and in 1988 s
a law degree at the prestigious Harvard Law School, after which she worked at Sidley Austin, a Chicago corporate law firm of high repute. Though Sidley didn't usually take on first-year law students as associates, in 1989 they asked Michelle to mentor a summer associate named Barack Obama. When he finished his term as an associate and returned to Harvard, their relationship continued long distance, and in 1992 they married. At the same time, Michelle was evaluating in those years whether a career in corporate law was really what she wanted. Corporate law, while lucrative, was not what she'd intended when she started college. She lost her father to kidney complications in 1991, which furthered her process of reflection; she was later quoted saying by the New York Times, "I wanted to have a career motivated by passion and not just money." She left Sidley Austin and went to work for Chicago, first for the Mayor and then providing her expertise to Valerie Jarrett, the head of the planning and development department. In that position she was working for job creation and to bring new life to Chicago's neighborhoods, and after this turning point, she never looked back.

After spending a few years working in hospital administration for the University of Chicago Hospitals, Michelle became First Lady of the United States when her husband won the presidential election of 2008. In this role, she advocated for military families, working women balancing family with career, and arts and arts education. Michelle also supported LGBT civil rights, working with her husband for the passage of the Employment Non-Discrimination Act and the repeal of Don't Ask Don't Tell. In 2010, she began to take steps to create a healthier lifestyle for the youth of America with the "Let's Move" campaign to prevent child obesity. These are just a few of many of her accomplishments as the first African American First Lady in the White House. Now that she has left it, she is preparing to continue her advocacy work and write a planned memoir as she and the Obama family settle into their new residence in Washington, D.C., where they will remain until daughter Sasha Obama finishes high school.

"There are still many causes worth sacrificing for, so much history yet to be made."

— Michelle Obama

To Learn More:

The National Archives for Black Women's History is the largest repository solely dedicated to the collection and preservation of material relating to African American women. The collection includes correspondence, photographs, and speeches. For further information, please contact 202-673-2402 or for more information, see its page in the Library of Congress web site: https://www.loc.gov/folklife/civilrights/survey/view_repository.php?rep_id=1667

• CHAPTER SIX •

They Resisted. They Persisted. They Are Awesome

The women's movement is, in essence, a social and political movement. Make that very political. While pioneering women have been blazing trails in every field, some of the work that has made for the most meaningful changes has taken place in the political arena for women's rights, civil rights, and rights for workers. Often, the first women that come to mind are Susan B. Anthony and Elizabeth Cady Stanton, who organized the first women's convention 150 years ago. But women all over the globe have sacrificed and soldiered in the trenches of bureaucracy and policy to open the world up for all women.

Although "breaking the chains" that oppress and limit women's lives might be a notion that is a bit hackneyed now as we head for the new millennium, the laws did bind. Women couldn't vote by law! Women were paid less than half of men's wages! Women couldn't inherit property by law! A woman didn't have rights over her own body, birth control, or pregnancy until January 22, 1973, with *Roe v. Wade* ("We recognize the right of the individual, married or single, to be free from unwarranted governmental intrusion into matters so fundamentally affecting a person as the decision whether to bear or beget a child. That right necessarily includes the right of a woman to decide whether or not to terminate her pregnancy"), a heated battle in the courts even now. Until the 1970s, a woman could be committed to an asylum with a mere piece of paper signed by her husband. Imagine! There are many cases of a woman being hauled off to the nuthouse so hubby could trade her in for a new, younger model. The work done to change these laws can never be forgotten. We're now free to pursue any dream, any career, even political power thanks to the sheroic foremothers who dismantled the walls brick by brick.

With a few born-to-the-throne exceptions, women have only begun to rule the world in the first years of the new millenium. But as these examples prove, we're making up for lost time! And when we can't get inside the seats of power, we rouse a great deal of rabble around the edges.

AND DON'T FORGET THESE WOMEN WHO RULED

Elizabeth I, daughter of Henry the Eighth, who vowed never to lose *her* head in love and reigned alone for forty-five years;

Margaret, who united three Scandinavian countries in 1387 and ruled for twenty-five years;

Sonduk, who presided over a war-torn Korea in the seventh century and sent her countrymen to China to be educated;

Eleanor of Aquitaine, who really knew how to get around—she was queen of France for fifteen years and queen of England for fifty (and she managed to have ten kids as well!);

Catherine the Great, who reigned over Mother Russia with an iron fist and unparalleled brilliance. *His*tory has attacked her for her unabashed lust for life; herstory shall, finally, acknowledge her as an extraordinary politician and pragmatist.

ANNE MARBURY HUTCHINSON: BANISHED FOR HAVING A BRAIN

One of the earliest American sheroes is Anne Hutchinson, who was banned from the Massachusetts Colony in 1637 for daring to have her own theological interpretations of the religious teaching of her day. Born in England, the daughter of an Anglican minister, she grew up in a household where religious discussion was encouraged. As an adult, Anne and her husband, William, heard the sermons of Cotton Mather in England (whose refinement of the Puritans' Covenant of Works)—that living "right" was the key to salvation of the soul—(which he called the Covenant of Grace)—and that redemption or salvation of the soul was possible only through God's grace.

Mather's "heresy" got him booted out of England. Declaring that God had told her to follow Mather, Anne and her henpecked hubby and their brood (they had fifteen children, twelve of whom survived) decamped to Massachusetts, where they were soon embraced by the monied set and started going to the right church and living in the right part of the colony. The trouble started when Anne made the mistake of displaying her deep understanding of various doctrines and started holding theological salons for women. Anne's parlor preachments were very popular, but when men began attending, the chauvinist colonial clergy got teed off. Anne was "ministering" and therefore, breaking the law in Massachusetts against women having such authority. Hutchinson was tried for the "sin of traduction," branded a heretic, and banished from the colony with high drama: "The Church consenting to it we will proceed to excommunicate. Forasmuch as you, Mrs. Hutchinson, have highly transgressed and offended...and troubled the Church with your Errors...I do cast you out...and deliver you up to Satan...I command you in the name of Christ

Jesus and of this Church as a Leper to withdraw yourself out of the Congregation."

Most people would have slunk away in shame, but Anne defended her philosophies: "I bless the Lord, He hath let me see which was the clear ministry and which the wrong," and told her prosecuting persecutors they would all "go to hell!" She so scared the church fathers that they ordered her supporters to turn in their guns. She then hooked up with a freethinking Samuel Groton outside the colony and started a religious rebellion. Then Groton was banished. Anne Hutchinson established a religious settlement in Rhode Island, emphasizing a personal relationship with God rather than obedience to church doctrine. After the death of her husband, she and her children moved to a remote colony in the New Netherlands (now the location of Pelham Bay Park in the Bronx) Doubtless the itinerant religious reformer would've stirred up yet another congregation among the Dutch settlers, except Anne Hutchinson and five of her children were killed in an Indian attack.

Although she is now credited with spearheading the first salvo in the development of religious tolerance, the few history books of the time that included information on Anne branded her as a wicked "New England Jezebel." A plaque at the former Old Corner Bookstore in Boston, now the site of the *Boston Globe*, reads "On this site stood the house of Anne Hutchinson, a religious leader, brilliant, fearless, unfortunate. Banished to Rhode Island 1637. Killed by Indians 1643."

BELVA ANN BENNETT MCNALL LOCKWOOD: SEE HOW SHE RAN

Victorian powerhouse Belva Lockwood was the first woman to plead before the U.S. Supreme Court and the first woman to run for president of the United States. After being blocked from the law department of Columbian College (Now George Washington University) for fear that her presence would distract the male students, this widow and former school teacher applied to the brand new National Law School. Upon her graduation in 1869 at the age of forty-three, Belva was refused her degree and took this affront to the attention of President Ulysses S. Grant, who arranged for the due delivery of Belva's diploma.

This was just the beginning of her struggles to be allowed to practice law. Admitted to the District of Columbia bar, Belva was barred from speaking to federal courts due to her gender. Not willing to take the exclusion lying down, she then rammed a bill through Congress allowing women lawyers in the federal courts, becoming in 1879 the first woman admitted to the bar of the Supreme Court. Proving that Belva wasn't just in it for herself, she took up many cases for the underdog—championing, for example, the first southern black lawyer to argue before the Supreme Court. And in her most spectacular case, she won a famous $5 million judgment (an unheard of amount in the nineteenth century) for the Cherokee Indians, forcing the U.S. government to pay them for their land. This spectacular victory prompted opposing lawyer Assistant Attorney General Louis A. Pratt to designate her "decidedly the most noted attorney in this country, if not in the world."

With her brilliant legal mind, Belva figured that, "If women in the states are not permitted to vote, there is no law against their being voted for, and if elected, filling the highest office in the gift of the people" and decided to run for president as the candidate of the Equal Rights Party in 1884 and 1888, with a hefty platform espousing rights for all minorities (including voting rights for women) along with temperance, peace, and universal education. Interestingly, she was opposed by Susan B. Anthony and Elizabeth Cady Stanton, who urged her to endorse the Republican candidate, James Blaine (he was in favor of women's rights). Both Blaine and Lockwood lost out to Grover Cleveland, but Lockwood surprised everyone by getting thousands of votes! Throughout her life, she continued to work and speak on behalf of her favored causes—women, peace, and minority rights—attaining a national reputation as a brilliant and powerful speaker. In her later years, she threw her energies into the Universal Peace Union, a precursor to the United Nations that advocated arbitration as a solution to internal conflicts. In 1912, she reflected back on her lengthy career and remarked, "I never stopped fighting. My cause was the cause of thousands of women."

"Were I a voice—a still small voice—an eloquent voice, I would whisper into the ear of every young woman, improve and exercise every talent that has been given to you; improve every opportunity, obey your inspiration, give no heed to the croakings of those narrow minds who take old hide bound and musty customs for religion and law, with which they have no affiliation, and who tell you with remarkable ease that these professions were never intended for women."

— Belva Ann Bennett McNall Lockwood

OUTSIDE THE LAW

Women had a long journey to gain entry to the courtroom. Here are some of the important steps along the way:

- The first known woman lawyer ever was a Babylonian who brought suit against her husband's brother, pleaded her own case, and won—in 550 B.C.!
- Biblical plaintiffs **Mahlah, Noah, Hoglah, Milcah,** and **Tizra** were five sisters who tried to fight the unfair treatment they were receiving after their father's death In Numbers 27:1–8, they waxed eloquent, "Why should the name of our father be done away from among his family, because he hath no son? Give unto us therefore a possession among the brethren of our father." The judge, in this case God, ruled in their favor according to his spokesperson Moses, "The inheritance of their father (was) to pass unto them... If a man die, and have no son, then ye shall cause his inheritance to pass unto his daughter."
- In 1239, **Bettista Gozzadini** sat in the juridical chair at the University of Bologna, highly unusual for the Dark Ages.
- America's first lawyer was **Margaret Brent**, one of the largest landholders in colonial Maryland and the most active attorney of her day; her name is in the court records 124 times for the years 1642 to 1650!
- Among Belva's contemporaries, **Arabella Mansfield**, in June 1869, became the first woman in the United States to be admitted to the bar, but for reasons we don't know (but can easily guess) never practiced. Ada H. Kepley was the first American woman to actually receive a law degree—from Union College in 1870.

- In the 1860s, **Myra Colby Bradwell** tried to get into the legal profession, but was barred, even by the Illinois Supreme Court, who stated "this step...would mean...that it is in harmony with the Constitution and laws that women should be made governors, judges, and sheriffs." Myra tried to take it higher, but the appeal didn't get off the ground. Such a hue and cry erupted over Myra's case, the state of Illinois passed a law in 1872 forbidding sex discrimination in employment. Bradwell gained admittance to the bar in 1890, but by then was more interested in her new profession—working full time for women's civil rights!
- **Charlotte Ray** was the first black woman in America to be allowed to practice law in 1872, but couldn't because of threats from bigots.

ANGELINA EMILY GRIMKÉ AND SARAH MOORE GRIMKÉ: SISTER SOLDIERS

The Grimké sisters were raised like Scarlett and her sisters in *Gone with the Wind*, but, unlike the fictional characters, grew up hating slavery. The privileged duo, two of twelve children, had all the southern advantages of private tutors and training in the arts at their palatial Charleston, South Carolina, home and were brought up to be good, high church Episcopalians. But they first showed their abolitionist spunk when Sarah was twelve; she was caught teaching a slave to read and write, a criminal offense. Because Angelica supported her, they were both punished.

As soon as they could, they high-tailed it out of there. Sarah bailed in 1821, moving north to The City of Brotherly Love and converting to Quakerism because of its antislavery beliefs. Angelina followed eight years later and repeated her sister's religious switch and "lefty" leanings, going so far as to join the Philadelphia Anti-Slavery Society.

Angelina had a nose for publicity and got her passionate condemnation of slavery published in William Lloyd Garrison's magazine *The Liberator*. Spurred by this break, Angelina followed up with a pamphlet entitled "An Appeal to the Christian Women of the South," which tried to appeal to women's consciences in opposing slavery: "But, perhaps you will be ready to query, why appeal to women on this subject? We do not make the law which perpetuates slavery. No legislative power is vested in us; we can do nothing to overthrow the system, even if we wished to do so. To this I reply, I know you do not make the laws, but I also know that *you are the wives and mothers, the sisters and the daughters of those who do*; and if you really suppose *you* can do nothing to overthrow slavery, you are greatly mistaken...1st. You can read on this subject. 2nd. You can pray over this subject. 3rd. You can speak on this subject. 4th. You can *act* on this subject."

Her appeal created a storm of controversy. In her hometown of Charleston, the postmaster burned all copies and put out a warning that Angelina better never show her face again in the South. At that point, sister Sarah took up the charge and attacked the slavers with a shot below their biblical belts with a refutation of the lame excuse that slavery was "OK" according to the Bible in her "Epistle to the Clergy of the Southern States."

The fearless siblings took their abolitionist act on the road, speaking to mixed crowds of both men and women. This really raised the dander of so-called "proper" society—ladies were not supposed to appear in public with men who were not their husbands and women were not supposed to lecture or preach—and they returned fire with a printed attack from the Massachusetts clergy that was preached to every available congregation in 1837. The clergy condemned women reformers and preachers, issuing a caution regarding any female who "assumed the place and tone of man as public reformer...

her character becomes unnatural." This was followed by other pious publications assaulting the Grimké sisters for overstepping their place.

As a result of the churches' attack, the sisters found themselves in the middle of the women's rights movement and are generally credited with being the first to make a link between the abolitionist cause and women's rights. The irrepressible duo fired back in grand style with letters in the *Spectator* and in Sarah's book, published in 1838, *Letters on the Equality of the Sexes and the Condition of Women* where she took the panty-waisted preachers down with her brilliant manifesto declaring women as absolutely and naturally endowed with equal rights, and that the only "unnatural" behaviors being performed in American society were those of men suppressing women!

Later, Angelina became the first woman in America to speak to a legislature with the presentation of her antislavery petition signed by 20,000 women to the Massachusetts state legislative body. The Grimkés were ahead of their time in many other ways as well, embracing new health fads and intellectual movements and running with a pretty arty crowd, including Henry David Thoreau who was intrigued by their up-to-the-minute fashion sense, describing them as "two elderly gray-haired ladies, the former in extreme Bloomer costume, which was what you might call remarkable." Go Grimkés!

"I ask for no favors for my sex. I surrender no claim to equality. All I ask our brethren is, that they will take their feet from off our necks and permit us to stand upright on the ground which God designed us to occupy."

— **Sarah Moore Grimké**

AMELIA BLOOMER: FREE YOUR *** AND YOUR MIND WILL FOLLOW

"Drag" had a whole different meaning for nineteenth-century fashion plates! Women were wearing fifteen pounds worth of skirts and petticoats until, in the 1850s, Amelia Bloomer started advocating a radical new undergarment in her new circular, *The Lily*, the first journal by and for women. Amelia was inspired to try this liberating new costume when she was visited by Elizabeth Cady Stanton and her cousin, Elizabeth Miller. While abroad, Miller was motivated to unburden herself of several pounds of skirts and created a Turkish-inspired short skirt and pantaloon combo that offered much comfort and freedom of movement. Stanton and Bloomer jumped into pairs of drawers with both feet, and Bloomer sang the praises of their new couture option in her magazine, "Fit yourselves for a higher sphere and cease groveling in the dirt. Let there be no stain of earth upon your soul or apparel." The pantaloons proved to an overnight sensation with scores of women sending in requests for patterns. The regular press lampooned the 'loons as "Bloomerism," and thus were born "bloomers."

SUSAN B. ANTHONY AND ELIZABETH CADY STANTON: FEMINIST FOREMOTHERS

The pioneer crusader for women's right to vote started life as a precocious child. Raised in the 1820s by a Quaker father who believed in independent thinking and education for women, Susan learned to read and write by the time she was three. Her first career was as a schoolteacher, but she soon found her niche as a political reformer, taking up the cause of temperance, then abolition. In 1869, she and Elizabeth Cady Stanton organized the National Women's Suffrage Association and put out a pro-feminist paper, *The Revolution*.

When the Fourteenth Amendment to the Constitution was passed in 1872 guaranteeing equal rights for African Americans, including the right, as citizens, to vote, Anthony and Cady Stanton kicked into action demanding the right to vote for women as well. Susan and a dozen other suffragists were jailed for trying to vote in the presidential election of that year. Undeterred, they began to work for a separate amendment giving this right to women. However, Congress patently ignored the amendments put before them each year on the vote for women until fifty years later.

Susan B. Anthony

Both Stanton and Anthony were real hell-raisers. Stanton, along with Lucretia Mott, organized the first women's rights convention in 1848 with a platform on women's rights to property, equal pay for equal work, and the right to vote. Stanton was introduced to Susan B. Anthony three years later. They were a "dream team," combining Elizabeth's political theories and her ability to strike people's emotions, with Susan's unmatched skill as a logician and organizer par excellence. They founded the first temperance society for women and amazed everybody with their drastic call for drunkenness to be recognized as a legal basis for divorce. Reviled during her lifetime, she learned to live with the taunts and heckles; critics claimed, among other traits, that she had "the proportions of a file and the voice of a hurdy-gurdy." Nonetheless, the "Napoleon" of the women's rights movement, as William Henry Channing called her, tirelessly lectured around the country for women's rights until her dying day in 1906.

Elizabeth Cady Stanton

Although she didn't get to realize her dream of voting rights for women, the successors she and Stanton trained did finally win this landmark victory for the women of America. Of the 260 women who attended the foremothers' historic first women's rights convention in 1848, only one woman lived long enough to see the passing of the victorious 1920 amendment grating women the right to vote—Charlotte Woodward. She declared at the time, "We little dreamed when we began this context that half a century later we would be compelled to leave the finish of the battle to another generation of women. But our hearts are filled with joy to know that they enter this task equipped with a college education, with business experience, with the freely admitted right to speak in public—all of which were denied to women fifty years ago."

"Failure is impossible."

— **Susan B. Anthony**

BREAKING THE CONCRETE CEILING

Lucretia Mott worked with Elizabeth Cady Stanton in planning the Seneca Falls Convention. Mott was an electrifying speaker, coming from Europe where she was a well known Quaker preacher. She didn't mince words and spoke powerfully and directly to women's rights, adding the radical note needed to light the fires of equal rights and abolition: "the world has never seen a truly great nation because in the degradation of women the very foundations of life are poisoned at the source."

Women legislators worked for years to get a statue of Susan B. Anthony, Lucretia Mott, and Elizabeth Cady Stanton in the Capitol rotunda. In spring of 1977, they finally succeeded. At the dedication ceremony, Representative Louise Slaughter (D., N.Y.) quipped to the statue, "Well sisters, it's going to be very hard to put you back in the basement now."

POLITICAL CORRECTION

At the Seneca Falls suffragette convention on July 19, 1848, the Declaration of Independence was rewritten to include women, and a slew of resolutions were passed designed to promote gender equality. Among them are:

"Resolved, That all laws which prevent women from occupying such a station in society as her conscience shall dictate, or which place her in a position inferior to that of man, are contrary to the great precept of nature, and therefore of no force or authority.

"Resolved, That woman is man's equal—was intended to be so by the Creator, and the highest good of the race demands that she should be recognized as such.

"Resolved, That the women of this country ought to be enlightened in regard to the laws under which they live, that they may no longer publish their degradation by declaring themselves satisfied with their present position, nor their ignorance, by asserting that they have all the rights they want.

"Resolved, That it is the duty of the women of this country to secure themselves their sacred right to the elective franchise.

Resolved, That the equality of human rights results necessarily from the fact of the identity of the race in capacities and responsibilities.

Resolved, That...[these] being...self-evident truth[s] growing out of the divinely implanted principles of human nature, any custom or authority adverse to it, whether modern or wearing the hoary sanction of antiquity, is to be regarded as...self-evident falsehood[s], and at war with mankind."

MOTHER JONES: MOJO RISING

In the 1960s, big business came to be known as "The Man." A hundred years before the hippie revolution, Mother Jones was giving The Man a kick in the wallet every chance she got. She organized her first labor strike at the midpoint of her life, age forty-seven, and devoted the rest of her life to establishing unions in coal mines, breweries, factories, and cotton mills over a span of forty years. Armed with steel-trap smarts, a tough, no-nonsense manner and endless courage, she fought her way to the forefront of the labor movement and paved the way for safer, more humane conditions for workers, including child labor laws and the eight-hour work day.

A charismatic leader who helped the underpaid and overworked laborers of America fight for their rights, Mary Harris Jones came to be known as Mother Jones because of her concern for the workers she came across. Portrayed in the many photos taken, as the sweetest of grandmothers in her proper Victorian gowns, hats, and spectacles, she was however, in her own words, "a hell-raiser." Doubtless, she enjoyed the epithet once hurled at her by a prosecutor in West Virginia—"the most dangerous woman in America."

She was born into a working-class family of revolutionaries. Her father and his father before him were both soldiers in the battle for Irish independence. Her grandfather was hanged for his participation in the revolution; her father escaped to North America to avoid arrest. Young Mary attended public school and trained both as a seamstress and a teacher. She taught at a convent in Monroe, Michigan, for a year before deciding to set up a dressmaker's shop in Chicago. The year 1860 found her in Memphis teaching; there she met and married George Jones, an ironworker, union member, and labor organizer, who died seven years later of yellow fever. This was enough to send her back to Chicago, where she applied her skill as a seamstress, making fancy dresses for the wealthy of Lake Shore Drive. Anger welled up inside her at the selfish wealthy folks she sewed for who blithely ignored the needy and basked in their sumptuous comforts.

Four years after losing George to yellow fever, Mary lost her shop to Chicago's great fire, and she joined the ranks of the homeless. Her anger at the selfish wealthy class incited her to attend Knights of Labor meetings where she quickly became admired for her orations and argumentation. Mary Harris had found her true calling—as a labor activist, agitator, and activist. She was nothing short of brilliant. Her passionate calls to action were heard by thousands of Americans who were inspired by her to fight for basic human rights and respect as workers. She had an almost magical ability to band people together to fight against incredible odds.

"Women are the foundation of the nation," she declared as she put her heart and soul into helping the condition of working women in rural areas and mountainous towns of West Virginia, Pennsylvania, Illinois, Ohio, and as far west as Colorado, Utah, and Arizona. She forged a powerful sisterhood with these women and saw behind the shy faces a steely strength that she helped them tap. "Women have great power, if only they knew how to use it," she would declare often, urging women to focus their eyes on the prize of better pay, decent working conditions, and reduction of the soul-killing hours. "This is the fighting age. Put on your fighting clothes. You are too sentimental!"

Mother Jones labored in the trenches alongside the workers, sleeping on their floors in cold mountain shacks and sharing their scant food. While intellectuals theorized about class struggles and economic ideals, Mother Jones worked in the gritty reality of these people's daily lives. She saw herself as one of the struggling, too, and babysat, cared for the sick, held the dying, and scavenged for food, clothing, coal, and money during strikes. Her distrust of the suffragette movement came from her total allegiance to the uneducated working poor; many of the suffragettes were of the monied, educated, upper class she so resented. She let them worry about getting the right to vote for women; she was making sure they could survive the business of making a living.

A victim of sexism, Mother Jones was never allowed to participate in the United Mine Workers of America she fought so hard for. Men completely ran the union; she was allowed no part of it. From the sidelines, she tried her best to advise in impassioned letters these men for whom she had built a powerful membership. Late in life, she was saddened by the infighting and corruption she was powerless to prevent.

Mother Jones championed the underdog at her own expense and often at enormous personal risk. Ahead of her time, she amazed West Virginia mine workers she had organized when she implored them to be more understanding of the foreign-born "scabs" who were sent to work the mines during strikes. She also lobbied on behalf of African American workers who suffered bigotry from the unions.

Born in the Victorian Age and brought up to be subservient, Mother Jones was a first generation Irish American who fought the good fight and left the world a better place for her class, for women, and for the ethnic groups trying to find their place among the workers of America. Mary Harris Jones was fortunate to live long enough to see many of the great changes she fought for in improving the lot of the working class. Iron-willed and lion-hearted, Mother Jones lived by her principles. A shero in both words and action, she reminds us all, "it is the militant, not the meek, who shall inherit the earth."

"This Jeanne d'Arc of the miners was a benevolent fanatic, a Celtic blend of sentiment and fire, of sweetness and fight...(who) captured the imagination of the American worker as no other woman—perhaps no other leader—ever has."

— **Dale Fetherling** *on Mother Jones*

EMMA GOLDMAN: RADICAL RHETORICIAN

Teenage immigrant Emma Goldman had escaped from Russia in 1885 after witnessing the wholesale slaughter of the idealist political rebel anarchists who called themselves the Nihilists. Two years later in America, the young woman "born to ride the whirlwinds" as someone once said, saw it happen again with the new trial and killings of the Haymarket anarchists who had opposed Chicago's power elite. Rather than scare her off the politics of idealism forever, young Emma was drawn even more toward the kind of political passion that risked death for principles. She "devoured every line on anarchism I could get," she notes in her autobiography *Living My Life*, "and headed for New York City, command central in the 1890s for radicals of many stripes."

In New York, Emma met one of the anarchists whose writing she'd been devouring, Johann Most, who encouraged her to develop her gift for public speaking. Emma worked as a practical nurse in New York's ghettos where she saw the price women paid for want of any birth control. Soon she was taking to the soapbox to air her views on this lack of available contraception and the resulting reliance on back-room abortions: "Thanks to this Puritan tyranny, the majority of women soon find themselves at the ebb of their physical resources. Ill and worn, they are utterly unable to give their children even elementary care. That, added to economic pressure, forces many women to risk utmost danger rather than continue to bring forth life." Her campaign reached the ears of Margaret Sanger and influenced the development of a national birth control campaign.

But birth control was only one of her bailiwicks; what she was really advocating was anarchism: a classless, governmentless society made up of small groups in free, humanistic cooperation with one another. She had a tremendous gift for verbal rhetoric. Nicknamed "Red Emma," she traveled the United States lecturing—often six months of the year, five nights a week—making frequent stops at Mabel Dodge's infamous salon, and publishing her monthly magazine, *Mother Earth*, a vehicle for her twin concerns of women's liberation and the rights of the working class. Reporter Nellie Bly was delighted to note that "Red Emma" was very pretty "with a saucy turned up nose and very expressive blue-gray eyes...(brown hair) falling loosely over her forehead, full lips, strong white teeth, a mild, pleasant voice, with a fetching accent."

In 1893, she was jailed for a year for exhorting a crowd of unemployed men who believed "it was their sacred right" to take bread if they were starving. Later she came to believe that the ends do not always justify the means, and she repudiated violence as a tool to create change. She continued to mesmerize crowds with her impassioned speeches until 1917 when her opposition to World War I led to a two-year imprisonment. She was subsequently deported, the Justice Department fearful of allowing her to continue her antiwar campaign: "She is womanly, a remarkable orator, tremendously sincere, and carries conviction. If she is allowed to continue here she cannot help but have great influence."

She continued to exercise influence from abroad; in 1922 *Nation* magazine proclaimed that she was one of "the twelve greatest living women." She was allowed back into the country after her death when the government decided that her silenced corpse posed no risk, and she was buried in Chicago with the Haymarket martyrs.

"The more opposition I encountered, the more I was in my element and the more caustic I became with my opponents."

— Emma Goldman

THE MABEL DODGE SALON

Anybody who was anybody in the intellectual and art worlds of the early twentieth century hung out at Mabel's salon, among them: D.H. Lawrence, Gertrude Stein, Alice B. Toklas, Andrew Dassburg, Georgia O'Keefe, Leon Gaspard, Ansel Adams, and Robinson Jeffers. Beginning in New York's Greenwich Village after a stint in a Medici villa in Florence, Mabel Dodge worked for her vision of a "New World Plan" to bring the world's greatest thinkers, writers, artists, musicians, and social reformers together to whet each other's minds and create a second renaissance. Lois Palken Rudnick, a historian specializing in this era, says this about Mabel, "When she came

back to the States, she landed in New York City amidst America's first great social and political revolution. She became one of the rebels of Greenwich Village and was involved with the Armory Show, the first show of post-impressionist art to come to the States. She supported anarchists and socialists and their projects, like Emma Goldman and Margaret Sanger...She was an artist of life."

DOLORES IBARRURI: LA PASIONARIA

The shero of the Spanish Civil War, Dolores Ibarruri was born in 1895 to a Basque miner. She worked as a servant until she joined the Partido Socialista and began writing incendiary political diatribes under the pseudonym, *La Pasionaria:* "The Passion Flower." She and her husband Julian Ruiz helped found the first Communist parties in Spain in 1920. The mother of six children with Ruiz, Ibarruri didn't let motherhood slow her down; not only did she continue writing for the *El Mundo Obrero* workers' newspaper, in 1934, she organized a women's group called *Agrupacion de Mujereres Antifascistas.*

Noted for her keen political mind, fearlessness, and charisma, Ibarruri was elected to Parliament in 1936 and was freed from a stint in jail so that she could serve. She began making speeches on behalf of the Popular Front Government, rousing audiences with her impassioned pleas to halt the tide of Fascism. When full-scale civil war broke out in Spain, La Pasionaria exhorted her fellow loyalists to remain steadfast with cries of *"No Pasaran!"* (They shall not pass!) When Franco grabbed the power seat, she left the Spain she had fought for to live in the USSR. During the mass exodus of Communists from Spain, the great Spanish matriarch met photographer Tina Modotti. Modotti was so trusted by the exiled Spaniards, she was one of two people guarding Ibarruri's hospital room when she fell ill with a bad case of hepatitis.

In Soviet Russia, Ibarruri served as a Secretary-General of the Spanish Communist Party from 1942 until she assumed the presidency in 1960, a post she held until 1977. When Franco died later that year, La Pasionaria moved back home to Spain, and in Spain's first elections in forty years, was reelected to Parliament. She was eighty-one years old, fierce as ever, and accorded a shero's welcome back to the country that lionized her. La Pasionaria, whose career was based on dedication to her crusade for freedom, received much recognition for her incredible courage and self-sacrifice; she won the Lenin Peace Prize and was named honorary vice president of the International Democratic Federation of Women. She will always be remembered for her valor in the face of great danger and for her belief that, "It is better to die on your feet than live on your knees!"

ROSA LUXEMBURG: RED ROSA

"Emancipate!" That was the cry of socialist revolutionary Rosa Luxemburg who was born a Polish Jew and devoted her life to improving the plight of workers around the world through her political theories. She helped found the Spartacus League in Germany and worked ceaselessly toward change, cranking out more than 700 books, pamphlets, and treatises.

She dazzled everyone she encountered with her fierce intelligence; Lenin himself became one of her biggest fans even though she publicly disagreed with him. In 1905, Rosa staged a worker's revolt in Poland and protested World War I very vocally, prompting the authorities to throw her in jail for the entire war. Shortly before her fiftieth birthday, Rosa Luxemburg was murdered in 1919 by political opponents during the German revolution she helped create.

Rosa Luxemburg's standing as one of the great intellectuals of the turn of the century is in danger of obscurity. The Nazis set about to obliterate her writings and Stalinists undertook a smear campaign to distort Luxemburg's theories. But she was a great political theoretician, one who sought to bring equality to the working class.

INTERNATIONAL WARRIOR WOMEN TAKING CHARGE

Hawaii's last queen was **Lili'uokalani**. She was raised by American missionaries in the nineteenth century and married an Englishman before taking her up her role as the ruler of the beautiful island chain. She was quite accomplished as a stateswoman and also as a singer who treasured her island's culture and feared the loss of it with the Western invasion. It is daunting to realize she was imprisoned and held in isolation after her brother King Kalakaua's death so white annexationists could take over Hawaii and incorporate it into the United States. Think about that the next time you hear somebody complain about what a tourist trap the once pristine paradise has become!

Maria de la Mercedes Barbudo was a Puerto Rican rebel who fought for emancipation and abolition circa 1800 and was exiled and murdered for her efforts toward her country's independence.

Nana Yaa Asantewa was born in 1863 and went on to become the national shero of Ghana, known as the Queen Mother. British colonists stole Ghana's sacred treasure; going to war against the Brits, Nana (at the age of fifty) led an uprising to take back the Golden Stool. Nana and her army of women were defeated, but her valor and that of her women warriors was legendary. She died in prison at seventy after being a captive exile for twenty years.

Sorjini Chattophyaya Naidu was a nineteenth-century Indian-born Brahmin, the highest caste, and rebelled by marrying a man from a lower caste. This was just the beginning of her activist actions; she went against her family's orders by discarding the academics of math and science her father had chosen for her, becoming a poet instead. She joined Gandhi's movement for peaceful independence and was jailed many times ("I was born a rebel and I expect to die a rebel unless I free India!") for civil disobedience, and later ran a salon in Bombay open to all races, castes, and religions. Upon India's independence in 1947, she became governor of her province and worked for women's rights.

In March 1928, **Chen Tiejun** was arrested, jailed, tortured, and executed at the age of twenty-four for her radical feminism. A founding member of the Chinese Communist Party, she organized a women's underground army of rebels and weapons smugglers. Forced to marry by her provincial parents, she left her husband immediately and attended college to become a teacher. Betrayed by a fellow Red Guard, her courageous refusal to divulge any information to her captors made her a shero of the Communist movement and Chinese feminists.

Founder of the Egyptian Feminist Union, **Huda Sha'Rawi** was part of the last generation of Egyptian women to come of age under the harem system in the late eighteenth century. Born to a wealthy family, she was at the forefront of Egyptian feminism and led the movement to free Egypt from British colonial rule.

ELEANOR ROOSEVELT: THE GREATEST OF ALL?

No book on awesome women would be complete without a profile of Eleanor Roosevelt, named by historian Deborah G. Felder as the most influential woman in history.

Though she was born to the privileged class, Eleanor reached out to all women, regardless of economic status, and they responded, knowing she was a kindred soul. Eleanor was born Anne Eleanor Roosevelt and came from colonial Roosevelt stock on both sides of her family. Eleanor remembered being "like a little old woman" and all her life was keenly aware of what she called "a lack of beauty." She seems to have survived the pre-*Reviving Ophelia* batterings to her self-esteem fairly well, despite a vain and selfish mother who nicknamed Eleanor "Granny" and never passed up the opportunity to remind her that she didn't inherit her mother's beauty. Fortunately, her dashing humanitarian father, Elliott, loved her dearly and instilled in his "little Nell" a strong sense of the importance of giving to others.

By the age of ten, Eleanor was an orphan and was made to live with her stern matriarch of a grandmother, then sent to the very exclusive Allenswood girls school in London. Allenswood was run by a forthright liberal activist, Marie Souvestre, who took Eleanor under her wing and lavished affection and attention on her. Eleanor recalled these days as the best of her life.

Returning home in 1902, she had the obligatory debutante ball, but preferred doing good works at the settlement houses among the working class to partying at snooty, upper-class salons. She also sneaked in an engagement to her fifth cousin, political aspirant Franklin Delano Roosevelt; the blushing Eleanor's hand was given in marriage by then-President Roosevelt, otherwise known as "Uncle Teddy." Eleanor and Franklin quickly had six children, losing one baby shortly after birth. Eleanor was painfully shy, a terrible issue to deal with when she had to constantly entertain to advance her husband's political career, even harder to do with a bossy mother-in-law hovering over the children and trying to take over the household.

The burgeoning young Roosevelt clan soon found themselves in the District of Columbia while FDR served as Assistant Secretary of the Navy. It is there that Eleanor found out about his affair with Lucy Mercer, Eleanor's social secretary. Eleanor was devastated, but found an inner resolve to withstand the pain and became even more dedicated to positive social change. She joined the League of Women's Voters and the Women's Trade Union League, working toward reform for women's pay and limiting the hours of the working day. In 1921, FDR fell ill with polio. Leaving the tending of him to others, Eleanor served as FDR's eyes and ears out in the world, traveling all over the country listening to people, discerning what Americans of all walks of life wanted and needed. For the rest of her life, she strove tirelessly to advance the cause of getting more women into government office and was deeply concerned with unemployment, poverty, education, housing, day care, health care, and civil rights. (Of her, Franklin once prayed, "Dear God, make Eleanor a little tired." But he never ceased relying on her sage advice.)

When FDR was elected president, Eleanor was less than thrilled with her status as First Lady: "Now I'll have no identity," she proclaimed. But she took on the job and made it her own. She held a press conference, the first First Lady to do so, and regularly spoke with a corp of women reporters. While FDR had his fireside chats, Eleanor had "My Day," a newspaper column and radio show that she used as a pulpit for many social justice issues, including the time Marian Anderson was blocked from singing in D.C. by the Daughters of the American Revolution because she was black. When Eleanor announced her resignation from the DAR in protest, their ranks dwindled in shame.

After her husband's death, she continued on with her work, including becoming a delegate to the United Nations, where she is credited with drafting and pushing through to adoption the *Universal Declaration of Human Rights* and launching UNICEF. For all the good she did, this humanitarian whom Harry Truman dubbed "The First Lady of the World" is still, nearly fifty years after her death, one of the most cherished figures in herstory.

"You get more joy out of the giving to others, and should put a good deal of thought into the happiness you are able to give."

— Eleanor Roosevelt

FRANCES PERKINS: DEAR TO HER HEART

Frances Perkins joined Franklin Delano Roosevelt's cabinet in 1933 as secretary of labor when America was reeling from The Great Depression. She remained in this office as long as FDR himself did, serving her country well during its worst-ever economic crisis. Frances also worked on behalf of reform for workers and on many other issues dear to the First Lady, Eleanor's, heart. She was responsible for the creation of many jobs and work corps, for the development of better minimum wages, and for benefits such as Social Security and unemployment insurance. Frances' zeal as an industrial reformer came from a tragedy she witnessed in 1911, when 146 women working at the Triangle Shirtwaist company died in a fire because there were no fire escapes. This was a real turning point for Perkins, "I felt I must seal it not only on my mind but on my heart as a never-to-be-forgotten reminder of why I had to spend my life fighting conditions that could permit such a tragedy."

CLARE BOOTHE LUCE: LUCE CANNON

Clare Boothe Luce, "the woman with the serpent's tongue," was the anti-Eleanor Roosevelt, a sort of alternate universe doppelganger who used her razor-sharp wit to oppose while "faintly praising" the First Lady and other unrepentant New Dealers. A virulent Republican and FDR basher, Clare was both a smart and tough cookie, albeit not to everyone's taste. Clare, however, had a wholly unique way of asserting her woman power. As a young woman, one of her summer jobs during college was dropping feminist tracts out of an airplane for some elderly but unstoppable suffragists. Her next job was writing photo captions for *Vogue*; there the renowned beauty quickly ascended to the position as *Vanity Fair's* managing editor. She was the first woman to hold this post for the glamour glossy and soon proved she could hold her own with the boys, even managing to be welcomed in to their cigarettes and brandy ritual.

Then she met *Time* and *Fortune* magnate Henry R. Luce, married, and quit the day job to write plays, starting with the stinker *Abide with Me* and then surprising everyone with the all-female *To the Women*, a take-no-prisoners satire of snooty society ladies, which went on to become a very successful movie. Clare became an international cause celebre with the success of *To the Women*, penning a few more stage plays including *Kiss the Boys Goodbye* before she pulled another switcheroo: war correspondent for *Life* magazine on the battle fronts of Burma, India, and China during the early years of World War II. She even interviewed Madame Chiang Kai-shek and Prime Minister Nehru.

Clare's next incarnation was politician and she went on the stump, dissing FDR, Winston Churchill, and a herd of other such sacred cows. She stunned everyone with her gift for rhetoric of the biting, stinging sort. Her next move was to run for a seat in Connecticut's Congress with a very hawkish platform—her slogan was "Let's Fight a Hard War Instead of a Soft War"—and she campaigned for the rights of women, blacks, and workers. Easily winning a seat, she served for four years and then retired while she was ahead. Clare then took her domestic campaigns abroad, convincing the Italian Prime Minister to give Italian women the vote! Her good relations with Italy garnered a post for Clare as the ambassador to Italy in 1953, becoming the United States' second woman ambassador and the first woman chief of mission to a major European power. In 1953, she was fourth in the Gallup poll of the most admired women in the world. Clare became the grande dame of the Grand Old Party from the Goldwater sixties until her death of cancer in 1987. Clare will be best remembered for her quick wit and verbal virtuosity. She was absolutely one of a kind; she never luxuriated in her husband's great wealth, but instead worked her behind off for many causes and made great strides for women in her wake.

"Because I am a woman, I must make unusual efforts to succeed. If I fail, no one will say 'She doesn't have what it takes.' They will say, 'Women don't have what it takes.'"

— Clare Boothe Luce

LUCE LIPS

- From the diary Clare kept her psychedelic-inspired musings in when she and hubby Henry dropped acid in 1960: "Capture green bugs for future reference," "Feel all true paths to glory lead but to the grave," and "The futility of the search to be someone. Do you hear the drum?"

- On Veep Henry Wallace: "his global thinking is, no matter how you slice it, globaloney!"
- On Franklin Delano Roosevelt: "Now I do not for a moment believe that Mr. Roosevelt is a real dictator. Rather, he is a sort of super-duper, highly cultured political boss."
- On Harry Truman: "A gone goose."
- On Eleanor Roosevelt: "No woman in American history has ever so comforted the distressed or so distressed the comfortable."
- On Mississippi senator Theodore Bilbo: "the high muckamuck in America of that muckiest and most vulgar of all modern pagan cults: racism!
- On the environment: "I am bewildered by the paradox presented by a nation that can land on the moon, orbit satellites 190 million miles from earth, but can't find a way to rid its own landscape of broken-down automobiles."

LEE TAI-YOUNG: WOMAN WARRIOR

Lee Tai-Young was the first Korean woman ever to become a lawyer and a judge as well as the founder of the first Korean legal aid center. She was born in what is now North Korea in 1914, the daughter of a gold miner. She received a degree in home economics from Ewha Womans University, a Methodist college, and married a Methodist minister in 1936. Lee had dreams of becoming a lawyer when she came to Seoul to study at Ewha, but when her husband fell under suspicion of being a spy for the U.S. and was jailed for sedition by the Japanese colonial government in the early 1940s, she had to go to work to maintain her family. She took jobs as a school teacher and a radio singer, and took in sewing and washing as well.

After the war, Lee continued her studies with the support of her husband. In 1946, she became the first woman to attend Seoul National University and earned her law degree in 1949. She was the first woman ever to pass the National Judicial Examination in 1952. Five years later she founded the Women's Legal Counseling Center, a law practice that provided services to poor women. Lee, along with her husband, were participants in the 1976 Myongdong Declaration, which called for the return of civil liberties to Korean citizens. Because of her political views, she was arrested as an enemy of President Park Chung-hee, and in 1977 received a three-year suspended sentence along with a loss of civil liberties including being automatically disbarred for ten years.

Her law practice evolved into the Korea Legal Aid Center for Family Relations and served more than 10,000 clients per year. She authored 15 books on women's issues, beginning with a 1957 guide to Korea's divorce system. In 1972, she published *Commonsense in Law for Women*; other notable titles include *Born A Woman* and *The Woman of North Korea*. She also translated Eleanor Roosevelt's book *On My Own* into Korean. In 1975, the Ramon Magsaysay Award Foundation chose her as the recipient of their Community Leadership Award; she was given an award by the International Legal Aid Association in 1978. She received international recognition from many quarters, including an honorary law doctorate from Drew University in Madison, NJ in 1981. In 1984, she published a memoir, *Dipping the Han River Out with a Gourd*, four years before she passed away at the ripe old age of 84.

"No society can or will prosper without the cooperation of women."

— Lee Tai-Young

BETTY FRIEDAN: MAD HOUSEWIFE

When Betty Friedan submitted her article in 1956 about the frustrations women experience in their traditional roles as housewife and mother, she received rejections from *McCalls, The Ladies's Home Journal,* and every other publication she approached. The editors, all men at that day and age, were pretty disapproving, too, going so far as to say any woman would have to be "sick" not to be completely satisfied in her rightful role!

But Betty knew that she and millions of women like her were not sick, just stifled. Betty nee Goldstein Friedan put aside her dream of being a psychologist for fear of becoming a spinster, instead choosing to marry and work for a small newspaper. She was fired from her job when she got pregnant for the second time, and began, like most middle-class women of her day and age, to devote herself full-time to the work of running a home and family, what she called "the dream of life, supposedly, of American women at that time." But after a decade of such devotion, she still wasn't happy and theorized she wasn't alone. A graduate of Smith College, she decided to poll her fellow alumnae. Most of her classmates, who had given up promising careers to devote themselves to their families, felt incomplete; many were deeply depressed. They felt guilty for not being completely content sacrificing their individual dreams for their families, each woman certain that her dissatisfaction was a personal failing. Betty called this "the problem that has no name" and so she gave it one, "the feminine mystique."

Over the next five years, her rejected article evolved into a book as she interviewed hundreds of women around the country. *The Feminine Mystique* explored the issue, criticizing American advertisers' exclusively domestic portrayal of women and issuing a call to action for women to say no to the housewife role and adopt a "new life

plan" in which they could have both families and careers. With its publication in 1963, *The Feminine Mystique* hit America like a thunderbolt; the publisher W.W.I. Norton had printed only 2,000 copies, never anticipating the sale of 3 million copies in hardcover alone!

Unintentionally, Betty had started a revolution; she began to be flooded with letters from women saying her book gave them the courage to change their lives and pursue equal access to employment opportunities and other equality issues. Ultimately, the response to Betty's challenge created the momentum that led to the formalization of the second wave of the U.S. women's movement in 1966 with the organization of NOW—the National Organization for Women.

Betty was NOW's first president and took her role as a leader in the women's movement seriously, traveling to lectures and campaigns for change, engendering many of the freedoms women now enjoy. She pushed for equal pay for equal work, equal job opportunities, and access to birth control and legalized abortion. In 1970, she quit NOW to fight for the Equal Rights Amendment, and in 1975, was named Humanist of the Year. Of her, author Barbara Seaman wrote, "Betty Friedan is to the women's movement what Martin Luther King was to blacks."

In 1981, responding to critics who claimed feminism ignored the importance of relationships and families to most women, she penned *The Second Stage*, in which she called on men and women to work together to make both the home and the workplace havens for both genders. Before her death in 2006, Betty was making another revolution with her book, *The Fountain of Age*, raising consciousness about society's stereotypes about aging thirty years after she, as futurist Alvin Toffler so aptly put it, "pulled the trigger of history" with *The Feminine Mystique*.

"It's been a lot of fun making the revolution."

— Betty Friedan

BETTY'S PERSONAL SHEROES

From a 1984 radio interview: "I admire Barbara Jordan [and] Martha Griffiths, the lieutenant governor of Michigan...I have in some ways, great admiration for Indira Gandhi...After the winning of the vote in 1920, until my *Feminine Mystique* in 1963, women's history was almost blotted out of the national consciousness. We didn't study it in school. So, the women that are now, in my opinion, heroines of history before me: Mary Wollstonecraft in England, Elizabeth Cady Stanton, Margaret Fuller, Susan B. Anthony, [and] Charlotte Perkins Gilman in the United States, and their like in other countries...Eleanor Roosevelt, of course...I criticized, but also admired a great deal; Margaret Mead, Abigail Adams, the wife of John Adams, one of the first Presidents of the United States...I always adored Collette, and the idea of Collette and the writings of Collette. I love the imagery of Madame de Stael, who would be doing all the things at once the way women have to do them. She would be having a pedicure, having her nails polished, nursing her baby at her breast, dictating a menu to her cook, waving goodbye to her lover going off to the Napoleonic Wars and writing at the same time, writing her stories, her memoirs...I love that image. But the images of women we are beginning to have now, we are only [now] discovering that they are as a result of the women's movement. We, who have made the women's movement, had to create ourselves and help each other create ourselves as a new kind of woman."

BELLA ABZUG: BATTLING BELLA

When brilliant young attorney and editor of the *Columbia Law Review* Bella Abzug graduated from Columbia in 1947, she headed straight back home to New York City to represent labor interests and civil rights. The daughter of a Bronx butcher, Bella credits her interest in social change to her grandfather, a Russian Jewish immigrant. In the fifties, she had ample opportunity to pursue her passionate causes during the McCarthy hearings, defending many on trial for leftist leanings.

For decades, if there was action to be taken or change to be made, Bella Abzug was in there with her considerable charisma, impressive rhetoric, and intense desire to make the world a better place, particularly for women and minorities. She is regarded as having been influential in the passage of the 1954 Civil Rights Act and the Voting Rights Act of 1965. Unstoppable Bella also took on the Vietnam War issue in the sixties and founded Women Strike for Peace.

In 1969, the die-hard Democrat jumped into politics herself, running for New York City's 19th Congressional District with the catchy slogan, "This Woman Belongs in the House!" and winning a showdown against Barry Farber. Bella Abzug didn't disappoint her backers one bit when she started in, hammer and nails, constructing her platform of change. Her very first day, Bella put out a call for withdrawal of all troops from Vietnam by July, 1971, and went on from there with dramatic pursuits of her ultraliberal agenda. Almost as famous for her hats as her flamboyant rhetoric, she never backed away from the chance to fight for one of her causes, a trait that earned her a number of nicknames: Battling Bella, Hurricane Bella, and Mother Courage, to name three.

In her signature large hats, she was easily recognized as one of the preeminent feminists among a core group including Betty Friedan, Shirley Chisholm, and Gloria Steinem, with whom she founded the National Women's Political Caucus in 1971, whose mission was the dispersement of political power to include the women, the poor, the working class, racial minorities, and other groups previously shut out from politics.

She lost a bid for the Senate by a narrow margin in 1976 and lost the chance to become the mayor of New York City the following year. In the nineties, she was the co-chair of the Women's Environment and Development Organization, an international network dedicated to protecting the planet as well as furthering the causes of social justice and women's rights. Until her death in 1998, this plain-spoken strong-headed shero never backed away from a chance to fight for one of her causes.

Bella, who insisted on being called "Ms.," continued to attract considerable controversy as well as virulent defenders and supporters throughout her life. One thing for sure is that she never failed to put everything she had on the line for the pursuit of a better world for women and minorities. In her autobiography, *Bella! Ms. Abzug Goes to Washington*, she says, "There are those who say I'm impatient, impetuous, uppity, rude, profane, brash, and overbearing. Whether I'm any of those things or all of them, you can decide for yourself. But whatever I am—and this ought to be made very clear at the outset—I am a very serious woman."

"We were meant to advise, not just consent."

— Bella Abzug

KATE MILLETT: THE "LAVENDER MENACE"

The second wave of feminism had many facets. While Betty Friedan argued for economic equality, in her 1970s book *Sexual Politics*, Kate Millett advocated a more militant revolution and boldly decried patriarchy with a call for a radical revision of roles for women. Millett represented the "lavender menace" uptight Americans feared—lesbians! Wild woman politico Millett minced no words in her crusade against sexism, even criticizing missionary style intercourse as one of the evils of keeping women down. She has gone on to write several more books guaranteed to shock in some form or fashion: *The Prostitution Papers*, an exploration and defense of hooking; *Flying*, a frank account of her love life; and *Sita*, about the death of a lesbian affair. She has also made a well-regarded film, *Three Lives*, and revealed her institutionalization for mental illness in an eye-opening account. According to Gayle Graham Yates in *Makers of Modern Culture*, Kate Millett is the best known American feminist outside America because of her newsmaking trip to Iran to work on behalf of Iranian women's rights ending in her expulsion from the country by the Ayatollah Khomeni.

"Patriarchy decrees that the status of both child and mother is primarily or ultimately dependent on the male."

— **Kate Millett**

GLORIA STEINEM: WONDER WOMAN

Gloria Steinem's name is synonymous with feminism. As a leader of the second wave of feminism, she brought a new concern to the fore—the importance of self-esteem for women. Her childhood did little to bolster her sense of self or predict the successful course her life would take. Her father, an antique dealer, traveled a lot for work, and her mother suffered from severe depression and was often bedridden and self-destructive. Because they moved so often, Gloria didn't attend school until she was ten, after her family was deserted by her father and Gloria assumed the roles of housewife and mother to her mother and sister. Escaping through books and movies, Gloria did well at school and eventually was accepted to Smith College, where her interest in women's rights, sparked by her awareness that her mother's illness had not been taken seriously because "her functioning was not necessary to the world" began to take hold.

After a junket in India, she started freelancing; her goal was to be a political reporter. Soon she hit the glass ceiling; while she made enough money to get by, she wasn't getting the kind of serious assignments her male colleagues were—interviewing presidential candidates and writing on foreign policy. Instead she was assigned in 1963 to go undercover as a Playboy Bunny and write about it. She agreed, seeing it as an investigative journalism piece, a way to expose sexual harassment. However, after the story appeared, no editors would take her seriously; she was the girl who had worked as a Bunny.

But she kept pushing for political assignments and finally, in 1968, came on board the newly founded *New York* magazine as a contributing editor. When the magazine sent her to cover a radical feminist meeting, no one guessed the assignment would be transformational. After attending the meeting, she moved from the sidelines to stage center of the feminist movement, cofounding the National Women's Political Caucus and the Women's Action Alliance.

The next year, Steinem, with her background in journalism, was the impetus for the founding of *Ms.*, the first mainstream feminist magazine in America's history. The first issue, with shero Wonder Woman on the cover, sold out the entire first printing of 300,000 in an unprecedented eight days, and *Ms.* received an astonishing 20,000 letters soon after the magazine hit the newsstands, indicating it had really struck a chord with the women of America. Steinem's personal essay, "Sisterhood," spoke of her reluctance to join the movement at first because of "lack of esteem for women—black women, Chicana women, white women—and for myself."

The self-described "itinerant speaker and feminist organizer" continued at the helm of *Ms.* for fifteen years, publishing articles such as the one that posited Marilyn Monroe as the embodiment of fifties women's struggle to keep up the expectations of society. She penned *Outrageous Acts and Everyday Rebellions* in 1983, urging women to take up the charge as progenitors of change. This was followed by *Revolution from Within* in 1992, illuminating her despair at having to take care of her emotionally disturbed mother as well as her struggles with self-image, feeling like "a plump brunette from Toledo, too tall and much too pudding-faced, with...a voice that felt constantly on the verge of revealing some unacceptable emotion." Steinem stunned her reading public with such self-revelatory confessions. Who would have guessed that this crack editor and leading beauty of the feminist movement had zero self-image?

Gloria Steinem's real genius lies in her ability to relate to other women, creating the bond of sisterhood with shared feelings, even in her heralded memoir. Still a phenomenally popular speaker and writer, Gloria Steinem crystallizes the seemingly complicated issues and challenges of her work by defining feminism as simply, "the belief that women are full human beings."

"The sex and race caste systems are very intertwined and the revolutions have always come together, whether it was the suffragist and abolitionist movements or whether it's the feminist and civil rights movements. They must come together because one can't succeed without the other."

— Gloria Steinem

STEINEM'S SHEROES

- The Grimké Sisters whom she sees as the roots of "new feminism"
- Shirley Temple
- Louisa May Alcott

KATHERINE GRAHAM: KATHERINE THE GREAT

Although Katherine Graham was not a politician, she wielded enormous power in the political arena as owner of the *Washington Post*, still one of the most important and respected newspapers in the world today. Born Katherine

Meyer, she was the daughter of Eugene Meyer, a brilliant French Jew who moved to America and attended Yale, made a fortune in banking and on the stock exchange, and retired a multimillionaire before he was thirty years old!

Katherine's childhood is a classic silver spoon story, raised by domestic help while her parents maintained the lifestyle of the glittery successes they were. A staunch Republican, Eugene Meyer took on a second career as a public servant and served as an independent thinker, swung to the opposite pole on the left, and earned a degree in journalism. After a brief stint in San Francisco reporting for the now defunct *News*, Katherine accepted an offer of $29 a week to go and work for the paper Eugene Meyer had bought five years before—the *Washington Post*.

Katherine fell in love with the publisher of the *Post*, Philip Graham, and after they wed, they bought the paper from her father for a million dollars. Philip was brilliant and bipolar. He was keenly interested in building a publishing empire, and soon they added the magazine *Newsweek* to their holdings. Philip also dabbled in the high stakes game of politics and became involved in the very inner circles of power on Capitol Hill, convincing the young John Fitzgerald Kennedy to go with Lyndon Johnson from Texas as his running mate for the presidency. Then, in 1963, he committed suicide after a manic depressive episode. Katherine became a widow and responsible for both *Newsweek* and the *Post* in one day.

Katherine battled her shyness and rose to the occasion, becoming the publisher of the *Post*. Diving in feet first, she saw that the *Post* had been drifting along listlessly. It needed, Katherine believed, a charismatic editor to become a first-rate example of journalistic excellence. She found him in Ben Bradlee, a hard charging investigative reporter whom she quickly named managing editor.

In 1971, the *Post* received worldwide attention when President Richard Nixon slapped a restraining order on the paper for the publishing of the Pentagon Papers, revealing the United States government's involvement in the political machinery of Southeast Asia. Graham refused to back down and later emerged the victor in the skirmish when the Supreme Court decided in the *Post's* favor.

One year later, the *Post* took the spotlight again for breaking the story of the Watergate scandal. Graham financed the Watergate investigation and stood firmly behind her editor and reporters against the White House's retaliatory measures. Her sheroism in the face of enormous pressure from friends and political players to back off from Watergate was simply astounding. She remained steadfast while the *Post's* stock plummeted and so-called friends disappeared rather than be associated with the woman who challenged Richard Nixon and, ultimately, brought him and his house of cards down. When she retired in 1991, she was one of only two women heads of *Fortune 500* companies.

BARBARA WALTERS: THE "TODAY GIRL" WHO BECAME A LEGENDARY JOURNALIST

Barbara Walters once said, "I was the kind nobody thought could make it. I had a funny Boston accent. I couldn't pronounce my Rs. I wasn't a beauty." For decades, she has proven everyone who doubted her to be utterly wrong. Born September 25, 1929, Barbara is an American broadcast journalist, author, and television personality who has hosted shows including The Today Show, The View, 20/20, and the ABC Evening News. Barbara attended Sarah Lawrence College in 1951; she obtained a B.A. in English and then worked at a small advertising agency for a year. After that, she went to work at the NBC network affiliate in New York City doing

publicity and writing press releases. Barbara continued on to produce a number of shows, including the Eloise McElhone Show until its cancellation in 1954. She then started as a writer on the CBS Morning Show in 1955.

Barbara's career began to skyrocket in 1961 when she became a writer and researcher for the Today Show; she later moved up to be the show's "Today Girl", a position in which she presented the weather and light news items. At that time, it was still early in the second wave of the women's movement, and no one took a woman presenting hard news seriously, and there were difficulties with news anchors like Frank McGee who demanded preferential treatment as she started to cross over into news anchor territory. After McGee passed away in 1974, NBC at last promoted Barbara to the position of co-host – the first woman ever to rise to such a position on any U.S. news program.

Barbara was on a roll. Two years later, she became the first woman to co-anchor any American evening news show on a major network when she joined the ABC Evening News, ABC's flagship news program. Walters had a difficult relationship with her co-anchor Harry Reasoner, because he didn't want to have to work with a co-anchor. This led to their team-up lasting only from 1976–78. Walters became a household name while a co-host and producer at the ABC newsmagazine 20/20 from 1979 to 2004, as well as for her appearances on special reports as a commentator, including presidential inaugurations and coverage of 9/11. She was also a moderator for the final debate between presidential candidates Jimmy Carter and Gerald Ford. Barbara is famous for her interviews with memorable people, including Fidel Castro, Vladimir Putin, Michael Jackson, Katharine Hepburn, Anna Wintour, and Monica Lewinsky. In addition to her work at 20/20, Walters co-created The View, a current events talk show hosted solely by women, in 1997. She was a co-host on the show until May 2014 but continues as an executive producer. Barbara Walters was inducted into the Television Hall of Fame in 1989, and in 2007 received a star on the Hollywood Walk of Fame. She has also won Daytime and Prime Time Emmy Awards, the Women in Film Lucy Award, the GLAAD Excellence in Media Award, and a Lifetime Achievement Award from the New York Women's Agenda.

SHIRLEY CHISHOLM: "UNBOUGHT AND UNBOSSED"

Shirley Chisholm was a nonstop shero whose own sense of empowerment spread to everyone who came in contact with her. In 1968, Shirley Chisholm was the first black woman to be elected to Congress, a historic triumph for her gender and race. Four years later, she ran for president in the primaries.

Born in the borough of Brooklyn, New York, in 1924, she spent seven years in Barbados with her grandmother, Emily Seale. She credits the "stiff upper lip" yet excellent education she received in Barbados as giving her an advantage when she returned to the United States. Shirley garnered many scholarship offers upon high school graduation, choosing Brooklyn College to study psychology and Spanish with the intention of becoming a teacher. She got involved with the Harriet Tubman Society, where she developed a keen sense of black pride. Acing every course, she received a lot of encouragement to "do something" with her life. A Caucasian political science professor urged her to pursue politics, a daunting idea at the time. But the seed was planted.

After an arduous job search, Shirley finally found work at the Mount Cavalry Child Center; her magna cum laude degree didn't seem to offset her color for many potential employers. She also took night classes at Columbia, where she met Conrad Chisholm. They married soon after, giving her a stable foundation upon which to build her house of dreams. She continued to work in early childhood education, becoming director of several day care centers and private schools.

In the sixties, Shirley stepped into the political arena, campaigning for a seat in the state assembly in her district. She won the Democratic seat in 1964 and began the first step in a history-making career, winning again in '65 and '66. Then she decided to run for the U.S. Assembly. Even though she was up against a much more experienced candidate with deep-pocketed financial backing, Shirley prevailed; she was aware that there were 13,000 more women than men in the district and quickly mobilized the female vote. She also underwent surgery for a tumor at this time, but went back to work immediately, quickly earning a reputation as one of the most hard charging black members of the Assembly.

Even in Congress, the race issue reared its head. She was assigned to the Agricultural Committee to work with food stamp distribution because she was a black woman. Shirley didn't take this lying down and fought to get off that committee, moving on to Veteran's Affairs and, finally, Education and Labor where she believed she could really do some good. Known for her straight-shooting verbal style and maverick political ways, she always saw herself as an advocate for her constituency, seeking to be the voice of those traditionally overlooked by politics: Hispanics, Native Americans, drug addicts, and gay activists.

As a presidential candidate for the 1972 Democratic nomination, she placed women's rights at the center of her campaign, claiming that she was not a "gimmick" candidate, but a serious contender. Although she failed to get the nod, it did make her a national spokesperson for the civil and women's rights movements. Since then, she helped create the National Political Congress of Black Women and taught, lectured, and authored two books, *Unbought and Unbossed* and *The Good Fight*. Shirley Chisholm was at the forefront of obtaining real political power for African American woman.

"I'm the only one among you who has the balls to run for president."

— **Shirley Chisholm** *to the Black Caucus members at the Democratic convention*

YVONNE BRAITHWAITE BURKE: POLITICAL STANDOUT

Yvonne Burke was the first black woman elected to the U.S. House of Representatives from California, serving from 1973–1978. The daughter of a janitor and a real estate agent, the Angeleno native was noted as exceptionally bright by her teachers and was sent to a "model" UCLA college prep school. The only African American student at the school, Yvonne was treated viciously by the other students, but didn't let that stop her from turning in a stellar performance. Everywhere Yvonne went, she encountered more bigotry, including the women's law sorority she was turned down by, compelling her to form an alternative women's law sorority with two Jewish law students. Starting with her election in 1972, Yvonne Brathwaite's career in Congress was equally outstanding; she was unfailingly supportive of the causes of desegregation, equal employment, and better housing. In '78, she chose to run for California State Attorney General rather than seek reelection. She currently practices law in Los Angeles. Yvonne is a visionary with the smarts and dignity to rise above the hatred she has personally experienced just for being black, saying, "It's just a matter of time until we have a black governor and, yes, a black president." With the election of Barack Obama, she was proven right.

INDIRA GANDHI: DAUGHTER OF DESTINY

Indira Nehru Gandhi's life mirrors the divided country she governed as the first woman Prime Minister of India. She inherited a political consciousness from her nationalist grandfather Motilal Nehru and her father, India's first Prime Minister, Jawaharlal Nehru. The Nehrus are sometimes called India's royal dynasty, but this is a contradiction of the very ideals the Nehru family and the peaceful revolutionary Mohandas K. Gandhi believed in as they worked to end England's colonial rule over India.

As a girl, Indira witnessed up close the birth of modern, independent India under the leadership of Gandhi and her relatives. The Nehrus were a wealthy family who were moved by meeting Mohandas in 1919 to give up all their possessions and join in the struggle for independence. Indira endured the frequent jailings of Jawaharlal (and later, her mother) for nationalist activities. The young girl's role model was Joan of Arc; later she told of playing with dolls to whom she assigned patriotic roles in the fight to free India from their foreign rulers. Indira's childhood was unusual, by any means, often accompanying her father in his travels and meeting luminaries such as Albert Einstein and Ernst Toller. Indira also organized The Monkey Brigade for preteen revolutionaries and was later beaten cruelly for marching carrying India's flag. She and her family often visited Gandhi, who was "always present in my life; he played an enormous role in my development."

Indira suffered depression, anxiety, and illness from her unsettled life, and at age twenty-two married Feroze Gandhi, a family friend who was a Parsee, a member of a small religious sect, and not considered appropriate for Indira, who was of the Brahmin, or priestly, caste. Arrested for their nationalist activities, both Indira and Feroze spent nine months in jail, which, Indira claimed, was the most important event of her life, strengthening her political resolve.

Upon the deaths of their great leader Gandhi and the continued bloodshed during the Partition dividing India into Hindu India and the new Muslim state of Pakistan, Indira joined India's Congress party and began to forge her own political sensibility. When India gained independence in 1947, her father became Prime Minister; because he was a widower, he needed Indira to act as his official hostess. During the time of her father's multiple strokes, Indira was tacitly acting as Prime Minister. Upon his death in 1964, Indira became president of the India National Congress. After her father's successor Lal Bahdur Shastri's brief ministry and death from heart failure, Indira won the election by a landslide and became the leader of the world's largest democracy, a leader of a country where women's rights were not a top priority. Immediately she became a role model for millions of India's women, traditionally subservient to men.

Indira inherited a land where starvation, civil wars, severe inflation, and religious revolts were a daily reality. She constantly endangered her health by working sixteen hour days trying to meet the needs of the second most populated country on earth. Her political fortunes rose and fell; she was booted out of office in 1977, only to be reelected a few years later to her fourth term as prime minister. Her controversial birth-control program is overlooked oftentimes in the criticisms that she traded political favors in order to hang onto the ministry.

Indira was constantly caught in between the warring factions and divisions of India's various provinces and interests, and the history of her ministry reads like a veritable laundry list of riots, uprisings, and revolutions all played out on partisan quicksand. Her assassination demonstrates this fully. In 1919, British troops had massacred thousands of Sikhs, a proud warrior caste, in their sacred place of worship—the Golden Temple of Amritsar Sixty-five years later, Amritsar again ran red with the blood of Sikh extremists attempting to create a stronghold in which to make their demand for greater autonomy. When the Indian army invaded and seized back the temple, the sparks of anger blazed out of control. Across India, Sikhs were cursing the name of Ghandi, including some of her personal security guards. Four months later, Indira was shot to death by a Sikh in her garden, where she was about to be interviewed by Peter Ustinov. Her son, Rajiv, became the next Prime Minister and met an equally violent end when a Sri Lankan Tamil woman leapt onto him and detonated a bomb she had strapped to herself.

Indira Gandhi's life is difficult to fully comprehend without a grasp of Indian history. Perhaps the deepest understanding of her comes through consideration of her chosen role model, Joan of Arc, a model for self-sacrifice who places the interests of her country above the value of her own life, and as a woman warrior in a battle of religious politics pitting men against men. Indira Gandhi's own insistence to reporters who wanted to talk about her uniqueness as a woman Prime Minister speaks volumes as well: "I am not a woman. I am a human being."

MARGARET THATCHER: IRON MAIDEN

Margaret Thatcher may have drawn fire from critics for her staunch conservativism, but she has the respect of the world for her no-nonsense strength and for her rise from greengrocer's daughter to the first woman Prime Minister of Great Britain. MT earned all her laurels through sheer hard work, studying diligently to get into Oxford where she studied chemistry and got her first taste of politics. Upon graduation, she got a law degree, married Dennis Thatcher, and had twins in short order. Her passion for conservative politics increased, and she impressed party members with her zeal and talent for debate. She won a seat in the House of Commons in 1959, and her rise in the party ranks was steady and sure, leading to her election in the eighties as Prime Minister, the first woman ever to head a major Western democracy. Vehemently anti-Communist and anti-waste, she curtailed government with a singular fervor, surprising everyone by going to war with Argentina over the Falkland Islands. Tough as nails, Margaret explains her modus operandi thusly: "I've got a fantastic stamina and great physical strength, and I have a woman's abilitiy to stick to a job and get on with it when everyone else walks off and leaves."

ELIZABETH WARREN: NEVERTHELESS, SHE PERSISTED

Born in 1949, Elizabeth Warren grew up in a middle-class Oklahoma City family with three older brothers. At age 13, young Elizabeth started waiting tables to help her parents out after her father had a heart attack. A star member of her high school debate team, she won the title of "Oklahoma's top high school debater." This took her to George Washington University on a debate scholarship, but two years later she left to marry Jim Warren, her high school sweetheart. The couple moved to Texas when he found a job as an engineer at NASA, and Elizabeth graduated from the University of Houston in 1970 with a degree in speech pathology and audiology. She taught disabled children at a Texas school for a year before again relocating for her husband's work, this time to New Jersey.

After the arrival of daughter Amelia, Elizabeth enrolled at Rutgers School of Law–Newark when her daughter turned two. Shortly before receiving her J.D. in 1976, she became pregnant with their second child. After passing the bar, Elizabeth worked from home, specializing in real estate closings and wills in her new law practice. They divorced in 1978; Elizabeth later remarried but kept her surname (under which she was practicing law at that time).

Warren lectured at Rutgers School of Law–Newark for a couple of years, then moved to the University of Houston Law Center where she became the Associate Dean for Academic Affairs in 1980. In 1987 she became a fulltime professor at U. Penn's law school, where she obtained an endowed chair in 1990. She became the Leo Gottlieb Professor of Law at Harvard Law School in 1995; by 2011, she was the only tenured professor of law there who had gone to law school at a public university in the U.S. Warren assumed an advisory role at the National Bankruptcy Review Commission in 1995, and with others worked to oppose proposed laws which would severely limit consumers' rights to file for bankruptcy, efforts which in the end did not prove successful. From 2006–2010, she was on the FDIC Advisory Committee on Economic Inclusion. Warren is also a member of the National Bankruptcy Conference, an independent group which advises Congress on bankruptcy law. Her work in academia and as an advocate spurred the formation of the Consumer Financial Protection Bureau in 2011, the year that she declared her intention to seek nomination as the Democratic candidate for the U.S. Senate in 2012; she won the nomination and the election, and became the first woman ever elected to the U.S. Senate from Massachusetts.

While campaigning, Warren made a speech at Andover that went viral; she replied to a charge that asking the rich to pay more taxes is "class warfare" by pointing out that no one becomes wealthy in the U.S. without the benefit of infrastructure funded by the taxpayers: "There is nobody in this country who got rich on his own. Nobody. ...You moved your goods to market on the roads the rest of us paid for; you hired workers the rest of us paid to educate; you were safe in your factory because of police forces and fire forces that the rest of us paid for. You didn't have to worry that marauding bands would come and seize everything at your factory, and hire someone to protect against this, because of the work that the rest of us paid for. Now look, you built a factory and it turned into something terrific, or a great idea. God bless. Keep a big hunk of it. But part of the underlying social contract is, you take a hunk of that and pay it forward for the next kid who comes along."

PHOOLAN DEVI: INDIA'S BANDIT QUEEN

While many Indians reviled their own elected Prime Minister Indira Gandhi, they embraced Phoolan Devi, an outlaw believed to have killed sixty people in central India's Chambal Valley. It is difficult to separate fact from fiction in the story; the male outlaw figure is a common subject of North Indian folklore, and Phoolan's tale has many of the same elements. This version is based on the story reported by Mala Sen, in her fascinating and assiduously researched biography of Devi.

Born in 1956 into a boatman subcaste, Phoolan's (which means "flowerlike" in Hindi, but she was more like a steel magnolia!) first insurrection took place when she and her sister wanted to sit in the mustard field they had worked in all day to "stop and smell the mustard blossoms." When their higher caste landlord beat them up because they wouldn't instantly leave, Phoolan watched her sister and parents nearly bleed to death. When she refused at age ten to put up with an arranged marriage to a man twenty years older, her traditionally minded village couldn't deal with it, and Phoolan fell victim to kidnapping by a group of *dacoits*; bandits to you and me. The kidnapping was just as violent as you might expect a gang of marauders to be, and she was dragged, kicked, slapped, and suffered indignities of guns aimed at her private parts and a threat to cut off her nose. It is a real testament to Phoolan's strength that she wasn't utterly broken by the repeated rapes. Phoolan's family was unable to get any help from authorities, who refused to waste their time looking for their rebellious "good-for-nothing" daughter. Meanwhile, the press had a field day with the story, inventing sensational details of their own to make for a good read in the papers. One such tall tale involved Phoolan engineering her own kidnapping because she *wanted* to be with the dacoits.

Whatever happened, one year later, Phoolan took charge of the gang through her own strength of will and personal power. Mala Sen also reports that the gang (thanks to the execution of the rapists by Phoolan's champion, Vikram Mallah) turned into post-Raj Robin Hoods, giving stolen money to elderly and poor Indians. Well-embroidered accounts of Phoolan Devi's exploits were soon making her the second most famous woman in India after Indira Gandhi, who urged peaceful measures in dealing with the headline-grabbing outlaw girl.

Soon, songs about the "Rebel of the Ravines" were being composed, statues of Phoolan Devi were sold in the market next to Krishna and Kali, and millions of Indians begged for her life to be spared in the "manhunt" to bring "The Bandit Queen" in after the alleged massacre of twenty-two Hindu men by Devi's gang. Thanks to the national attention, Phoolan's capture took place safely in front of thousands of witnesses, and she kept up her spirits in prison, where she gave interviews, prayed, and walked unshackled. (She spent eleven years in prison without ever being charged.) India was even more delighted when they finally saw the Phoolan Devi they'd heard so much about; she is strikingly beautiful, with dark, commanding eyes and a magnificent smile. (Phoolan's fairy tale–like story contains a tragic footnote, exemplifying the place of women in a societal admixture of medieval and modern. In prison, she suffered a ruptured ovarian cyst and the presiding doctor performed a hysterectomy, admittedly to prevent "Phoolan Devi breeding more Phoolan Devis!")

Her legend lives on around the globe and Mala Sen's excellent biography has been made into an acclaimed feature film. In India and England, she has become a folk shero. At her surrender, she is reported to have said, "If I had money, I would build a house with rooms as large as the hall of this prison. But I know this is all a dream. If any woman were to go through my experience, then she too would not be able to think of a normal life. What do I know, except cutting grass, and using a rifle?"

Phoolan was freed and all charges against her were dropped in 1994. In 1996, she ran for and was elected to the Samajwadi Party, but the prejudicial odds against a lower caste woman, even an internationally famous one, were against her in the subcontinent. In August of 1997, Phoolan threatened to kill herself when the criminal charges against her were again raised. Though, tragically, she was assassinated in 2001, her colorful legend lives on.

"She was walking tall, taunting them all,
answering the call...with her rifle by her side"

— a popular Indian Phoolan Devi street song

CORAZON AQUINO: MOTHER IN THE LIMELIGHT

Hot on the heels of anti-shero Imelda Marcos (or should I saw hot on the 1,600 heels; remember the 800 pairs of shoe scandal?) came Corazon Aquino, a political neophyte who quietly and competently took the helm of the volatile islands nation in the aftermath of the Marcos regime.

Cory didn't set out to run a country. Educated in the Catholic school system in the United States and the Philippines, she abandoned higher education to marry Benigno Aquino, a promising politician, and served as his helpmate and mother of their five children. Benigno opposed the martial law of Marcos and was jailed in 1972; when he was released, the family fled to the United States, where they lived until 1983. By this time Marcos was losing control of the reins of power, and Benigno decided to return to help agitate for his resignation. As the Aquinos stepped off the plane, Benigno was assassinated. In that moment, Cory had to decide—turn tail or take up the mantle of her slain husband. She chose the latter, uniting the dissidents against Marcos. In 1986, she ran for the presidency of the Philippines, abandoning the speeches that had been prepared for her to talk of the suffering that Marcos had caused her in life. Although both sides declared victory, Marcos soon fled and Cory assumed power.

After the tabloid dictatorship style of the Marcos family, the widow-turned-stateswoman stunned the world with her no-nonsense manner and absolute fearlessness. Corazon Cojuangco Aquino stood fast amid the corrupt circus of Filipino politics even though coup after coup attempted to remove her from office. She quickly earned the respect of her enemies when they discovered it wasn't so easy to knock the homemaker and mother of five from her post as president of the explosively unstable nation. And she refused to live in the opulent palace the Marcos had built, proclaiming it a symbol of oppression of the poor masses by the wealthy few, and chose to live in a modest residence nearby.

However, longterm leadership proved difficult. Although she was credited with drafting a new democratic constitution that was ratified by a landslide popular vote, her support dwindled in the face of chronic poverty, an overstrong military, and governmental corruption. Her presidency ended in 1992.

For her achievements and courage, Cory Aquino has received numerous honorary degrees from sources as diverse as Fordham University and Waseda University in Tokyo. Named *Time* magazine's Woman of the Year, Cory is also the recipient of many awards and distinctions, including the Eleanor Roosevelt Human Rights Award, the United Nations Silver Medal, and the Canadian International Prize for Freedom. Acknowledged by the Women's International Center for her "perseverance and dedication," Corazon Aquino was honored as an International Leadership Living Legacy who "faced adversity with courage and directness."

ESTHER IBANGA: THE PEACEMAKER

Esther Ibanga is a Nigerian pastor and dedicated community organizer for peace in conflict-ridden regions who has received the Niwano Peace Prize for her advocacy of peace and unity in Jos, Nigeria. She was born in 1961 in Kagbu, Nigeria, the seventh of ten children, eight of them girls. Both of her parents were very religious; her father was a policeman who won awards for his honesty and bravery, and her mother went on many mission trips as part of her involvement with her church. Ibanga earned a degree in business administration in 1983 from Ahmadu Bello University, and after serving the mandatory year in the National Youth Service Corps, she went to work for the Central Bank of Nigeria, where she eventually gained a position as a manager. She left the bank to become the first female church leader in the city of Jos, Nigeria, in 1995.

In 2010, Pastor Ibanga founded the Women Without Walls Initiative in response to the constant state of crisis in Plateau State Nigeria since 2000. WoWWI is an NGO that includes Nigerian women from all walks of life and provides advocacy, training for women in building peace, mediation between warring parties, help for people displaced within Nigeria, assistance to the poor, empowerment of women and youth, and development projects in underprivileged areas to prevent grievances from sparking violent conflicts. Her hard work and dedication has helped to restore peace between Christian and Muslim communities in Jos North, a potentially volatile flashpoint. Her approach is to empower women, both inside and outside of Nigeria, to successfully strive to advance the status of women and children of all ethnicities, religions, and political leanings – to allow women to realize themselves as "natural agents of change".

Pastor Ibanga was the leader of a march in February 2010 to the Jos government house in protest of the Dogon Nahawa ethno-religious crisis, in which many lives, including those of women and children, had been lost; more than 100,000 women dressed in black participated. When 276 teenaged girls were kidnapped by Boko Haram terrorists from their school in Chibok, Nigeria, WoWWI joined in the Bring Back Our Girls campaign with other women leaders. Rallies crossing religious and cultural lines were held to demand that the government expedite the girls' release. Pastor Ibanga continues to campaign for the freeing of the 113 girls who are still held captive and speaks internationally on the issue.

MEGYN KELLY: TRUTH TELLER

Megyn Kelly, born in 1970, is a journalist and political commentator. She earned a degree in political science from Syracuse University, and while an undergraduate, investigated sexual harassment cases. She then went on to obtain a J.D. from Albany Law School. After some time as an associate at a Chicago corporate defense firm, Kelly moved to Washington D.C. and was hired by ABC affiliate WJLA in 2003 as a general assignment television reporter. In 2004 she made a move to Fox News, where she was the contributor of legal segments to *Special Report with Brit Hume* as well as hosting her own segment during *Weekend Live*, *Kelly's Court*. In 2010 she became the host of her own afternoon show, *America Live*. During the 2012 presidential election contest, in the evening of election day, Fox News made a projection that Obama would win re-election after partial returns had been released. When Republican strategist Karl Rove took issue with the projection, Kelly asked him, "Is this just math that you do as a Republican to make yourself feel better? Or is this real?" This drew attention to political independent Kelly. She left *America Live* in 2013, but after the birth of her third child that year, returned to Fox News as the host of her new nightly program, *The Kelly File*, which has at times occupied the number one ratings spot among Fox News shows. Megyn Kelly has drawn a lot of controversy over the years due to her outspoken persona, including sparring with candidate Trump; she responded to his criticism of her by saying that she would not "apologize for doing good journalism".

ANITA HILL: WE ALWAYS BELIEVED YOU

Nobody could have guessed that the televised Senate hearings on the nominations of Clarence Thomas to the U.S. Supreme Court would be the top-rated show of 1991. America's collective mouth hung open in amazement at the brouhaha that brewed up around Judge Thomas' worthiness based on the charges of sexual harassment by one Anita Hill. The hearings catapulted the issue of sexual harassment in the workplace into the most hotly debated and analyzed topic of the day, one that still reverberates years later. Prior to Anita's brave stand, sexual harassment was mainly swept under the industrial gray carpeting of most offices, but she singlehandedly forced it to the very center of the national agenda.

The nation and, indeed, the world, watched transfixed as the incredibly poised Anita revealed her experiences with Clarence Thomas as a coworker. With great dignity, she testified that Thomas kept after her to go out with him, referred to himself as "an individual who had a very large penis and...used a name...in pornographic material," and asked her to see "this woman (who) has this kind of breasts that measure this size," in a seemingly endless barrage of ludicrous and lugubrious insults to her as a fellow professional. Senate hearings, usually desert dry and devoid of tabloid titillation, suddenly featured long discussions including the terms "penis" and "pubic hair."

The prelude to the media circus took place when the president announced his choice of "black Horatio Alger" Clarence Thomas as the Supreme Court replacement for the retiring Thurgood Marshall. Anita Hill, a law professor at the University of Oklahoma, contacted Harriet Grant, the Judiciary Committee's nominations counsel. She told Grant that Thomas had harassed her in a sexual and inappropriate manner when she had worked as his assistant at the Equal Employment Opportunity Commission. She had, in fact, quit the EEOC because of his behavior and gone into academia. Grant cc'd the senatorial committee on the allegations, but the Senate whipped through the approval process with nary a word about Hill's report and prepared to vote for confirmation of Thomas. Then journalist shero Nina Totenberg of National Public Radio and New York *Newsday's* Timothy Phelps broke the story wide open to a shocked public. Seven women from the House of Representatives marched in protest to the Senate building, demanding of the sheepish Senate committee to know why the committee had ignored Hill's complaint.

Nothing in Hill's background could have prepared her for the media onslaught. Born in 1956 as the youngest of thirteen children, she was raised in rural Oklahoma in a deeply religious family. An outstanding student, she graduated as valedictorian of her integrated high school, earned top honors in college, and was one of only eleven black students out of a class of 160 at Yale University Law School.

Even through Anita Hill had been promised immunity and total confidentiality, she appeared before the committee in a special session before the scrutiny of the nation. The Judiciary Committee was dismissive, as only Old Boys can be, of Anita Hill and her testimony, even going so far as to ask her if she was taking her revenge as the "woman scorned," and they suggested that she was a patsy for radical liberals and feminists. While Anita's allegations were ultimately disregarded and Clarence Thomas was voted in, Anita's grace under pressure won many admirers who protested the Thomas appointment. The controversy remained headline news for months; polls of public opinion showed Anita Hill gaining and Bush losing points as I Believe You Anita! bumper stickers appeared on thousands of cars across America. For her outspokenness, she was awarded the Ida B. Wells Award from the National Coalition of 100 Black Women and named one of *Glamour's* Ten Women of the Year in 1991.

Anita Hill's courage of conviction made her a shero of the late twentieth century. In her words, "I felt I had to tell the truth. I could not keep silent."

"You just have to tell the truth and that's the most anyone can expect from you and if you get that opportunity, you will have accomplished something."

— **Anita Hill**

HILDA SOLIS: PIONEERING POLITICIAN

Hilda Solis was born in 1957 and raised in La Puente, CA; her Nicaraguan and Mexican immigrant parents had met in citizenship class and married in 1953. Her father had been a Teamsters shop steward in Mexico; he again organized for the union at the Quemetco battery recycling plant, but his efforts for the workers did not prevent him from being poisoned there by lead. Hilda's mother was also active in the union during her years working at Mattel once all the children were in school.

At La Puente High School, students were not necessarily expected to try to better themselves through higher education; one of Hilda's guidance counselors told her mother, "Your daughter is not college material. Maybe she should follow the career of her older sister and become a secretary." Fortunately, another counselor supported Hilda's applying to college, and went so far as to visit her at her house to help her fill out a college application. Hilda earned a bachelor's in political science from California State Polytechnic University and went on to obtain a Master's in public administration at USC.

Solis interned and edited a newsletter in the Carter Administration's White House Office of Hispanic Affairs. In Washington, DC, she met her future husband, Sam Sayyad. She returned to the west coast, and in 1982 became the Director of the California Student Opportunity and Access Program, which helped disadvantaged young people prepare for college. Friends urged her to consider running for elective office, and after a successful run in 1985, she served for some years on the Rio Hondo Community College District. Solis also became State Senator Art Torres' chief of staff. In 1992 she ran for the California State Assembly and won with the support of Barbara Boxer, Gloria Molina, and her mother, who notably fed her campaign volunteers on homemade burritos.

In 1994, Art Torres was nominated to a statewide position as insurance commissioner, and Solis ran for and won the State Senate seat he vacated. She was the first woman of Hispanic descent ever to serve in the State Senate as well as the youngest member of the Senate at the time. She authored domestic violence prevention bills, and she stood up for workers with a bill to raise the minimum wage from $4.25 to $5.75, which was massively opposed by business and vetoed by Governor Pete Wilson. Solis didn't let that stop her; she successfully led a ballot initiative drive, using $50,000 from her own campaign money. When the initiative passed, others knew that she was someone to be reckoned with. Similar initiatives were enacted in other states on the wave of this victory. Solis worked to enact an environmental justice law to protect low-income and minority neighborhoods from being repeatedly targeted for new landfills and pollution sources, and in 2000, she received the JFK Library Profile in Courage Award for this work, the first woman ever to win it. She also called out garment sweatshop operators for their violations of labor conditions, and was an advocate for the people on education and health care issues; 2000 was also the year that she successfully ran for Congress. In 2008, she became the first Hispanic woman to serve in the U.S. Cabinet when President Obama tapped her for the position of Labor Secretary. After serving for the duration of his first term, she decided to resign and returned to California, where she is presently an L.A. County Supervisor.

RASHMI MISRA: TEACHING FOR CHANGE

Rashmi Misra grew up in a military family, so she moved around, attending several schools, but completed her schooling in Delhi, India. She went to Lady Sri Ram College and studied German and public relations. Concurrently, she also studied Odissi dance, an ancient form of Indian classical dance that came originally from Hindu temples. As a young woman, she was employed as a member of the ground staff by Lufthansa Airlines. In 1985, she began teaching a class for five girls at her home, which was then on the campus of IIT Delhi; this was the beginning of what would become VIDYA. As she describes it, "...I realized that the children were thirsty to learn, but the opportunities and means were missing. I went to slums to find children and educate them... Educating the underprivileged kept me motivated."

After she married, she emigrated to the United States. She built the small education project she had started into VIDYA, a major nonprofit that employs over 300 people and has made a difference to more than 220,000 families in the three decades since then. The NGO works with people in the extremely disadvantaged neighborhoods of Delhi, Bangalore, and Mumbai, supplying schools as well as remedial education; literacy, computer, and other skills training; and microfinance and other support on behalf of social entrepreneurship. Much of VIDYA's work still focuses on helping children, as well as women entrepreneurs; but supporting women and children transforms entire communities. Misra found – and inspired – many volunteers and carried out fundraising over the years to sustain VIDYA's efforts. Visit their web page to learn more about the fruits of her work – and never doubt that one woman who cares can make a difference: http://vidya-india.org/

ASIEH AMINI: TAKING ACTION FOR A CAUSE

Asieh Amini is a renowned expatriate Iranian poet and journalist living in Norway. From her birth in 1973 until 1979, she lived a fairly privileged life, as her landed-gentry family was well-to-do and employed servants; but they lost much of their wealth during the Iranian Revolution in 1979. Besides adapting to her family becoming no more than middle class, young Amini despised the fact that females now had to wear the mandatory black hijab covering. As a child, she thought the hijab was ugly and would cry when she was required to wear it like other girls. In 1993, Amini started journalism school at Tabataba'i University in Teheran. While still just a freshman, she started writing for the hardline daily Kayhan, then wrote for Iran, a larger newspaper. Iran started publishing a youth supplement and tapped Amini to be the cultural editor of the 28-page section; this was an unusually high position for a woman to have in Iran, and there was pushback from male staff who didn't like her being in charge of men as a section editor – men older than she was, no less. She refused to give in and focused on working hard, up to 14 hours a day.

As the political winds shifted in Iran, censorship relaxed somewhat, and more young women started to work in the field of journalism. Amini worked at a paper that covered women's affairs, though she opposed the concept of separating news by gender; then she became a freelancer, covering Kurdish demonstrations and a Shirazi earthquake. In 2006, she started investigating killings of young women after learning of the horrific execution of a 16-year-old girl. She worked to publish what she discovered, but lost a job at one newspaper and was turned down by various others. The editor-in-chief who fired her said it was impossible for their paper to publish the story, since she was fighting Sharia law and the Iranian judicial system. Finally a women's journal agreed to publish an abridged version of the story. Amini soon learned of a 19-year-old young woman named Leyla with the mental age of an 8-year-old child who had been abused as well as prostituted by her mother since childhood and was sentenced to die by hanging. Amini wrote about and advocated for her, gaining international attention, which at last led to a new trial for Leyla and after that a safe place for Leyla to live and be cared for. In the course of what she then thought of as organizing for children's rights, Amini learned about stonings, which were still going on in secret even though they had been officially illegal since 2002.

When she discovered that the most hardline judges in Iran were continuing to sentence women and others to death by stoning because they thought they answered to a higher authority than the law of the land, Amini co-created the "Stop Stoning Forever" campaign in 2006. Her role was to amass evidence that stonings were still taking place. She worked ceaselessly with her group and managed to find 14 people who had been sentenced to be stoned; then they reached out for international support, even going so far as smuggling facts to Amnesty International, which put the information into the public eye, even back in Iran. In 2007 she was detained in prison for five days following a silent women's rights sit-in at a courthouse; after that, it became clear that she was under surveillance. At last she fled with her daughter to Sweden in 2009 after a warning that several female prisoners had been interrogated about her and that she would likely soon be among the many "disappeared". She moved to Norway and pursued her longtime interest in writing poetry, and she is presently working on a new documentary book while completing a Master's degree in Equality and Diversity at NTNU.

AMAL ALAMUDDIN CLOONEY: ADVOCATE FOR INTERNATIONAL JUSTICE

Amal was born in Beirut, Lebanon, in 1978; when she was two, the Alamuddin family left Lebanon for Buckinghamshire, England. In 1991 her father returned to Lebanon, while Amal and her three siblings stayed with their mother, a foreign editor of a Pan-Arab newspaper who also founded a PR company. Amal graduated with a degree in jurisprudence from Oxford in 2000, and continued to study law at New York University. While at NYU, she clerked for a semester in the office of Sonia Sotomayor, who was at the time a U.S. Court of Appeals judge for the Second Circuit, long before she rose to become an Associate Justice of the U.S. Supreme Court. She went on to pass the bar in 2002 in the U.S. and in 2010 for England and Wales; she went on to a judicial clerkship at the International Court of Justice at The Hague, and continued at the International Criminal Tribunal for the former nation of Yugoslavia and at the Office of the Prosecutor at the UN Special Tribunal for Lebanon. In 2010, Amal returned to Britain to practice in London as a barrister. In 2013, she was appointed to various UN commissions, both as an advisor to Special Envoy Kofi Annan on Syria, and as Counsel to UN human rights rapporteur Ben Emmerson on the 2013 Drone Inquiry into the use of drones in counter-terrorism operations. In the last few years, she has taught at schools including Columbia Law School's Human Rights Institute, UNC-Chapel Hill, New York's New School, The Hague Academy of International Law, and the University of London, on interesting subjects such as international criminal law and human rights litigation. Amal is a lawyer for the people and has worked on many cases, including the effort for recognition of the Armenian Genocide of 1915; she cares about speaking for the voiceless and fighting for what is fair. She also co-founded the Clooney Foundation for Justice in 2016 with her husband, actor George Clooney.

LIZZIE VELASQUEZ: BRAVE HEART

Lizzie Velasquez was born prematurely, weighing in at less than three pounds, in 1989 in Austin, Texas, and was diagnosed with a genetic disorder that leaves her unable to gain weight. To this day she has never weighed in at

more 64 pounds, despite frequent and carefully timed intake of food. She is also blind in her right eye and vision-impaired in her left eye. In 2006, when she was 17, Lizzie was named the "World's Ugliest Woman"; ever since then, she has been a spokesperson against bullying. In January 2014 she gave a TED talk titled, "How Do YOU Define Yourself". Her YouTube channel has garnered 54 million views. Lizzie has also self-published a book with her mother called *Lizzie Beautiful: The Lizzie Velasquez Story*, and has also written two other books that offer personal stories and advice to teenagers. A documentary film about her life called *A Brave Heart: The Lizzie Velasquez Story* premiered at SXSW in 2015 and later aired on Lifetime. Lizzie continues to be a motivational speaker and author.

MALALA YOUSAFZAI: A FORCE FOR GOOD IN THE WORLD

Malala Yousafzai is a Pakistani activist for female education and the rights of girls, as well as the youngest person ever to receive the Nobel prize. She was born in Mingora, Pakistan in the country's Swat Valley in 1997. Her father, Ziauddin Yousafzai, believed that she would one day become a politician, and would let her stay up late at night to discuss politics. She spoke about education rights for the first time at age 11, when her father took her to the local press club in Peshawar, on the topic, "How dare the Taliban take away my basic right to education?" At this time, the Taliban were frequently blowing up girls' schools. When she heard that BBC Urdu news was looking for a schoolgirl to anonymously blog about her life and that the girl who had been about to do it had changed her mind due to her family's fear of the Taliban, Malala, who was only in the seventh grade at the time, took on the task. BBC staff insisted she use a pseudonym: she was called "Gul Makai", or "cornflower" in Urdu.

Malala hand-wrote notes which were then passed to a reporter to be scanned and sent to BBC Urdu by email. On January 3, 2009, her first post went up. Her descriptions continued to be published as military operations began, including the First Battle of Swat; eventually Malala's school was shut down. By January 15th, the Taliban had issued an edict in Mingora that no girl was allowed to go to school – and by this point, they had already destroyed over one hundred girls' schools. After the ban went into effect, they continued to destroy more schools. A few weeks later, girls were allowed to attend school, but only at coed schools; girls' schools were still banned, and very few girls went back to school in the atmosphere of impending violence that hung over the area. On February 18th, local Taliban leader Maulana Fazlulla announced he would lift the ban on education of females, and girls would be able to attend school until March 17th, when exams were scheduled, but they would have to wear burqas.

After Malala finished her series of blog posts for the BBC on March 12th, 2009, a New York Times reporter asked her and her father if she could appear in a documentary. At this point, military actions and regional unrest forced the evacuation of Mingora, and Malala was sent to stay with country relatives. In late July, her family was reunited and allowed to return home, and after the documentary, Malala began to do some major media interviews. By the end of 2009, her identity as the BBC blogger had been revealed by journalists. She started receiving international recognition and was awarded a National Youth Peace Prize – a first-time award in Pakistan – by her country's government. As things developed, she began to plan the Malala Education Foundation in 2012, whose purpose would be to help economically disadvantaged girls to be able to attend school. But in summer of that year, a group of Taliban leaders agreed to kill her – unanimously. As she rode the bus home in October, a masked gunman shot her; the

bullet passed through her head, neck, and shoulder, and wounded two other girls.

Malala barely survived, but was airlifted to a Peshawar hospital, where doctors removed the bullet from her head in five hours. She then received specialized treatment in Europe with the Pakistani government bearing the cost. Since her recovery, she has continued to speak out both for education for girls and for the rights of women in general. At age 17, she was the co-recipient of the 2014 Nobel Peace Prize for her work on behalf of children and young people, sharing the prize with Kailash Satyarthi, a children's rights activist from India. Malala is the youngest Nobel laureate ever. That year she also received an honorary doctorate from University of King's College in Halifax, Nova Scotia. On her 18th birthday, she opened a school in Lebanon not far from the Syrian border for Syrian refugees, specifically teenage girls, funded by the nonprofit Malala Fund. She is continuing her schooling as well as her activism. Learn more about her work at https://www.malala.org/

TEN NOBEL WOMEN: SHEROES OF PEACE

The Nobel Peace Prize is one of the highest honors a human being can receive; I like to think of it as the designation for the truly evolved! The lore behind the prize is that Alfred Nobel was always interested in the cause of peace, but he was moved to do something about it by his friend, baroness Bertha von Suttner. She became involved in the international movement against war founded in the 1890s and inspired Nobel to back it financially. By January 1893, Alfred wrote the good baroness a letter of his intentions to establish a prize for "him or her who would have brought about the greatest step toward advancing toward the pacification of Europe." Clearly this prestigious endowment has spread to include the whole world and includes women and men from many different ethnicities and backgrounds. Since 1901, over 100 Peace Prizes have been awarded. So far, women recipients have received the laurel for a 10 percent average, but as of the last decade, women are catching up. Here are ten priestesses of pacifism:

Baroness Bertha von Suttner was sheroic from the start when she went against her family's aristocratic ways and worked as a governess and nanny (Does that remind you of any other titled nanny turned peace activist?!), going on to write an antiwar novel *Die Waffen Nieder* (Lay Down Your Arms) and receiving the prize on the designated day of December 10, 1905.

Jane Addams received the Nobel Peace Prize in 1931 when she was near death. She had been a strong opponent of World War I and was a controversial choice for that reason; in fact, in an extremely strange pairing, her corecipient Nicholas Murray Butler had been her greatest critic. Her commitment to activism was so great she requested that the organizations she founded, Hull House and the Women's International League for Peace and Freedom (WILPF), be listed on her gravestone!
One of Jane Addams' partners in pacifism was **Emily Greene Balch**, who worked with her in WILPF and took over leadership of the league upon Addams' death in 1935. In 1946, Balch received the illustrious honor wherein she was acknowledged for her practical, solution-oriented approach to peace in her special work with Slav immigrants, her staunchness in the face of being fired from Wellesley for her war protests, and her key role in obtaining the withdrawal of U.S. troops from Haiti in 1926 after a decade-long occupation.

After a gap of *thirty years* in which no women won, two sheroes took the prize for peace in 1976—**Betty Williams** and **Mairead Corrigan**. Williams, a Belfast housewife, and Corrigan, who had lost two children in her family to the war between the Irish Republican Army and the British soldiers, were leaders in the movement to stop the senseless violence in Northern Ireland. They were cited as having demonstrated "what ordinary people can do to promote peace."

In 1979, **Mother Teresa** was awarded the highest honor for her incredible contribution to social justice. By the age of twelve, the devout Catholic girl from Albania knew she wanted to devote her life to the poor and went to India soon after, teaching and working in the Calcutta slums. She founded a new order, The Missionaries of Charity, and continued the work that crossed all boundaries of race and religion. Her image came to symbolize kindness and spirit in action. Her tragic death one week after Princess Diana's in September of 1997 saw the loss of two great advocates for the poor, the sick, and the disenfranchised.

The 1982 Nobel Peace Prize went to **Alva Myrdal** of Mexico, who shared it with her countryman Alfonso Garcia Robles, both of whose work in the disarmament movement has gone far to lessen the threat of global destruction. Myrdal has worked with peace and social justice since the thirties, and she has written one of the most important books on the subject. She had been passed over (along with many other peaceful sheroes) by the Nobel Committee for mostly male choices until such a hue and cry arose that the prize pickers listened! Alva described her Nobel moment as her "peak" but said the "Norwegian People's Prize" was "dear to her heart."

Aside from Mother Teresa, the Nobel shero receiving the most publicity has to be Burmese Buddhist and political prisoner **Aung San Suu Kyi**, who won in 1991. Deeply inspired by the work of Mahatma Gandhi, Aung San based her life and actions on what she calls "a profound simplicity," delineated beautifully in her book *Freedom From Fear*. Her dedication to freeing the people of

Burma from their government under a brutally oppressive dictatorship has gained the respect of the world. Aung San was jailed after winning an election that opposed the military government of Myanmar (Burma). She is not only the national shero of her country but of the world, for her unswerving courage in the face of a cruel and corrupt power.

Rigoberta Menchu Tum was a controversial choice the Nobel committee made in 1992. A Mayan Indian and Guatemalan native, Tum was criticized by many conservative pundits for her involvement in the guerilla rebel group of her country; they saw it as being in conflict with the Nobel ethics of commitment to nonviolence. The truth is, however, that even though her father and many friends and fellow *campesinos* were burned alive in a peaceful protest at the Mexican embassy, she never participated in violence and has always worked toward peace and justice for her country within the social political arenas, explaining, "we understood revolutionary in the real meaning of the word 'transformation.' If I had chosen the armed struggle, I would be in the mountains now."

Jody Williams received the Nobel Peace Prize for her work with the International Campaign to Ban Landmines (ICBL) on October 10, 1997, the day after her forty-seventh birthday. Jody, a frank, down-to-earth New Englander has pulled off the impossible—getting governments around the world to agree to help in the cleanup of landmine fields across the globe. Unlike many other eco-political issues, this one has a very human face to it—hundreds of people, many children, are maimed and crippled for life with limbs simply blown off when they step on a landmine. The crisis has received international publicity that helped catapult it to resolution. Jody received some very important assistance in drawing the problem to the world's attention from another shero, Princess Diana, whose disastrous death

in Paris three months before the Nobel award prevented her from seeing the fruition of her landmine work in Jody's triumph.

• CHAPTER SEVEN •

Amazing Musicians and Muses: Taking Center Stage

The recent hype about women breaking onto the music scene in the mid-nineties is pretty tiresome. Women have been making music since hominid Lucy rattled the skulls and drummed with the bones of her ancestors in the grasslands of ancient Africa. The truth of the matter is more likely to be a scared and sagging music industry, running on the empty recycling of male-dominated rock, finally realizing that record-buying audiences want more. A definite paradigm shift is taking place, but the women on center stage today are standing on foundations built by women who fought to get the opportunity to perform, get recorded, get air play, and just get a chance. For example, Billie Holiday, an enormous talent, struggled throughout her career and paid the price for the ill-treatment she received as a black woman insisting on being taken seriously for her music. Janis Joplin, a similarly tragic and equally awe-inspiring figure, also met a tragic end with drugs and booze. She was another light who burned too brightly, surrounded by parasitic moths and living with the crushing pressure of maintaining authenticity as a superstar commodity.

Thankfully, things have changed. Women now keep the copyrights to their music, run their own record companies, call the shots, direct the videos, and manage their money with the strategic elan of MBAs. Madonna has gone from eating garbage and squatting in New York City to become an icon and mogul. Tina Turner turned the tables on an abusive Svengali Ike, started meditating, and came back with a vengeance for an amazing career as a seemingly ageless R&B goddess. Ani DiFranco took the "DIY" (do it yourself) credo all the way with Righteous Babe Records, her own label, which she started at age fifteen. The Lilith Fair, an all-woman traveling rock show, stunned the world with sold out shows in every city and a media firestorm that blew the other, mostly male festivals like Lollapalooza and Horde out of the water.

Offstage, the business of music has seen a power shift, as well. Sylvia Rhone was the first woman ever to run a record company, Elektra, by pushing up through the ranks of an industry she describes as having a "pimp mentality." Today, several women are at the top of the ranks of Sony, MTV, and Epic Records. However, these women's success stories are cautionary tales of working with the constraints of boy's club corporations where women are mere window dressing or products are sold with an emphasis on sex. Pope-bashing radical feminist singer and proud mother Sinead O'Connor (whose record company tried to tell her she couldn't have children because it would interfere with record promotion and who withdrew from the Grammys when she discovered that misogynist comedian Andrew Dice Clay was a presenter) offers this advice to women: "Learn to say no straight off. You don't have to look like the makeup artist wants. Trust your instincts. One can't make an omelet without breaking eggs..." Rapper shero Mary J. Blige puts it most succinctly with her cut-to-the-chase wisdom for women: "Don't let anybody stomp you out!"

BIG MAMA THORNTON: "STRONGER THAN DIRT"

Willie Mae "Big Mama" Thornton checked out for good when the New Wave washed onto the music scene, dying

of heart and liver failure in 1984. After fifty-seven years of hard living and a good deal of hard drinking, she was a mere shadow of herself in her last year, weighing only ninety-seven pounds. At the height of her careers, Thornton held center stage singing, drumming, and blowing harmonica with rhythm n' blues luminaries Muddy Waters, B.B. King, Eddie Vinson, and Janis Joplin.

Her most remembered contribution to music history will always be the song "Hound Dog," a number one hit in 1953 written especially for her by Jerry Leiber and Mike Stoller. It was as much her appearance as her blues style that influenced the writing of "Hound Dog." "We wanted her to growl it," Stoller later told *Rolling Stone*. Three years later, Elvis Presley covered Big Mama's tune and took her signature song for his own. Like so many other black blues stars, she wasn't mainstream enough; by 1957, her star had fallen so low she was dropped by her record label. And, like many other blues stars of the day, she was inadequately compensated for her work; although her incredible, soul-ripping rendition of "Hound Dog" sold two million copies, Big Mama received only one royalty check for $500.

Unstoppable, however, she hit the road, jamming with fellow blues masters, amazing audiences across America. Big Mama's success came from her powerful presence on stage. She had begun performing publicly in the forties as an Atlanta teen where she danced in variety shows and in Sammy Green's Hot Harlem Review. Thornton's own musical heroes were Bessie Smith and Memphis Minnie, whom she always held as great inspirations for her decision to pursue music as a career. Thornton was a completely self-taught musician who learned through watching, "I never had no one teach me nothing. I taught myself to sing and to blow the harmonica and even to play drums, by watching other people."

James Brown, Otis Redding, the Rolling Stones, and Janis Joplin helped create a resurgence of interest in the blues in the sixties. Janis covered "Ball and Chain," making that a huge hit to millions of fans who never knew Thornton's version. In a sad repetition of history, the royalties to Big Mama's "Ball and Chain" were contracted to her record company, meaning she didn't get a dime from the sales of Joplin's cover of the tune. However, because of the popularization, artists like Big Mama began to enjoy a crossover audience, and the spotlight they had previously been denied by a record-buying public producers believed preferred black music sanitized by singers such as Presley.

With a new interest in the real thing, Big Mama started performing at blues festivals around the world, resulting in classic recordings such as "Big Mama in Europe," and "Stronger than Dirt," where she was backed by Muddy Waters, James Cotton, and Otis Spann. "Stronger than Dirt" featured Thornton's interpretations of Wilson Pickett's "Funky Broadway" and Bob Dylan's "I Shall Be Released." Big Mama's final albums were "Sassy Mama!" and "Jail," a live album recorded in prisons. In 1980, Thornton, Sippie Wallace, and Koko Taylor headlined at the unforgettable "Blues Is a Woman" show at the Newport Jazz Festival. Although Big Mama barely made enough money to live on through her music, her contribution to blues was enormous. She died penniless and alone in a Los Angeles boardinghouse, decimated by drink and disappointed by her ill-treatment from the music industry. But she received tremendous respect from her peers and influences dozens of musicians, even to this day.

"At what point did rhythm n' blues start becoming rock and roll? When the white kids started to dance to it."

— Ruth Brown

PEGGY JONES: LADY BO

A woman who followed her own star and in so doing shattered several music stereotypes, Peggy Jones had music in her soul from the beginning; a dancer in her toddler years, she had performed in Carnegie Hall by the age of nine. As a youngster, the New Yorker was intrigued by the ukelele and moved onto the guitar. It never occurred to her that it would seem unusual for a woman to play guitar in the forties. "Little did I know that a female playing any instrument was like a new thing. I was breaking a lot of barriers."

By the age of seventeen, she was producing and cutting singles such as "Honey Bunny Baby/Why Do I Love You?" and "Everybody's Talking/I'm Gonna Love My Way." In the late fifties, she and her friends and future husband Bobby Bakersfield formed The Jewels, a band made up of men and women, which was very unusual for the time; even more unique, the band included both black and white members. The Jewels got a lot of flack for their disregard for gender and racial boundaries, but they persisted in performing to enthusiastic audiences. Jones recalls fighting past the objections, "I just hung in there because this is what I wanted to do, and I had a real strong constitution as to the way I thought I should go about it."

Peggy's singular instrumentation is one of the components of Bo Diddley's successful albums and national tours throughout the fifties and sixties. Diddley, famous for his signature rhythm, saw Jones walking down the street with her guitar one day, and, ever the savvy showman, recognized that having a pretty girl playing guitar in his band would be a very good thing for ticket and record sales. Peggy was ushered into the world of professional musicianship full-time with Diddley's touring band. She learned a great deal, perfecting her guitar playing to the point where Diddley himself was a bit threatened by her hot licks. She also saw the hardships of the road and experienced firsthand the color line that existed even for music stars. When they hit the South in the hearses they toured in, the band often had to stay in nonwhite hotels and had to use separate bathrooms for "coloreds." They even figured out a way to cook in the car when they couldn't find a restaurant that would serve black people.

However, Jones wasn't content with just backup and liner note credits and took a hiatus from the nonstop Bo Diddley road show. She again wrote her own material and performed with The Jewels again. In the late sixties, she formed her own band and went out on the road. Peggy Jones was a true pioneer for women in music. Because of her, the idea of a woman playing guitar—or any instrument in a band—became much more acceptable.

"I don't think I went in with any attitude that 'Oh, oh, I'm a girl, they're not going to like my playing.' So probably that might have been my savior, because I just went in as a musician and expected to be accepted as a musician."

— **Peggy Jones**

JOAN BAEZ: NOT JUST BLOWIN' IN THE WIND

Folk shero and guitarist Joan Baez was one of the women musicians who benefitted from Peggy Jones' career. Joan tapped her muse young —as a college tapped her muse young—as a college student at Boston University. In 1960, at age nineteen, she became a household name overnight with her album *Joan Baez*. Fiercely political, her recordings such as "We Shall Overcome" point to her alignment with civil rights, and she was one of the best known Vietnam

War protestors and worked for the No Nukes campaign as well. Oddly enough, one of the causes Joan never aligned herself with was feminism. "I don't relate with feminism. I see the whole human race as being broken and terribly in need, not just women." With her inspirational voice and her long dark hair, she gave a generation of women a model of activism, personal freedom, and self-determination. Baez lives by her own light—and in so doing, encourages us all to follow our consciences.

YOKO ONO: AVANT SAVANT

One of the most controversial figures in rock history, Yoko Ono was an acquired taste for those willing to go with her past the edge of musical experimentalism. Unfairly maligned as the woman who broke up the Beatles, she is a classically trained musician and was one of New York's most cutting edge artists before the Fab Four even cut a record. Born in Tokyo in 1933, she moved to New York in 1953 and attended Sarah Lawrence, but even then had trouble finding a form to fit into; her poetry was criticized for being too long, her short stories too short. Then she was befriended by avant-garde composers such as Arnold Schoenberg and John Cage.

Soon, Yoko was making a splash with her originality in post-Beatnik Greenwich Village, going places even Andy Warhol hadn't dared with her films of 365 nude derrieres, her performance art (inviting people to cut her clothes off her), and her bizarre collages and constructions. Called the "High Priestess of the Happening," she enthralled visitors to her loft with such art installations as tossing dried peas at the audience while whirling her long hair. Yoko Ono had an ability to shock, endless imagination, and a way of attracting publicity that P.T. Barnum himself would've envied!

When John Lennon climbed the ladder on that fateful day to peer at the artful affirmation Yoko created in her piece "Yes," rock history was made. Their collaborations—The Plastic Ono Band, Bed-Ins, Love-Ins, Peace-Ins, and son Sean Lennon—have created a legacy that continues to fascinate a world that has finally grudgingly accepted and respected this bona fide original. Yoko's singing style—howling and shrieking in a dissonant barrage—has been a major influence on the B52s and a generation of riot grrl bands.

Now Yoko Ono and her talented son, Sean, tour together and work on behalf of causes they are committed to—the environment, peace, and Tibet. Ono, whose sweet speaking voice belies the steely strength underneath that has enabled her to endure for so long, explains her sheroic journey in the preface she contributed to Gillian G. Gaar's excellent book on women in music, *She's a Rebel*. In it, she relates her pain at her father's discouragement of her dream of becoming a composer, doubting her "aptitude" because of her gender. "'Women may not be good creators of music, but they're good at interpreting music' was what he said." Happy that times have changed, she points to the valiant efforts made by "women artists who kept making music despite overwhelming odds till finally the music industry had to realize that women were there to stay."

In retrospect, Yoko Ono was breaking real musical ground when others were cranking out bubble gum pop and imitating—who else—The Beatles. Yoko's feminism gets lost in the shuffle of the attention to her as an iconoclast.

She was an enormous influence on awakening John's interest in the women's movement, and together they attended the international feminist conference in June of 1973 and together wrote songs inspired by the women's movement, including "Woman is the Nigger of the World." Much of Yoko's musical output in the seventies was on the theme of feminism; her song "Sisters O Sisters" is one of her finest works, a reggae-rhythm number. Yoko's sheroism lies in her intense idealism and her commitment to making this a better world.

"I'm a Witch. I'm a Bitch. I don't care what you say."

— **Yoko Ono** *in 1973*

ARETHA FRANKLIN: EARNING OUR RESPECT

A preacher's daughter, Aretha Franklin started her musical career early, appearing with her famous dad, Revered Clarence LaVaugh Franklin, at Detroit's New Baptist Church. She is a talented musician who eschewed piano lessons so she could experiment with her own style of playing. By the age of eight, in 1950, Aretha electrified her father's congregation with her first gospel solo; by fourteen, she'd cut her first gospel record, "Songs of Faith." Encouraged by her father and his circle of friends and acquaintances, which included Dinah Washington, Reverend James Cleveland, Mahalia Jackson, Clara Ward, Sam Cooke, and Art Tatum, the budding gospel great had her eyes on the glittery prize of pop stardom. She decided to move to New York to pursue her dream in 1960.

The following year she had an album, *Aretha*, on Columbia, which positioned her as a jazz artist, covering classics like "God Bless the Child," "Ol' Man River," and "Over the Rainbow." Franklin went on to record ten albums with Columbia, while record execs waffled about how to package her. Jerry Wexler of Atlantic records was a fan of Aretha and signed her immediately when her contract with Columbia ran out. Wexler rightly saw Aretha as an R&B singer. She agreed. Her debut album on Atlantic, *I Never Loved a Man*, contained the hit "Respect," which catapulted Franklin to number one on both the pop and the R&B charts. "Respect" became an anthem in 1967 for both feminists and black activists.

"Respect" was just the beginning of a chain of hits for the singer: "Baby, I Love You," "Natural Woman," and "Chain of Fools" came hot on the heels of the international smash hit, and soon Aretha was dubbed the "Queen of Soul" and reigned over the music world with the power and authority of her god-given gift.

Aretha was inspired to sing, rather than be a church pianist, when she heard Clara Ward. "From then on I knew what I wanted to do—sing! I liked all of Miss Ward's records." She also idolized Dinah Washington and recorded a tribute album in 1964 after Washington's tragic death at the peak of her prime. Much like Washington did for Bessie Smith, Aretha did an amazing and moving set of covers to honor the brilliance and glory of the Detroit diva entitled "Unforgettable." And it is—as is her 1985 duet with Annie Lennox, summing up the sherodom of legends of women: "Sisters Are Doin' It for Themselves." Amen, Sisters!

DINAH WASHINGTON: LEGENDARY VOICE

Rolling Stone journalist Gerry Hershey makes the claim, "If there is a paramount body for evidence to support the feminist poster 'Sisterhood is powerful,' it is Dinah Washington's 1958 LP tribute to the Empress, *The Bessie*

Smith Songbook." Dinah Washington is one of the all-time great vocalists who immediately took ownership of any song she sang. In addition to a great set of pipes, she had a good head for business, running a restaurant in Detroit and a booking agency, Queen Attractions, where she signed talent like Muhammad Ali and Sammy Davis, Jr. Able to juggle many different gambits, Washington also dominated the stage of the Flame Show Bar and Detroit's Twenty Grand Club, where future superstars Marvin Gaye, Diana Ross, and Aretha Franklin sat enthralled, watching a master at work. Motown was just gearing up when Dinah Washington died accidentally of an unfortunate combination of pills and alcohol. A legend in her own time, she is rumored to have married as many as nine times before her untimely demise at age thirty-nine. Dinah Washington, one of the most gifted singers to have ever held a microphone, lived large, predated the excess of rock stars with peroxide wigs, and a home filled with gorgeous cut crystal chandeliers, and toilet-seat covers made from mink!

JONI MITCHELL: THE LADY OF THE CANYON

Nearly every significant contemporary musician, male or female, cites Joni Mitchell as a major influence. Born in Alberta to a Royal Canadian officer and a school teacher in 1943, Roberta Joan Anderson contracted polio at nine and spent much time inside her own head during her lonely convalescence. She remained introspective throughout her life and developed a love of the arts that informs her sensibility still. Like other fifties teens, Joni danced to Elvis, Chuck Berry, and the Kingston Trio, buying a guitar to sing at Wednesday dance parties. She lost her taste for art school when the classes appeared to be assembly-line training for commercial artists. Instead she started singing in Toronto cafes where she met and married fellow singer Chuck Mitchell, a liaison that lasted for two years. Upon the breakup of their marriage, she rebounded to New York where she tried her hand at professional songwriting. She was soon successful; her material was selected by Tom Rush, Judy Collins, and Buffy Saint-Marie.

Like sister-shero Carole King in her opus *Tapestry*, the songwriter recorded some tracks of her own with great success. Joni Mitchell's late sixties album *Ladies of the Canyon* was a moody sensation, followed immediately by *Blue, Court and Spark* and a subsequent catalog of impressive diversity and size. She branched out from her folk origins into jazz, blues, and electronic music, composing, singing, and recording, among other eclectic works, a vocal tribute to Charles Mingus. Joni Mitchell became a musician's and critic's darling (though some dismissed her more avant-garde work as self-indulgent noise) and a favorite with progressive radio listeners.

Cool and ethereally beautiful, Joni's personal life drew much attention from the press, embarrassing her and her lovers with exposes tracking her numerous liaisons, including those with rockers Graham Nash, Jackson Browne, and horn player Tom Scott. This was echoed recently in extensive coverage of her reunion with the daughter she gave up for adoption in infancy.

Joni Mitchell, who thinks of herself as a poet of the prairies, has left an indelible mark on twentieth-century music herstory. Her smart, ironic, saturnine music is played by the serious listeners and musicians of each generation that comes along. For her part, Joni prefers simplicity, clarity, truth. "For a while it was assumed that I was writing women's music. Then men began to notice that they saw themselves in the songs, too. A good piece of art should be androgynous."

"A man in the promotion department criticized my music for its lack of masculinity. They said I didn't have any balls. Since when do women have balls anyway? Why do I have to be like that?"

— Joni Mitchell

ALISON STEELE: SONG OF THE NIGHTBIRD

Alison broke important ground for women in radio when she took wing on the airwaves in the 1960s as the first female disc jockey at a major radio station. "I listened to her faithfully," says author Joan Steinau Lester. "She was absolutely fantastic. At the time, I only knew I liked her and the show. It was only years later that I realized she'd broken ground for women in a male-dominated industry."

Progressive rock radio was becoming the hottest sound across the nation, and WNEW was one of the top stations in the nation. Alison was well on her way to a very Mary Tyler Moore-type career in TV, starting by leading a morning exercise program and climbing her way up the ladder to "weather girl." When AM and FM radio stations split apart instead of simulcasting, competitive radio stations were forced to hire another staff to man the FM stations, putting many in a bind for salaries. Alison recalls that the standard rate for AM jocks at the time was $150,000 a year, while the FM scale was a mere $125 a week. Management at WNEW figured they could hire an all-woman FM crew and stay within the standard FM pay scale.

Alison and her companion women disc jockeys, mostly actresses and models, made their debut on July 4, 1966. Alison was nearly the only one with any previous experience in any realm of broadcasting. By September 1967, the all-woman stable of jocks was out of a job for a reason that Alison herself puts most succinctly, "America, New York, was not ready for lady DJs!" Thanks to creativity and experience in the world of entertainment, Alison wasn't let go—the only woman to have survived. She had been experimenting within her on-air time, trying angles that kept the listeners' interest high—theater reviews, celebrity interviews, and lots of high energy personality. When management found in a pre-purge survey that 90 percent of listeners knew her name and enjoyed her show, they made the smart decision to keep her on board.

Along with drastic personnel changes, the station management also made a format change to progressive rock. Alison was out of familiar terrain with rock music, as was the remaining all-male staff and the all-male management. When Alison asked for guidance, she was given the precise and, as it turned out, appropriate advice to simply "do her thing." They gave her the graveyard shift, too—midnight to 6:00 A.M. The ever-intrepid Alison figured her nighttime listeners were a special breed of insomniacs, lonely people, and assorted other nocturnal types. "I felt that night was a very special time." She knew from personal experience that emotions intensify at night—loneliness, depression, and illness. Alison's sensitivity to people paid in spades; she reached out and connected to her listeners by creating this special persona, The Nightbird, and the listeners responded overwhelmingly. "I felt that if I could make this bond visible between people who are feeling things at night, then I'd have something going." She put all of her creativity into her alter ego with high drama, fantasy, and many completely unique elements the likes of which nighttime radio had never heard. Listeners were hooked after her jazzy intro with the sound of softly fluttering wings and the poetic intro Alison had written ending with "as the Nightbird lifts her wings and soars above the earth into another level of comprehension, where we

exist only to feel. Come fly with me, Alison Steele, The Nightbird at WNEW-FM until dawn."

The phones at the station rang off the hook that first night. Station management told her that she had a "little hit" and then her male boss told her he would tell her how to do it. Instead of being congratulated for originality and the instant popularity of her new show, Alison was treated like a loose cannon, and they tried really hard to mold her and her show into something less unique and more like the shows all the other DJs, men at this point, were doing. Alison stuck to her guns and refused to change the Nightbird, only to be buried even further into the night hours, beginning at 2:00 A.M.! Alison's stories include the station's refusal to buy a step stool so she could reach the records on the top shelf. The response to the most popular DJ at the station was a threat to hire "a taller person."

Alison went on to win Billboard's "FM Personality of the Year" in 1978, the first woman to receive this honor. Although she was enormously popular, she was regarded with resentment by many of her fellow jocks. In fact, the station made very little effort to clue Alison in to just how important she was to the station. WNEW was the top station in the country in the hot new category of progressive rock. They were also beloved in their own backyard of New York and began doing public appearances, including one at a concert in Madison Square Garden. This was really the eye-opener. Alison loves to tell this story, "I was the last person be introduced. So they were all on stage when they introduced Alison Steele, 'The Nightbird,'" The six male DJs who had been introduced before her had to stand there and eat crow while the entire crowd stood and cheered and screamed and clapped for their favorite DJ, Alison, The Nightbird.

Sheroes don't always get to reap the rewards of their actions during their lifetimes. For Alison, this standing ovation from 20,000 fans who adored her courage and creativity was music to her ears. For proof of Alison Steele's popularity, look no further than the 70's TV show, "B.J. and the Bear," which boasted a female trucker character named Angie who worked as a radio DJ at night with the air name of "The Nightingale."

*"It was my moment of glory, I worked hard for it. I took a lot of s*** over it. And I enjoyed every minute of it."*

— Alison Steele

HELEN REDDY: "I AM STRONG. I AM INVINCIBLE."

Along with Led Zeppelin, art rockers Yes and Fairport Convention, one of the artists Alison Steele played on her nationally popular radio show was Helen Reddy. Both of these women struggled for years to make it. Reddy's songs were embraced as anthems for a nation of women collectively committed to shattering the glass ceiling. For the time, Helen Reddy's achievement was stunning. She wrote a hard-core feminist song and took it to the top of the charts; "I Am Woman" was the number one hit on the charts in 1972. In clear ringing tones, Helen declared a message that empowered and encouraged women around the world, "I am woman, hear me roar. I am too strong to ignore...if I have to, I can do anything. I am strong. I am invincible!"

Sing it, Sister

BONNIE RAITT: BORN TO SING THE BLUES

Born in 1949 in Burbank to a show biz family, Bonnie Raitt plays the slide guitar like she was born in the Blue Ridge Mountains. Her first exposure to the music scene was classical piano (her mother's forte), her father's Broadway show tunes, and the Beach Boy harmonies she grew up with. A Christmas gift changed Bonnie's life—at age eight, she received a guitar and worked diligently at getting good at playing it. The first time she heard Joan Baez, Bonnie went the way of folk and moved to Cambridge, Massachusetts, to be a part of the folkie coffeehouse scene. Unfortunately for her, folk music was on its last legs. Instead she hooked up with Dick Waterman, a beau who just happened to manage the careers of Bonnie's musical icons: Son House, Fred McDowell, Sippie Wallace, and Muddy Waters. By the age of twenty, she was playing with Buddy Guy and Junior Wells—opening for the Rolling Stones with two blue greats.

Bonnie's road to fame, however, was very long and winding. It had to come on her terms. Always more interested in artistic integrity than commercial success, she had exacting standards and tastes. She demanded authenticity in playing the blues she loved and reinterpreting those riffs through the influences of country and rock. She didn't play the game and, a musician's musician, she rarely got radio air play. Thus she made her living traveling the country, performing in small clubs. Bonnie was also very outspoken on political causes. Raised as a Quaker, she has always been involved in political causes, doing many benefit concerts; in 1979, she cofounded Musicians United for Safe Energy.

The stress of the road, and of being a novelty in the music industry—a female blues guitarist—eventually took its toll, and Bonnie drowned her sorrows for a time in drugs and booze. In the mid-eighties, when her record label dumped her, she bottomed out, became clean and sober, and made the climb back up. In 1989, her smash album "Nick of Time" won her a Grammy and garnered sales in excess of four million.

Since then, she hasn't stopped making her great earthy blend of blues, folk, pop, and R&B, or working on behalf of the causes that are meaningful to her. Bonnie Raitt is a consummate musician who loves to perform live, loves to pay homage to the blues greats, and continues to speak her mind. In an interview in *Rolling Stone*, she laid it on the line about the current looks-dominated music industry: "In the 70s, all these earthy women were getting record deals—you didn't have to be some gorgeous babe. There's been some backsliding since."

"Any guy who has a problem with feminists is signaling a shortage in his pants. If I had to be a woman before men and women were more equal, I would've shot somebody and been in jail."

— Bonnie Raitt

MELISSA ETHERIDGE: THE MOUTH THAT ROARED

Melissa is beloved for the great music she makes, but she achieved eternal sheroism with her album "Yes I Am," a public coming-out and celebration of her lesbianism. An ebullient spirit who can sing, play killer guitar, and write hit songs by the droves, Melissa Etheridge hails from Kansas; and at thirty-six, she embraced shared motherhood of her child with her partner of ten years, film maker Julie Cypher. Melissa's personal shero is Janis Joplin, and she hopes to portray the Texas rock legend on film one day. Etheridge, who has enjoyed the

changing tide for women in the music industry, delights in the success of musicians she respects: Edie Brickell, Tracy Chapman, Toni Childs, Natalie Merchant, Michelle Shocked, and the Indigo Girls, all who sell records by the millions. Even a few years ago, Etheridge remembers that rock radio jocks claimed they could only play one woman a day or risk losing their male listeners. "All of a sudden the whole lid was blown off...people were coming to our concerts, and they were requesting our songs on the radio, and radio changed. That's the way America works. The public ultimately says, 'This what we want.' The world was ready for strong women's inspired music." And Melissa Etheridge was at the forefront of the revolution!

MADONNA: THE CULTURAL CHAMELEON

Has there been anyone in American culture who has remade herself as often—or as well—as Madonna? Truly an artist of her own physical form and image, Madonna has been a vamp, tramp, scamp; a Brooke Shields look-alike, a Marilyn Monroe look-alike, an Evita look-alike, and a Madonna (the original) look-alike. Her well publicized romances with Sean Penn, Warren Beatty, and her trainer Carlos Leon and filmmaker Guy Ritchie; the Material Girl; Girlie Show; and Sex Kitten—these incarnations almost seem like different women's lives. And in each of them, Madonna has evoked controversy.

She's been a target for her open approach to sex and the presence of eroticism in her work. Her sheroism as a gay rights and AIDS activist received much less press than her pointy bras did. Madonna was threatened with jail on several occasions for her pro-gay stance; she took the challenge and remained steadfast in her solidarity with the gay community.

Madonna Louise Veronica Ciccone was born into a staunchly Catholic home in Michigan in 1958. Her mother was extremely Puritanical; before she died when Madonna was six, she taught her that pants that zip up the front were sinful. By the time Madonna was a teen, she had fame on the brain and escaped to New York City as soon as possible to make it happen. Struggling as a dancer, she lived as a squatter until she hit the big time with "Lucky Star" in 1984. Since then, she has sold more than 100 million records, has appeared in fifteen films, had dozens of top ten hits, and penned a very controversial book, *Sex*.

Now on the right side of forty, Madonna has matured into her full glory. Beautiful, powerful, and unflinchingly honest, Madonna has come into her own, removed the many masks, and dared to reveal her heart. Motherhood suits her well, and she has flourished as a businesswoman with her successful Maverick Records. After her highly praised performance as Evita in the musical drama, Madonna no longer has to prove herself in any arena and is relaxed, confident, and grounded. She is also more vibrant than ever, looking back over her Manhattan days as a starving squatter, her hard-earned stardom and musing at the changes daughter Lourdes Maria Ciccone Leon and son Rocco John Ritchie brought to her life. "Becoming a mother, I just have a whole new outlook on life. I see the world as a much more hopeful place." She has adopted several children from Africa and has recently been a voice for the Trump Resistance. What is next in store for the former Material Girl? Stay tuned.

"I knew every word to Court and Spark; I worshipped her when I was in high school. Blue is amazing. I would have to say of all the women I've heard, she had the most profound effect on me from a lyrical point of view."

—**Madonna** *on pensive poetess and musical shero Joni Mitchell*

QUEEN LATIFAH: PLAYING WITH THE BIG BOYS

When Jersey girl Dana Owens renamed herself Queen Latifah and started rapping, she broke barriers in the very male world of hip-hop. Taking up the mantle of an African Queen, her music efforts—*Ladies First, All Hail the Queen, Nature of Sistah,* and *Black Reign*—proved to everyone that women could rap, rap well, and find a huge audience across gender lines. Queen Latifah crossed over mediums, as well, starring in the popular television series *Living Single* and in feature films *Set It Off, Jungle Fever, Juice,* and *Chicago* for starters. She paved the way for a new wave of female rappers such as breakout hip-hop stars Foxy Brown and Lil' Kim, with the intention of establishing a woman-positive place within the musical style she claimed was to the eighties and nineties what rock and roll was to the fifties and sixties. "My thing was to start with the ladies and get the self-esteem up."

COURTNEY LOVE: THE GIRL WITH THE MOST CAKE

Compared to Madonna and Yoko Ono and vilified by none other than Camille Paglia, Courtney Love is another chameleon—punk turned glamour grrrl who set the world on its ear with her amazing portrayal of Althea Flynt in *The People vs Larry Flynt.*

Love had lived a lot of life in a short amount of time. Born to San Francisco hippies in 1964, Love renamed herself and traveled in the mid-80s international punk circuit, playing bit parts in the filmmaker Alex Cox's prophetic *Sid and Nancy* and *Straight to Hell* before settling in Los Angeles and stripping for a living. In 1989 she formed the band Hole. Ironically, Hole's album "Pretty on the Inside" was selling twice as well as husband Kurt Cobain's band Nirvana's debut "Bleach," although Nirvana got all the press.

With "Smells Like Teen Spirit" from Nirvana's second effort *Nevermind*, Courtney and Kurt became the gods of grunge and grappled with fame, authenticity, and drugs. Upon Cobain's Seattle suicide by gunshot in 1994, Courtney acted out her pain publicly. When Hole lost their excellent bassist Kirsten Pfaff to a heroin overdose, Love hired Melissa Auf der Maur to play bass guitar. The world watched Courtney Love's catharsis in the tour for Hole's second album, appropriately titled *Live Through This*. The world started to listen, too, in a big way. Hole started selling records and getting the long overdue respect for Love's songwriting, raw and powerful singing, and fearless stage diving.

Love, whose post-modern "*Whatever Happened to Baby Jane*" tatters had been her trademark, surprised everyone recently with a 180-degree style-switch and much-hyped "makeover." Courtney responded by saying, "Somebody wrote, 'How can she rock in a Versace gown?' Well, easy, let me show you." No one should really have been surprised, though. Courtney Love is the best at throwing the unexpected left-curve. A bundle of contradictions, she is a searcher, a doer, a thinker, a self-described "militant feminist," who can quote Dickens or Dickenson, deconstruct Camille Paglia's occasionally obtuse critical theory, and can hold forth on any subject from her daughter Frances Bean Cobain (whom she dotes on) to Buddhism (which she practices) to Jungian archetypes (which fascinate her) rather eloquently, punctuated of course with a healthy dose of expletives. Courtney Love has courted controversy all her life in her quest to express

herself and her creativity with complete, unvarnished honesty. Her phoenix-like rise from the ashes of a traumatic and abusive childhood as well as a tragic superstar marriage to become the leader of a successful "third-wave" feminist band and a critically acclaimed actress has been awesome. Clearly, she's one to watch!

WILD WORDS FROM A WILD THING- THE BEST OF COURTNEY LOVE

"I've sought the feminine all my life. I looked for female protagonists in everything. My first record was a Joan Baez record my parents gave me. [And there were] Julie London and Patsy Cline and Loretta Lynn and Tammy Wynette and Joni Mitchell—the seminal."

"When I heard my first Patti Smith record, *Horses*, it was like, the ticket's right here in my hand; I can write it. It's a free zone."

"Are you in a Bette Davis mood? Are you in a Stevie Nicks mood? They're like goddesses."

"In the pinnacle of my rock stardom, I was probably part of this archetype...almost like Artemis: that very androgynous archetype. Amazonian."

"There have always been female gladiators of some sort."

PATTI SMITH: HARD ROCKING WOMAN

A poet who also makes music, Patti Smith has more in common with Jim Morrison than she does with Courtney Love. Like Morrison, Patti Smith was a Romantic, steeped in Byronic passion, Baudelaire's dark beauty, and Rilke's angel-haunted obsessions who lived in a world of grand imaginings far from her working-class Jersey. Self-schooled and self-styled, the former factory worker found New York in the late '60s to be the perfect canvas for her artistic ambitions. She also found a soulmate in photographer Robert Mapplethorpe, who turned their friendship into art with his now-famous monotints. Patti read poetry at Max's Kansas City to audiences of glittery night creatures like Andy Warhol, Edie Sedgewick and her boyfriend Sam Shepard, and hosts of hookers and actresses, in a coked-up atmosphere somewhere between William Blake's Hell and an uber-noir Berlin nightclub. She started by accompanying her ripping poems on a toy piano and graduated to a full band where she astonished everyone with her singing. Her song "Because the Night" became a Top 40 hit and made her a rock star. Then in 1978, she fell off stage one night, shattering her neck.

Soon after, she pulled one of the greatest disappearing acts of music history when she moved to Detroit to raise two children and run a household with her husband, Fred "Sonic" Smith, the guitarist for MC5. The deaths of both Robert Mapplethorpe and Fred Smith moved Patti to music again. Her album *Gone Again* and sold-out tour established Patti as a survivor. She still reads poetry at her shows, to rapt audiences who understand her as she screams out, "Jesus died for somebody's sins, but not mine."

ANI DIFRANCO: RIGHTEOUS BABE

Ani DiFranco has achieved incredible success entirely on her terms without the benefit of a record label by touring, working hard at her distinctive music. A folk punk phenom, DiFranco writes about her own life, offering strength, honesty, and courage to other women—who have responded in droves. Adored by thousands of devoted fans, DiFranco is slightly uncomfortable with being idolized as a role model of female empowerment, writing about it in her "I'm No Hero." Living on her own by the age of fifteen, the guitarist-songwriter who, in her own words has "indie cred" as a "stompy-booted, butch, folk-singer chick," remembers the irritation of walking into music stores and having the clerk assume she was there to pick something up for her boyfriend. She's gladdened to see these same music stores now packed with teenage girls inspired by the success and long-overdue acceptance of women in rock. "I don't feel like the superhero that sometimes I'm made out to be, but I guess I do feel responsible to other young women, and I do feel fortunate."

BEYONCE KNOWLES-CARTER: FLAWLESS

Born in 1981 in Houston, Texas, in 1990 Beyonce joined the all-girl R&B group Girl's Tyme, which after a few false starts under various names became Destiny's Child in 1996. After success with several chart-topping Destiny's Child singles, she recorded a solo album released in 2003 and has never looked back. She married hip hop artist Jay-Z in 2008; they later had a daughter named Blue Ivy, and as of 2017, they are currently expecting twins. She has performed twice at the Super Bowl and sang the national anthem at President Obama's second inauguration. In a 2013 interview with Vogue, Beyonce said that she thought of herself as "a modern-day feminist". She also sampled "We should all be feminists" from a TEDx talk in 2013 by Nigerian author Chimamanda Ngozi Adichie in her song "Flawless" of that year, although she has critics who feel her racy performances are not supportive of women's empowerment.

Since the rise of the Black Lives Matter movement, Beyonce and her husband have donated millions to it, as well as contributing to the Ban Bossy campaign, which seeks to encourage leadership in girls via social and other media. She has also included the mothers of Trayvon Martin, Michael Brown, and Eric Garner in the video for the song "Freedom" holding pictures of their unjustly murdered sons. In April 2016 Beyonce released a visual album called *Lemonade* as an HBO special. In it, she showed the strength found in communities of African-American women as well as in women as a whole. *Lemonade* debuted at number one, making Beyonce the only artist in history to have all of her first six studio albums reach the top of Billboard's album charts.

• CHAPTER EIGHT •

Awesome Artists: Creative Woman Power

Creative women have the advantage, no doubt about it. Before penning a poem or mustering a masterpiece, women have no need to invoke any semi-divine beings to give them a good idea. Women embody their own muse. Tapping this inner resource has unleashed an artistry that has changed the world many times over. The impulse to make art, immortalize a moment in time with a photograph, or express the ineffable with poetry and fiction has led many women to make forceful statements. Some powerful truths that couldn't have been expressed in any other way have come through the artistic enterprise, say, of Diane Arbus shooting pictures of the mundane, the bizarre, and the unutterably human. Russian-born Louise Nevelson began sculpting and, in so doing, reshaped the art world, while Harriet Beecher Stowe is credited by none other than Honest Abe Lincoln himself with having picked up her pen and starting the Civil War!

Throughout history, with rooms of their own or not, women have written, painted, danced, composed, and shot (as in a shutter), expressing both inner feelings and artistic vision. Eighteenth-century British novelist Jane Austen, thanks to some sumptuously produced and well acted films, is being read more widely than ever with *Emma, Sense and Sensibility,* and *Persuasion* hitting best-seller lists nearly two hundred years after their publication! Renaissance woman Ethel Smyth lived in nineteenth-century London where she wrote philosophy including *What Matters Most in Life*, golfed pretty seriously, and composed the anthem for the suffrage women, "March of the Women." Katherine Dunham, an anthropologist and choreographer lived among the Jamaican Accompong people in 1935, researching the African roots of their diasporic culture and incorporating their traditions into interpretive and preservationist dance. The impact of these and countless other artistic women on our culture has been incredible. Their sphere of influence is the globe we inhabit! Fearless creativity and relentless pursuit of artistic truth on the part of these sheroes have freed the imagination to its limitless bounds. They have produced art that shocks, and poetry that pierces, created new ritual dances, designated fantastic fashions, and looked into the very heart of the darkness that is the feminine. The lives of these women suggest that real inspiration can come only from being true to yourself at any cost. Here are a few of the bravest, those who took tremendous risks, often physical, in the pursuit of art.

SAPPHO: THE LITERATI OF LESBOS

Lyric poet Sappho is universally regarded as the greatest ancient poet. She came to be known as the "tenth muse." Although scholars can't agree whether Homer even existed or not, Sappho's work was recorded and preserved by other writers. An unfortunate destruction of a volume of all her work—nine books of lyric poetry and one of elegiac verse—occurred in the early Middle Ages, engendering a search for her writing that continues even now. The Catholic Church deemed her work to be far too erotic and obscene, so they burned the volume containing her complete body of work, thus erasing what could only be some of the finest poetry in all of herstory. Known for her powerful phrasing and the intensity of feeling, erotic and otherwise, Sappho's poetry is immediate and accessible to the reader. Upon reading Sappho, you can feel that you know her, her ecstatic highs as well as the depth of her pain and longings.

Sappho is believed to have been married to a wealthy man from the island of Andros, and she had one daughter. She taught at a small college for women and was also an athlete. One haiku-like fragment reports that she "taught poetry to Hero, a girl athlete from the island of Gyra." She was banished to Sicily for some time, but the majority of her life was lived on the island of Lesbos. Much of her work, her most lustful in fact, is written to other women, whom she exalts for their beauty, often achieving a poetic frenzy of desire. She also writes for her brother Charaxus and makes the occasional reference to the political arena of the ancient world she inhabited. Although Sappho is one of the earliest and best known poets of either gender, she is actually regarded, stylistically, as the first modern poet

To Atthis
Though in Sardis now,
she thinks of us constantly
and of the life we shared.
She saw you as a goddess
and above all your dancing gave deep joy.

Now she shines among Lydian women like
the rose fingered moon
rising after sundown, erasing all

stars around her, and pouring light equally
across the salt sea
and over densely flowered fields

lucent under dew. Her light spreads
on roses and tender thyme
and the blooming honey-lotus

Often while she wanders she remembers you,
gentle Atthis,
and desire eats away at her heart
for us to come.

BEAUTIFUL MINDS: WOMEN NOBEL PRIZE WINNERS IN LITERATURE

Selma Ottilia Lovisa Lagerlof, 1909, "in appreciation of the lofty idealism, vivid imagination, and spiritual perception that characterize her writings."

Deledda Grazia, 1926, "for her idealistically inspired writings which with plastic clarity picture the life on her native island and with depth and sympathy deal with human problems in general."

Sigrid Undset, 1928, "principally for her powerful descriptions of Northern life during the Middle Ages."

Pearl Buck, 1938, "for her rich and truly epic descriptions of peasant life in China and for her biographical masterpieces."

Gabriela Mistral, 1945, "for her lyric poetry, which, inspired by powerful emotions, has made her name a symbol of the idealistic aspirations of the entire Latin American world."

Nelly Sachs, 1966 (shared), "for her outstanding lyrical and dramatic writing, which interprets Israel's destiny with touching strength."

Nadine Gordimer, 1991, "who through her magnificent epic writing has—in the words of Alfred Nobel—been of a very great benefit to humanity."

Toni Morrison, 1993, "who in novels characterized by visionary force and poetic import, gives life to an essential aspect of American reality."

Wislawa Szymborska, 1996, "for poetry that with ironic precision allows the historical and biological context to come to light in fragments of human reality."

HARRIET BEECHER STOWE: CIVIL WARRIOR

Most schoolchildren are taught that Harriet Beecher Stowe was an extremely creative young woman who, almost accidentally, wrote a book that tore America apart. In this insidiously watered down and sugarcoated version of history we were spoon-fed as children, the most important aspects of Stowe's story are completely omitted. The truth is, and let us please let it be known far and wide, Harriet's opus, *Uncle Tom's Cabin*, was written with precisely the intent to publicize the cruelty of slavery and give it a human name and face so people could relate, sympathize, and, most importantly, ACT!

Extremely bright, Harriet was keenly interested in improving humanity even as a child. She lived in a large family of nine children; her father was a Calvinist minister and her mother died when she was five. She was very attached to her older sister, Catherine, who founded the Hartford Female Seminary. The year 1832 found the Beecher family leaving their longtime home of Litchfield, Connecticut, and moving to Cincinnati, right across the

Ohio River from Kentucky. From this vantage point so much closer to the south, Harriet had much greater exposure to slavery. A young, idealistic student of theology, Harriet did not like what she was seeing at all. Her father, Lyman Beecher, was the president of Lane Theological Seminary. Her brothers became involved in the antislavery movement and were extremely vocal about their feelings. Harriet, for her part, aided a runaway slave.

In 1836, Harriet met one of the professors of religion at her father's seminary, Calvin Stowe, married him, and bore six children. Around this time, she discovered her love of writing, contributing articles to numerous religious magazines and papers. She also began working on her first novel, *The Mayflower: Sketches and Scenes and Characters Among the Descendants of the Puritans*. After too many years across the river from the slave state of Kentucky, Harriet Beecher Stowe finally returned to the Northeast with her husband and children.

In 1850, the Fugitive Slave Acts passed Congress. It was this event that moved Harriet to write *Uncle Tom's Cabin*. She couldn't abide the inhumanity of slaves being hunted down and forcibly returned to their former owners after struggling so hard for the freedom that was their birthright. Horror stories of the torture of runaway slaves galvanized the sensitive Harriet to action, and she wrote the book with the full intention of sending out a cry against the whipping, maiming, and hanging of slaves.

Uncle Tom's Cabin or Life Among the Lonely was first run as a series of installments in the national *Era*, an abolitionist newspaper. Upon publication in book form in 1852, Stowe's work was very well received. Harriet had expected her novel to be a nonevent outside the circle of abolitionists, but she was very surprised. The entire printing of 5,000 sold out in two days, and the book sold three million copies around the world before the Civil

War! Harriet had outstripped her wildest dreams and had truly fired the shot that started what was to become the War Between the States. She also received critical acclaim from such literary luminaries as MacCauley, Longfellow, and Leo Tolstoy, who declared *Uncle Tom's Cabin* the "highest moral art." Abraham Lincoln himself called Harriet "the little lady who made this big war." Harriet's strategy was to show the extremes of slavery, culminating in the savage beating of the gentle old slave, Tom. The world was captivated by Stowe's dramatic story. Reviled in the south, Stowe met all her pro-slavery detractors with dignity, even going so far as to publish a critical *Key to Uncle Tom's Cabin*, and wrote a second novel about the plight of slaves in *Dred: A Tale of the Great Dismal Swamp*. Harriet Beecher Stowe is a shining example of courage and conviction; her life is proof of how passion and purpose can change the world.

"I won't be any properer than I have a mind to be."

— **Harriet Beecher Stowe**

CHARLOTTE PERKINS GILMAN : HER LAND IS YOUR LAND

Niece of Catherine Beecher and Harriet Beecher Stowe, Charlotte Perkins Gilman also felt, in her own words, "the Beecher urge to social service, the Beecher wit and gift of words." Born in 1860, Charlotte attended the Rhode Island School of Design and worked after graduation as a commercial artist. Exposed to the "domestic feminism" of the Beechers, the extremely sensitive and imaginative young woman had resolved to avoid her mother's fate of penniless desertion by her father and assiduously avoided marriage, but after two years of relentless wooing, Charlotte reluctantly agreed to marry artist Walter Stetson. After she bore her daughter Katherine, she had a nervous breakdown that inspired her famous story *The Yellow Wallpaper* and subsequent nonfiction accounts of her struggle with manic-depressive episodes. She wrote *The Yellow Wallpaper* for humanistic reasons: "It was not intended to drive people crazy," she said, "but to save people from being driven crazy, and it worked." Attributing her emotional problems in part to women's status in marriage, she divorced her husband and moved to California with her daughter (later, when Walter remarried, she sent Katherine to live with her father and stepmother, a move that was considered incredibly scandalous).

Although she suffered weakness and "extreme distress, shame, discouragement, and misery," her whole life, Charlotte's accomplishments are more than that of most healthy folks. A social reformer who wrote in order to push for equality for women, she lectured, founded the Women's Peace Party with Jane Addams in World War I, and wrote her best-known book, *Women and Economics* in only seventeen days. At one point, she undertook a well-publicized debate in the *New York Times* with Anna Howard Shaw, defending her contention that women are not "rewarded in proportion to their work" as "unpaid servant(s) merely a comfort and a luxury agreeable to have if a man can afford it." Gilman was unbelievably forward thinking for her time, even going so far as to devise architectural plans for houses without kitchens to end women's slavery to the stove so they could take up professional occupations.

Perkins Gilman wrote five more books pushing for economic change for women, a critically acclaimed autobiography, three utopian novels, and countless articles, stories, and poetry before her death by suicide after a long struggle with cancer in 1935. With the passing of time, Charlotte Perkins Gilman is usually remembered only for *The Yellow Wallpaper* and for her feminist utopian novel *Herland*, in which three American men enter Herland, an all-female society that reproduces through parthenogenesis, the development of an unfertilized egg. Less known is her impact as a nationally recognized speaker, political theorist, and tireless champion of women's causes at the turn of the century. She lived an unconventional life and suffered for it, revealing through her writing the often grim realities behind the Victorian ideals of womanhood and how it was possible to change the way men and women related to one another.

"I knew it was normal and right in general, and held that a woman should be able to have marriage and motherhood, and do her work in the world, also."

— Charlotte Perkins Gilman

CHARLOTTE PERKINS GILMAN ON SHEROISM

- In 1870, as a ten-year-old girl, Charlotte wrote a feminist tale of the sheroism of Princess Araphenia, only heir to the good King Ezephon. When the kingdom fell under attack from a wicked enemy, Princess Araphenia disguised herself as a warrior-prince with a magical sword supplied by an interplanetary visitor, Elmondine. Brave Princess Araphenia saved her father's kingdom and revealed herself after vanquishing the evil foes to the amazement and delight of her royal father.
- In 1911 on the subject of heroes: "strong, square, determined jaw. He may be cross-eyed, wide-eared, thick-necked, bandy-legged—what you please; but he must have a more or a less (protruding) jaw."
- On society run by women as depicted in Herland, written in 1915: "like a pleasant family—an old,

established, perfectly-run country place." Herland's society is made up entirely of women; therefore they have no enemies thanks to policies of "sister love" and "mother love."

MARY STEVENSON CASSATT: MAKING AN IMPRESSION

Mary Cassatt was the one American artist to be acknowledged and accepted by the French Impressionists. Born to privilege in Pennsylvania in 1844, Mary was lucky to have the opportunity to live abroad. Her father was president of the Pennsylvania Railroad; he relocated his family and lived in Germany so Mary's brother Alexander could study engineering. Later, they stayed in France. Mary was especially struck by Paris, and although she was self-identified as an American, she really did most of her work in the French capital. Her family wasn't supportive of her decision to be an artist. They tried to talk her out of studying at the Pennsylvania Academy of the Fine Arts; her father's reaction to her stated desire to pursue a career as an artist was "I'd rather have you dead!" (Although Father Cassatt's comment was extreme, it's important to remember that women simply weren't going off to foreign countries in 1865. Shero Mary did just that, helping knock down one more barrier for womankind.)

Cassatt was nothing if not persistent and managed to talk her difficult father into allowing her to study the Old Masters abroad. She made tracks for Spain, Italy, and then alighted in Paris for serious application of her training. by 1868, Mary had a painting accepted at the Paris Salon, to whom she submitted work until 1877 when Degas took a personal interest in her painting, asked her to join the Impressionist School, and encouraged the young woman to take up photography and Japanese print-making. Although Cassatt has her own distinctive style, she credits Degas as having been a wonderful encouragement,

inspiration, and influence on her art. As a counterpoint and reality check, Degas' remark upon seeing Cassatt's work for the first time should be kept in mind: "I am not willing to admit that a woman can draw well."
As if being the only woman Impressionist and the only American Impressionist weren't enough, Cassatt's contribtion to art herstory is even more sheroic in her choice of subject matter—young women and girls, mothers and their children. She approached her subjects with simplicity and directness, going about painting her models with no intent to glorify or sentimentalize. Unlike some of her fellow Impressionists, Mary drew her subjects prior to the application of pastels or oils. Her work has, to a certain degree, a great clarity because of this.

Mary Cassatt had a series of one-woman shows in Paris, establishing her reputation outside her immediate circle. She was also a discerning businesswoman, selling her own work and that of her artist friends, and advancing the cause of art a great deal when she convinced museums such as the Met and the Mavermeyer to exhibit contemporary art. She also very successfully advocated to American tourists to collect the bold new art; she was quite right when she told the visiting buyers it would be immensely valuable soon enough. She persuaded her wealthy brother Alexander to purchase paintings by Renoir, Degas, Monet, Pissarro, and Manet, making him the first real collector of this important school of art.

Eventually her reputation as an important artist crossed the Atlantic. In 1891, she accepted a commission from the Chicago World's Fair to paint a mural on "modern women." in 1904, she was given France's highest distinction when she was made Chevalier of the French Legion of Honor in 1904. As time went on, Mary had to take care of her sick sister and mother, cutting severely into her time to paint, and by 1913, she was so blinded by cataracts that she couldn't paint any longer.

Although some historians speculate that the relationship between Cassatt and Degas might have gone beyond platonic, Mary lived a very discreet public life, dedicated to her art, her family, and her independence. Toward the end of her life, she enjoyed hosting young would-be artists from America at her chateau with whom she passionately discussed art. She lived in France until her death in 1926, having accomplished more than she (or her doubting Thomas father) ever envisioned.

"Now I could work with absolute independence without considering the opinion of a jury. I had already recognized who were my true masters. I admired Manet, Courbet, and Degas. I took leave of conventional art. I began to live."

— **Mary Cassatt**

CAMILLE CLAUDEL: THE FEELER

Camille Claudel, born in France in 1864, is beginning to be accorded more respect for her sculpture, after being hidden in the looming shadow of August Rodin, best known for "The Thinker." Part of a creative clique in France that included Camille's brother Paul, who was a Catholic poet and playwright of note in the late nineteenth century, Camille was an artist of considerable talent. She studied with Rodin, becoming his model and mistress. Their relationship was stormy; the two artists' tempers would burn brightly and they were constantly breaking up and making up, but the relationship endured until 1898. When her brother Paul abandoned her, she committed an auto-de-fe. As was typical in that era, Camille was institutionalized for depression and hysteria starting in 1913, eroding her ability to continue forceful sculpting until her death in 1943. Anne Delbee's 1982 play "Une Femme: Camille Claudel" was the beginning of a revival of interest in Claudel. Controversially, the play posits the theory that Camille was more than a muse; indeed, she was the true artist of the two, infusing Rodin with creativity and ideas. In 1989, Isabella Adjani and Gerard Depardieu did a wonderful job of bringing the creative couple to the big screen. Despite the difficulties of her last years, Camille Claudel has become a French national sheroine and cause celebre.

KATHE KOLLWITZ: TORN FROM HER SOUL

German lithographer Kathe Kollwitz's art became the vehicle for her protest of the senselessness of war. She couldn't have found a more effective way to express her sentiments. The body of work she produced moved art historians the world over to classify Kollwitz as one of the four most important graphic artists of the twentieth century. Tragically, a great deal of her work was destroyed by the Nazis and by bombings in World War II, but what has survived is a record of her power. It is not only her powerful graphic technique that has provided lasting fame, but her subject matter—almost always a peasant woman with a strong body, often surrounded by children, different from the typical passive, sexualized women found in male-dominated art.

Born in 1867, Kollwitz became the first woman to be elected to Berlin's prestigious Academy of Art and became director there in 1928. She was also the only female of the *fin de siecle* group of left-wing liberal artists who founded To the Secession, an organization dedicated to opposing artists affiliated with the German establishment. When her son died in World War I, the focus of her art became graphic depiction of the effects on women and children of the social and political events of her lifetime. Her piece entitled "To the Weaver's Rebellion" portrayed the nightmarish conditions of the poor, along with the sequel of lithographs in "To the Peasant War" about the harsh lives of the working class in Germany. In her print "Outbreak" from this series, she created a portrait of a woman, "Black Anna," who singlehandedly started a revolution. "Raped" is one of the first pictures in Western art that dared to show the war of violence waged on women.

She was kicked out of the Academy of Art by the Nazis in 1933 who regarded her as a pariah—a political artist depicting poverty, reality, and less-than-uber-ideal peasantfolk! She died penniless and homeless in 1945, having been stripped of her sheroic lithographic art.

Amazingly, her surviving son discovered a diary she kept, describing her inner emotional life and her struggle to make art at the turn of the century, as a woman, a wife, and mother. Her entries, published as *To the Diary and Letters of Kathe Kollwitz* are a fascinating delineation of the emotional price women often have to pay to be creative, to be political, and to break new ground.

Her surviving art continues to affect people worldwide. In the cemetery in which she is buried there is a note in the visitors' book dated September 22, 1996: "God bless you Kathe. And all your children. We carry on what you have wished. Signed, A former enemy."

"It always comes back to this, that only one's inner feelings represent the truth. I have never done any work cold; I have always worked with my blood, so to speak."

— **Kathe Kollwitz**

ISADORA DUNCAN: DANCING FOR HER LIFE

Isadora nee Angela Duncan was born in San Francisco on a summer's day in 1877. Brought up in the manner of fallen aristocracy by her poor mother, a music teacher, young Angela studied classical ballet, but soon discarded the rules in favor of her own freer, interpretive dance.

Her public debut of this new style of dance was a total flop in New York City and Chicago, so she scraped together some savings and headed for Europe on board a cattle boat.

In London, she studied the sculptures of pagan Greece and integrated the sense of movement from these classical remnants into her dance practice. A grande dame of the British stage, Mrs. Patrick Campbell, became the young American's patron and set up private dance salons for Isadora at the homes of the most cultured creme de la creme. Soon, snooty Brits couldn't get enough of the barefoot and beautiful young nymph, dancing her heart out in a dryad costume that left very little guesswork as to Duncan's anatomy. Soon she was packing theaters and concert halls all over the continent. In 1905, she toured Russia as well.

Isadora Duncan was not only the dance diva of her day, but a woman who dared to flout social convention, bearing children out of wedlock (wedlock was a notion utterly repugnant to Duncan and her pack) to stage designer Gordon Craig and Paris Singer, of the sewing machine dynasty. But her life was not all roses—Duncan lost her two babies and their nurse when their car rolled into the Seine and all three drowned. Duncan tried to sublimate her grief with work, opening dance schools around Europe and touring South America, Germany, and France.

In 1920, she received an invitation to establish a school in the Soviet Union, where she fell in undying love with Sergey Aleksandrovish Yesenin, a respected poet half her age. The two married, despite Duncan's abhorrence of the institution, and were taken for Bolshevik spies as they traveled the globe. Upon being heckled mercilessly at a performance in Boston's Symphony Hall, Isadora Duncan bid her homeland adieu forever: "Goodbye America, I shall never see you again!" She was as good as her word; the honeymooners scuttled back to Europe, where their relationship crashed against the rocks of Yesenin's insanity. He committed suicide in 1925 and Duncan lived the remainder of her life on the French Riviera, where another auto accident ended her life. One of her dramatic Greek inspired scarves got tangled in the wheel of her car and she was strangled.

Though her life was sad and messy, Isadora Duncan's real triumph was her art. She changed the dance world forever, freeing the form from Victorian constriction to allow more natural movement. Duncan believed in celebrating the sculptural beauty of the female body and that dance, at its zenith, was "divine expression." Duncan is regarded by many to have been the chief pioneer of modern dance. She was a free spirit for whom "to dance is to live."

"If my art is symbolic of any one thing,
it is symbolic of the freedom of woman and
her emancipation."

— Isadora Duncan

GABRIELLE "COCO" CHANEL: FASHION SHERO

Considered by many to be the mother of modern fashion, Gabrielle "Coco" Chanel was the first fashion designer to create clothes that matched emerging attitudes of women for greater freedom and independence. Born in France around 1883, Coco's first step toward a life in the fashion industry was a job at a hatmaker's shop in Deauville, France, where she worked until 1912. At thirty-one years old, she struck out on her own, opening her very own shop featuring streamlined and unfussy wool jersey dresses. Strikingly new, her simple style caught on quickly. Chanel's success with the dresses and the celebratory atmosphere following World War I encouraged her to really go to town with smartly cut suits, sophisticated short skirts, and bold, chunky jewelry designed at her very own couture house in Paris!

In 1922, she created Chanel #5, the perfume every woman wanted, named for her lucky number; to this day, it remains one of the all-time favorite perfumes. Chanel's innovations are legendary—costume jewelry, evening scarves, short skirts, and the little black dress all came from the steel-trap mind of Coco Chanel. She retired in 1938, but got bored and staged a remarkably successful comeback in the mid-fifties.

Coco, the ultimate Frenchwoman, never married, but seemed to be utterly happy with her career as an independent businesswoman, in charge of her own time and her own life. She makes America's Horatio Alger look shabby—the daughter of a vagabond street peddler, she was raised in orphanages and went on to found an empire, live a busy glamorous life, and leave behind a legacy that will last forever. The idol of practically everyone in the industry, Coco Chanel was the epitome of the modern woman. Yves St. Laurent once called her "The Godmother of us all," and French surrealist Jean

Cocteau remarked, "(Coco Chanel) has, by a kind of miracle, worked in fashion according to rules that would seem to have value for painters, musicians, poets."

"There have been many Duchesses of Westminster, but there is only one Coco Chanel."

— **Coco Chanel** *on why she rejected a famous suitor*

SUPERMODELS TAKE ON ISSUES

- Coco Chanel, famous for her quote that "A woman doesn't become interesting until she reaches forty" would probably be amused with cartoon shero **Sandee**, the "SuperHero SuperModel" creation of designer Isaac Mizrahi. Sandee is a fun, enchanting, and good-hearted high-fashion model who has a mission. She's advocating for the acceptance of aging; to be specific, she wants it made perfectly clear that it is okay to be over thirty!
- Sandee's polar opposite in every way is real life supershero supermodel **Waris Dirie**, a resplendent Somali native who has come out of the closet about a horrific secret from her childhood—a female circumcision performed on her at the age of six. Waris saw her sister die from the same mutilation, and Waris has suffered tremendous health problems as a result. This only makes her all the more sheroic in stepping up to take on the role of spokesperson against this heinous crime against women that still happens all across the world. Waris is providing a human face to this twentieth-century atrocity. Since she took on the role, clitorectomies have already been outlawed in one African nation! "It was entirely my idea to reveal it publicly," says Waris, "No one

knew before. With my modeling exposure, I thought maybe now I've got the power to do something about it. To let people know about this terrible thing that happens to girls around the world."

LIYA KEBEDE: BEAUTY WITH A HEART

Liya Kebede was born in 1978 in Addis Ababa, Ethiopia. A film director noticed her distinctive features while she was still a schoolgirl attending Lycée Guebre-Mariam. Impressed by her unique look, the film director immediately recommended her to a French modeling agency. This opened up many opportunities for Liya, and at the age of 18, she moved to France to model for a Parisian agency before later relocating to New York City. Things started to really take off for her when she was offered an exclusive contract by designer Tom Ford for his fashion show for the Gucci Fall/Winter 2000 line, which was also the year she married Kassy Kebede. The cover of Paris *Vogue* followed; the entire issue was dedicated to her. She has modeled for designers including Dolce & Gabbana, Louis Vuitton, Yves Saint-Laurent, Emanuel Ungaro, Tommy Hilfiger, Shiatzy Chen, and Escada. But Liya Kebede is more than just another pretty face. She was selected to be the WHO's Goodwill Ambassador for Maternal, Newborn and Child Health in 2005, and soon started the Liya Kebede Foundation, which works for the health of mothers and infants and to prevent child mortality in her native Ethiopia and other African countries. The foundation has gone on to train health workers who have assisted in more than 10,000 births, as well as conducting global maternal health awareness campaigns that have reached millions. It also funds advocacy and supports low-cost technologies, training and medical programs, and community-based education. Kebede has also participated in Champions for an AIDS-Free Generation, a group of African heads of state and other leaders working to end the HIV epidemic. She has used her fame to help people look at the bigger picture and brought attention to the health of mothers and their children.

GEORGIA O'KEEFFE: AN AMERICAN ICON

Georgia O'Keeffe was born on a Wisconsin farm in 1887. The closest town was called Sun Prairie. O'Keeffe knew at a fairly early age that she wanted to be an artist and enrolled in the Art Institute of Chicago in 1904 until a bout of typhoid caused her to drop out. Upon her recovery, rather than returning to Chicago, she moved to New York, where she enrolled in the Art Students League. Feeling she didn't have what it took to be a painter, she moved to the south and made a living, first as a commercial artist and later as an art teacher. Rededicating herself to art in 1914, she took a teaching position at Columbia College in South Carolina, where she felt the easy teaching load would give her time to devote to drawing.

In 1916, Alfred Stieglitz came across her drawings and arranged for a show, exclaiming, "At last a woman on paper!" They married in 1924, and had a lifelong companionship documented by hundreds of photographs Stieglitz took of O'Keeffe. The relationship had many ups and downs, but through it all, Georgia painted, taking trips to the Southwest to give herself and her husband the emotional space they each needed. The terrain would increasingly come to dominate her work.

Upon Stieglitz's death in 1946, O'Keeffe moved to Santa Fe, where she purchased Ghost Ranch and opened her own gallery, An American Place. O'Keeffe loved the light and lines of her ranch, living there in her treasured privacy, painting up to her death at age ninety-nine. She won many awards, including the Medal of Freedom in 1977, and was elected to the American Academy of Arts and

Letters, and her works grace many of the most prestigious museums around the world.

Georgia O'Keeffe's style is unique; her paintings are at once both stark and rich. Her precise brush strokes applied to organic forms, flowers, skulls, and rocks overlaid with luminous color washes command the eye. Ever an iconoclast, Georgia O'Keeffe lived, and painted, by her own rules.

Regarded as one of the most important women artists of the twentieth century, she laid important groundwork for the ambitions of women artists simply by pursuing her singular vision. In 1930, O'Keeffe shared her thoughts on feminism, forty years before the second wave of activism. "I am interested in the oppression of women of all classes...though not nearly so definitely and so consistently as I am in the abstraction in my painting because the past has left us so small an inheritance of women's painting that has widened life...Before I put a brush to canvas I question, 'Is this mine? Is it all intrinsically of myself? Is it influenced by some idea or some photograph of an idea which I have acquired from some man?' That too implied a social consciousness, a social struggle. I am trying with all my skill to do painting that is all of a woman, as well as all of me."

"I am going to be an artist!"

— **Georgia O'Keeffe** *at age eight, when asked what she was going to be when she grew up*

GABRIELA MISTRAL: VOICE OF THE PEOPLE

The first Latin American woman to win a Nobel Peace Prize in literature, Gabriela Mistral was born in the Chilean village of Montegrande in 1889. Her mother,

Basque Petronila Alcayaga, was a teacher and her father was Jeronimo Villanueva. A teacher and a gypsy poet of Indian and Jewish birth, Jeronimo was overfond of wine and not quite so attached to his duties as a breadwinner and father; he deserted the family when Gabriela was three. As a schoolgirl, Gabriela discovered her call to poetry and also her own stubborn independence, switching her birth name, Lucila, for her choice, Gabriela. Several years later, as an adult, she chose a fitting surname, Mistral, hinting of a fragrant Mediterranean wind.
Her first love was a hopelessly romantic railroad worker who killed himself when the relationship faltered after two years. Her first book of poetry, *Sonetas de la Muerta* [Sonnets of Death] was written as a result of her sadness, guilt, and pain over the death of her ex-lover. When Gabriela published three of the Sonetas in 1914, she received Chile's top prize for poetry.

In the twenties and thirties, she wrote many volumes of poetry including *Desolacion* (Desolation), *Ternura* (Tenderness), *Questions, Tala*, and a mixed media anthology, *Readings for Women*. Mistral felt a special interest and sympathy for women and children, and worked to help the victims of World Wars I and II. Gabriela made real strides as an educator, as well. She initiated programs of schooling the poor, founded a mobile library system, and traveled the world, gleaning whatever she could to bring back and improve Chile's education system. In 1923, she was named "Teacher of the Nation." She became an international envoy and ambassador off and on for her country for twenty years, eventually serving the League of Nations and the United Nations.

In the late 1920s, a military government seized power in Chile and offered Mistral an ambassadorship to all the nations of Central America. Mistral refused to work for the military state and made a scathing public denouncement of the government machine. Her pension was revoked and, sheroically, Mistral had to support herself, her mother, and her sister through her writing. She lived in exile in France, eventually moving to the United States where she taught at Middlebury, Barnard, and the University of Puerto Rico.

She received the prestigious Nobel Prize in 1945. Upon accepting the revered award, Gabriela Mistral made a sharp contrast with dashing Sweden's King Gustav in her plain black velvet. Pointedly, she didn't accept the prize for herself, but on behalf of the "poets of my race." Mistral died in 1957, mourned by her native Chile where she was revered as a national treasure. A poor, rural schoolteacher of mixed race, Gabriela Mistral achieved the top posts and honors in her mountainous country. She was the "people's poet," giving voice to the humble people to whom she belonged, the Indians, mestizos, and Campesanos, and scorning the rampant elitism and attempts at creating a racial hierarchy in Europe and in her beloved Chile.

"I consider myself to be among the children of that twisted thing that is called a racial experience, or better, a racial violence."

– Gabriela Mistral

GWENDOLYN BROOKS: POET OF THE BEAT

Gwendolyn Brooks is one of the most innovative poets in the literary landscape of America. Born in 1917 in Topeka, Kansas, Gwendolyn's family moved when she was young to the far more urbane city of Chicago, a street-smart influence that still informs her work. Brooks wanted to bring poetry to the poor black kids of the inner city. She did—rapid fire, tightly wound iambic pentameter that predated rap and won her the distinction of being the first black person to receive the Pulitzer Prize (for *Annie Allen* in 1950). In later life, she took a more radical bent, hooking up with revolutionary black Beat LeRoi Jones (now Amiri Baraka) and Don L. Lee, and jumping into the causes of African Americans with both feet. She became a tough and angry Black Power poet penning verses grounded in classical style deconstructed through the lens of her newfound racial awareness and commitment to cause. Forty years after her prize-winning feat, her poetry is still raw, fresh, and commanding.

"I want to clarify my language. I want these poems to be free. I want them to be directed without sacrificing the kind of music, the picture-making I've always been interested in."

— **Gwendolyn Brooks**

ZORA NEALE HURSTON: SERAPH OF THE SUN

Zora Neale Hurston's readership is much larger now than at the height of her career. Almost forty years after her death in 1960, her body of work has been reprinted hundreds of times, ensuring her legacy in our literary heritage. A writer of the Harlem Renaissance, Hurston spoke for the silenced—black women. Her work—five novels, more than fifty short stories and essays, a collection of short stories, and her autobiography—demonstrates her commitment to the culture of her people and her anthropological scholarship of black language and history.

Born in rural Florida in 1891, Zora was very outspoken, insisting upon equality and eschewing traditional roles for a black woman of her day. For this, she credits her precious mother, Lucy, who urged her to "jump at de sun!" when she was nine. Despite a bumpy childhood with a stepmother she didn't care for, Hurston thrived in the all-black town of Eatonville, where she saw the example of a peaceful and good government by and for blacks. Her father, a popular Baptist preacher, was mayor of the town several times and warned his daughter that the world outside would be vastly different. She bounced among various relatives until, at fourteen, she headed out to make her own way in the world, working as a maid for a group of Gilbert and Sullivan traveling players. Landing in New York City, Zora made some fateful connections with leaders of the Harlem Renaissance, including Langston Hughes, Alan Locke, and Montgomery Gregory.

With financial aid, Zora received an excellent education at Barnard College in New York City where she was mentored by Franz Boas, the leading anthropologist of the day, who also had mentored Margaret Mead. Boas saw Hurston's endless drive and curiosity and set her to the task of gathering the cultural history of her people. After graduation, Hurston returned to Florida to record black folklore. She married a man she met there, Herbert Sheen, but divorced not long after, one of three divorces. She got a fellowship in 1934 to collect more folklore and went on a quest for knowledge about her people that took her to New Orleans, Jamaica, Haiti, and the Bahamas, where she studied voodoo in addition to her usual linguistics and tall stories. The data she accrued on this epic trip constituted the foundations for *Mules and Men* and *Tell My Horse*. *Jonah's Gourd Vine* is regarded as one of her finest works of fiction, and *Their Eyes Were Watching God* is hailed as her masterpiece. One of Hurston's greatest proponents, novelist Alice Walker, offers a powerful endorsement of Hurston's opus, "There is no book more important to me than this one."

Unfortunately, her friendship with Langston Hughes broke down over a play they were collaborating on, *Mule Bone*. The forties saw a further decline of Zora Neale

Hurston's career. Her essay, "How it Feels to be Colored Me" drew fire for its inflammatory frankness regarding what Hurston saw as the wholly unfair system of Jim Crow injustice. In 1940s America, Hurston's literary protests fell on unwilling ears.

In 1948, she was the victim of a trumped-up charge of child molestation in New York City. The case was thrown out, but Hurston was devastated and headed back to Florida. Undaunted, she continued to act from her conscience, protesting 1954's *Brown vs. Topeka Board of Education*, taking the position that it smacked of a bias toward black students and southern schools as inferior. Hurston, one of America's most original literary scholars, linguists, mythographers, and novelists, had to work as a librarian, a substitute teacher, and even as a maid to try to pay her bills. She was working on a book and still submitting articles to the *Saturday Evening Post* and *American Legion Magazine* even in her most desperate of circumstances.

When she died of heart failure in January of 1960, she was penniless and homeless, taking shelter at the Saint Lucie Welfare Home. Hurston's work languished, almost forgotten, until her masterful writing was "rediscovered" in the 1970s. Zora saw black culture as a treasure to be celebrated and shared, considering Caucasian culture as feeble when placed next to the vitality of black idiom and storytelling, Alice Walker searched out Hurston's unmarked pauper's grave in Fort Pierce, Florida, and wrote about her pilgrimage to find her sheroic foresister for *Ms.* Magazine in 1975. Her article "In Search of Zora Neale Hurston" created an avalanche of renewed interest in the writer who had been at the very epicenter of her Harlem Renaissance. The gravestone Walker had made read, "Zora Neal Hurston, A Genius of the South. Novelist, Folklorist, Anthropologist."

"I was not comfortable to be around. Strange things must have looked out of my eyes like Lazarus after his resurrection...I have been in sorrow's kitchen and licked out all the pots...I have stood on the peaky mountain with a harp and a sword in my hands."

— **Zora Neale Hurston** from *Dust Tracks on a Road*, Hurston's autobiography in which she predicts her whole life in twelve visions, including her ultimate destitution.

MARTHA GRAHAM: GRANDE DAME OF DANCE

Modern dance innovator, Martha Graham was born into a medical family in 1894. Her physician father was fascinated by how the body expresses the psychological, and the young girl was an eager student, adopting this physiognomic approach in her work. Martha's family settled in Santa Barbara, California in 1908, where she was further influenced by the crashing of the ocean's waves and Eastern art. In 1916, she began dancing professionally at Denishawn, the Los Angeles dance school and troupe founded by Ruth St. Denis and Ted Shawn. Martha eagerly enveloped herself in the global dance tradition at Denishawn—native American tribal, classical, folk, and ecstatic religious mysticism. Shawn worked with Martha on "Xochitl," a stunning Aztec ballet that showcased Martha's hidden power and passion. She stayed with Denishawn until 1923 when she decided their eclectics bordered on scattered, heading east for the Greenwich Follies. The next year found Martha teaching and experimenting with dance at Rochester's Eastman School.

Martha Graham appeared in New York as an independent dancer and choreographer for the first time in 1926. Critics were pleased with her grace and elegance in

"The Three Gopi Maidens" and "Danse Languide." The following year, Graham had dug deeper into her own creative source. Her new dances were stripped-down, purer, less to the taste of New York's taste-makers who declared her work, "ugly, stark, and obscure." Her signature movements spiraled out from a contracting of the torso. She was compared to Nijinsky for being completely unafraid to appear unattractive in the passionate throes of expression.

In 1927, she performed "Revolt," perhaps the first protest dance staged in America. With Arthur Honegger's modern avant garde music, Graham's "Revolt" shocked audiences, causing a hue and cry of protest to her protest dance. The following period proved Martha's hard work and dedication to innovation with "Frontier," which featured sculptural set-pieces by Isamu Noguchi; "Primitive Mysteries," scored for Martha by a fine composer, Louis Horst; "Night Journey," a retelling of the Oedipus myth through the eyes of Jocasta; and "Letter to the World," interpretations of Emily Dickinson's poetry and life. In a career that spanned more than fifty years, Martha Graham went on to create nearly 200 original dances, choreograph over 160 ballets, form her own school and company, and attain recognition as one of the most influential dancers of all time. The first to present modern dance sessions in ballet houses, Graham danced "to objectify in physical form my beliefs..."

"[Graham created] a dance technique that has become the basis of the education of hundreds of thousands of dancers around the world and establishing a new form for dance and twentieth-century theater."

— from the Scripps American Dance Festival award honoring Martha Graham

RUKMINI DEVI ARUNDALE: TRANSFORMING TRADITION AND SPEAKING FOR THE SILENT

Rukmini Devi Arundale was a dancer and choreographer who revived and transformed a branch of classical Indian dance; she was also a theosophist and an activist for the welfare and rights of animals. Born to a high-caste Brahmin family in 1904 in Madurai, India, she was reared in Madras (modern Chennai), where she was exposed to theosophical thought not only by her father but by famed theosophist leader Annie Besant and others. She shocked the conservative society of the time by marrying prominent British theosophist Dr. George Arundale at age 16. Three years later, Rukmini became President of the All-India Federation of Young Theosophists, and then President of the World Federation of Young Theosophists in 1925.

She traveled extensively with her husband and Besant, working to further theosophy, and became drawn to Western classical dance. Famed Russian ballerina Anna Pavlova arranged ballet lessons for Rukmini and suggested that she seek inspiration in the traditional arts of India. After first witnessing the ancient Indian dance form "sadir" in 1933, she studied sadir and bharatanatyam extensively with various teachers, then gave her first performance at the Diamond Jubilee Convention of the Theosophical Society; this set a precedent for upper-class women to take up a dance form that had been long associated with women of the lower classes, who were looked down upon. Rukmini started two theosophical secondary schools in 1934. In 1936, she and her husband established an academy of dance and music called "Kalakshetra" near Madras; the three schools eventually combined to become the Kalakshetra Foundation, which still exists as a highly respected cultural academy dedicated to the preservation of traditional values in Indian art and crafts.

Rukmini, along with forerunner E. Krishna Iyer, aimed to reshape the form of the dance, which had fallen into disfavor due to its association with devadasi temple dancers and erotic temple practices, which were disapproved of by the colonizing British Christian culture. She worked as a choreographer to purge Bharatanatyam of its erotic content and refocus it on devotion, and also brought in new musical instruments like the violin, innovative costumes, new lighting, stage scenarios, and jewelry inspired by temple sculptures.

Rukmini was a member of the Indian Parliament from 1952–1962. She had a keen interest in animal welfare and was involved with a number of organizations working for humane treatment of animals; as an MP, she was instrumental in enacting the Prevention of Cruelty to Animals Act in 1960. In 1962, she set up and chaired India's Animal Welfare Board. Interestingly, in 1977 she was actually offered the presidency of India by Prime Minister Morarji – which she declined. Rukmini Devi Arundale is still a beloved figure in modern India.

"We must keep both our femininity and our strength."

— **Rukmini Devi Arundale**

PEARL PRIMUS: PEARL OF GREAT PRICE

Dancer wunderkind Pearl Primus was born in 1919 in Trinidad; she became the top interpreter of her African heritage via choreography and performance. She received international attention and respect even though she had no formal training in dance and had intended on being a physician. Pearl was a Jill of all trades, working as a switchboard operator, photographer, health counselor, and as a welder in New York's shipyards, as well as many blue-collar factory jobs. Once Pearl committed to dance as her profession, she went at it with fierce dedication and concentration, viewing dance as a way to express her ideas about social conditions and the state of humanity. She was incredibly innovative, mixing dance and musical styles constantly. Fairly quickly, her pieces, such as "Strange Fruit," became classics. She also recited African, West Indian, and African American poetry and literature during freestyle dance performances, such as Langston Hughes' "Our Spring Will Come" and "The Negro Speaks of Rivers." Pearl Primus really dug into the Afro-Indian culture, learning and in turn teaching through her dance about the cultures, tribes, and history of her people. She once said, "Dance is my medicine. It's the scream which eases for a while the terrible frustration common to all human beings who, because of race, creed, or color are 'invisible.'"

MARGARET BOURKE-WHITE: THE MIRROR'S EYE

I wonder what Margaret Bourke-White would think of her hauntingly beautiful photograph of Mohandas Gandhi at his spinning wheel being used in the Apple ad captioned "Think Different." As if the grammatical issue weren't irritating enough, it seems tragic for a work meant to preserve the memory and honor of a man dedicated to peace and simplicity (he's spinning his own cloth so as to not wear manufactured foreign goods) now being used to market computers.

Born in the Bronx in 1904, Margaret Bourke-White "dared to become an industrial photographer and a photojournalist at a time when men thought they had exclusive rights to those titles, then rose with startling speed to the top of both professions," writes her biographer Vicki Goldberg. Indeed, her abilities did much to contribute to the rise of photojournalism, and many of our memories of important twentieth-century history are thanks to her efforts to document them for posterity. Although the Gandhi photograph may end up being the most famous thanks to some fairly insidious marketing, others are seared onto our memory: the Indian holocaust that took place during the partition when all Hindus were forced to leave the new northern state of Pakistan and all Muslims traveled north to the new state. The dead are still unnumbered in this trail of tears, estimates are as high as three million. She also photographed the Moslem massacre in Calcutta, horrendous and powerful pictures of dead Hindus being devoured by vultures.

As a *Life* staff photographer, she traveled the globe. In Moscow, she caught on film the Nazi air invasion of the Russian city. In South Africa, she photographed apartheid-beleaguered blacks slaving in diamond and gold mines for the gain of their oppressors. In Korea, she photographed guerilla warfare. She covered the war fronts in Africa, Italy, and Germany, and was with the Allied force that entered the death camp of Buchenwald, where she shot some of her most painful and important work. "I saw and photographed the piles of naked, lifeless bodies, the human skeletons in furnaces, the living skeletons."

In America, the 1934 drought and Dust Bowl migration were her subjects, as well as an unvarnished view of the abject poverty in Appalachia and other parts of the rural South. She and her husband, writer Erskine Caldwell, collaborated on several photo essay books, including *You Have Seen Their Faces*, reminding an insular America about her own forgotten people. During World War II, she was the first Army Air Force woman photographer in action in Italy and North Africa.

Margaret Bourke-White's sheroic dedication to telling the truth with pictures has left us with a fascinating chronicle of the twentieth century. In her pursuit of visual verity, she often put herself in danger, walking on steel beams to get the height for the best shot, going deep into dangerous mines, flying with a bomb squad in Tunisia, and even going down in a shipwreck in World War II. She died in 1971 of Parkinson's disease. In her lifetime, Margaret Bourke-White returned to us our own history and gave us the opportunity to learn from it.

"The impersonality of modern war has become stupendous, grotesque."

– **Margaret Bourke-White,** who put a face on the horrors

LINA BO BARDI: UNCOMPROMISING MODERNIST

Many people are afraid of glass houses, but not this amazing architect, born Achillina Bo in Rome in 1914. At age 25, she graduated from the Rome College of Architecture with her final piece, "The Maternity and Infancy Care Centre". Lina then began working in partnership with architect Carlo Pagani at Studio Bo e Pagani. She also collaborated with architect and designer Gio Ponti on a home design magazine. She opened her own solo studio in 1942, but due to the war, architectural work was scarce, so Lina did illustrations for newspapers and magazines. A year later, her studio was destroyed by an aerial bombing; this led to her becoming more involved in the Italian Communist Party. Domus Magazine commissioned her to travel around taking pictures to document the destruction war had brought to Italy. Lina also took part in the First National Meeting for Reconstruction in Milan, highlighting public indifference on the issue; to her, reconstruction was not merely physical, but moral and cultural.

In 1946, Lina and her husband moved to Brazil; they were received in Rio by the IAB (Institute of Brazilian Architects). She again opened her own studio and found her creativity newly inspired by Brazil. She and her husband cofounded the seminal art magazine Habitat; then in 1947, her husband Pietro was asked to establish and run a Museum of Art. Lina designed the building's conversion into a museum as well as designing an office building for the Associated Newspapers. In 1951, Lina completed the Casa de Vidro or "Glass House", a design influenced by Italian rationalism. She became a lecturer at the University of São Paulo in 1955 and soon published a major paper on teaching the theory of architecture. At age 74, she was honored with a first-ever exhibition of her work at the University of São Paulo. Lina Bo Bardi died at the Casa de Vidro in 1992, leaving behind designs for a new City Hall for São Paulo and a Cultural Centre for Veracruz.

"Architecture and architectural freedom are above all a social issue that must be seen from inside a political structure, not from outside it."

— **Lina Bo Bardi**

DOROTHEA LANGE: ACTIVIST PHOTOGRAPHER

"The discrepancy between what I was working on in the printing frames and what was going on in the street was more than I could assimilate," wrote Dorothea Lange of the reason she quit her job as a society photographer to record the misery of the Depression of the 1930s. Lange's sympathy for human suffering shines through in her luminous photographs, including her famous "Migrant Mother" and "White Angel Breadline." Her compassion came under attack later, however, when she was viewed as being overly empathetic with the Japanese Americans' internment during World War II. Though she was hired to record this event for posterity, the photographs were impounded and not shown until 1972, seven years after her death. Nonetheless, Lange was not deterred from her personal mission to capture the essential and universal humanness shared around the world. Her genius was in documenting that which might be ignored if not for her artistic eye compelling us to look.

FRIDA KAHLO: POP CULTURE PIONEER

Frida Kahlo's posthumous pop culture deification has eclipsed that of her husband, Mexican muralist Diego Rivera. A total iconoclast, Frida's visceral painting style has an intensity matched by few artists. Her fleshy fruits, torn arteries, tortured birthings, and imago-packed surrealist dreamscapes terrify and mesmerize. Her burning eyes in both self-portraiture and photographs make her hard to forget. Her pain seems to emanate from many wounds—psychic, physical, and romantic.

Born Magdalena Carmen Frida Kahlo y Calderon outside of Mexico City in 1907, her exotic looks, which have mesmerized millions, are a product of her heritage. Frida's father, one of Mexico's preeminent photographers, was a first generation Mexican born of Hungarian Jews, while her mother, Matilde Calderon, was a Mexican of mixed Spanish and Indian ancestry. Frida contracted polio when she was seven, stunting her right leg. Her father took charge of her recovery from polio, encouraging her to play sports to build back the strength of her right foot and leg. At fifteen, Frida was in a horrendous trolley-car accident, crushing her spine, right foot, and pelvis, leaving her crippled forever. Later, she depicted the crash as the loss of her virginity when the trolley car's handbrake pierced her young body. In pain for the remainder of her life, she underwent thirty-five surgeries, the amputation of her gangrenous right foot, and what she deemed as imprisonment bedridden in body casts. Indeed, several of Kahlo's greatest works were done while flat on her back, using a special easel her mother had made for her.

Her tempestuous relationship with world renowned painter Diego Rivera was also a source of great suffering. Often described as "froglike" in aspect, the Mexican art star was quite a ladies' man. During a hiatus between marriage to each other, Frida hacked off her beautiful long hair and dressed in baggy men's suits. She bitterly rued her inability to bear Rivera a child, grieving over several miscarriages. They went about making art in very different ways—Rivera's huge paintings were political messages on the walls of public buildings; Frida's paintings were deeply personal, vibrant colored paintings often done on tiny pieces of tin.

Frida and Diego were a very public couple. Coming of age in the wake of the Mexican Revolution, they were both very political, becoming friends with Leon Trotsky, Pablo Picasso, Russian filmmaker Sergei Eisenstein, Andre Breton, and the Rockefellers. Both artists embraced "Mexicanismo," Frida going so far as to wear traditional Indian peasant costumes at all times, cutting a striking and memorable figure with the rustic formality. Frida's stalwart adherence to all things "of the people" made her a national shero, with papers commenting on her resemblance to an Indian princess or goddess. In his article, "Portrait of Frida Kahlo as Tehuana," art critic Hayden Herrera asserts that the Latina artist was "unrestrained by her native Mexico's male-dominated culture. Tehuantepec women are famous for being stately, beautiful, smart, brave, and strong; according to legend, theirs is a matriarchal society where women run the markets, handle fiscal matters, and dominate the men." More than sixty years after her death, Frida and her work hold a fascination that shows no sign of fading. Her dramatic personal style and wild paintings have captured the public's imagination. She has been hailed as a role model for women artists, a stylistic pioneer and idealist who pursued her craft despite physical handicaps that would have stopped many others. Her body was broken but her spirit was indomitable, like the Tehuana women she identified with. As Herrera notes, "she became famous for her heroic '*allegria.*'"

ARTISTIS INFLUENCES

Dancer **Anna Pavlova** adopted the "Frida look" when she came to Mexico City. She danced a Mexican ballet in a native Indian costume, causing a sensation. Soon, bohemian intellectual types the world over were sporting the garb of Mexican peasant women.

ANOTHER WILD WOMAN

Frida Kahlo met Diego Rivera, twenty years her senior, through photographer **Tina Modotti**. Tina was really the catalyst for the direction Frida's life took toward art and leftist politics. Frida met Tina after her hospitalization from the trolley wreck; Modotti urged her to join the Communist party and gave her a hammer and sickle brooch to better show her affinities.

Tina Modotti left her home in Italy and moved to San Francisco in 1913. Theatrical in every way, she gained the respect of the Italian theater community for her acting, marrying Roubaix de l'Abrie Richey, a famously romantic painter and poet. Seven short years later, she moved to southern California and set her sights on a career in Hollywood films. Seeking out the bohemians of the day, she met photographer Edwin Weston, who soon became her lover. Weston taught Modotti photography and took many hauntingly beautiful shots of her.

Ultimately finding movie-making boring, Tina turned to the melting-pot of Mexico City, where she had a quick fling with Diego Rivera and hooked up with other artists, writers, and revolutionaries. Tina Modotti straddled the line between popular and notorious; she was even accused of the murder of her Cuban lover, who was murdered in cold-blood as he and Modotti walked together in the streets of Mexico City. Maligned by the press, she was kicked out of Mexico in 1930. She went to Berlin and the Soviet Union, where she devoted herself full-time to political activism with radicals Sergei Eisenstein, Alexandra Kollontorai, La Pasionaria, Ernest Hemingway, and Robert Capa. Tina Modotti lived in constant danger from her espionage on behalf of Stalinism. She went on to play a major role in the Spanish Civil War before dying alone under mysterious circumstances in 1942. Pablo Neruda read a poem he had written especially for Tina Modotti at her funeral service.

SIMONE DE BEAUVOIR: INDIVIDUALITY AND INTELLECTUS

Existentialist writer Simone de Beauvoir was the leader of the feminist movement in France. Her book, *The Second Sex*, immediately took a place of importance in the feminist canon upon its publication in 1949 and established Beauvoir's reputation as a first-rate thinker. Although her brutally honest examination of the condition of women in the first half of the twentieth century

shocked some delicate sensibilities, others were gratified to have someone tell it like it was. Beauvoir described the traditional female roles of wife and mother as that of "relative beings" dependent on context. She urged women to go after careers and endeavor to achieve fulfillment through meaningful work.

Beauvoir avoided the trap of "relative being" (and nothingness) by remaining partners and lovers with Jean-Paul Sartre, whom she met in her early twenties in a salon study group at Paris' famed university, the Sorbonne. They recognized each other as soulmates immediately and stayed together for fifty-one years in a highly unorthodox partnership wherein they left openings for "contingent loves" so as not to limit their capacity for enriching experience. She eschewed motherhood and all forms of domesticity; the duo rarely dined at home, preferring cafes for all their meals. They lived together only very briefly during World War II and had difficulty protecting their privacy as word of the trendy new existentialist philosophy, ultimately espousing ambiguity, spread and their international prestige heightened. While Sartre is generally credited as the creator of existentialism, Simone was no philosophical slouch. Her treatise *Existentialism and the Wisdom of the Ages* postulates the human condition as neutral, neither inherently good nor evil: "[The individual] is nothing at first," she theorized, "it is up to him to make himself good or bad depending upon whether he assumes his freedom or denies it."

Beauvoir's first efforts toward her writing career were fictional, including her aptly titled maiden voyage as a novelist in 1943's *She Came to Stay*, a fictionalization of Sartre's youthful protegee Olga Kosakiewicz who entered into a triangular living relationship with the two French intellectuals. Next, she tackled the male point of view in her epic novel treatment of death in *All Men Are Mortal*, whose central character was an immortal she tracked for seven centuries. In 1954, after the success of her feminist classic *The Second Sex*, Beauvoir returned to fiction with *The Mandarins*, a novelization of the splintered and disenchanted French intelligentsia, which won the illustrious Goncourt Prize.

She continued to write and publish, creating a weighty body of work. She outlived Sartre and died on a Paris summer day in 1986 after a long and thoughtful life, leaving a legacy of significant contributions to gender and identity issues as well as philosophy and literature.

"One is not born a woman, one becomes a woman."

— the first line of *The Second Sex*

CLARA ISAACMAN: A LIFE IN HIDING

Clara's family moved to the Belgian city of Antwerp in 1932 to escape the Romanian persecution of Jews after her father was beaten just because he tried to vote. They got a good start in Antwerp, where they ran a bottle-packing operation from their home. As the talk of anti-Jewish activities started to spread through Europe, the family kept on working hard, trying to go on as best they could, always keeping on the lookout for trouble. Clara's first experience with the cause of her parents' frightened whispers came when a troop of Nazis came and searched her school.

After that, the nightmare accelerated. Clara was shunned by her former playmates for being Jewish and lived in constant fear of being taken away. The family ended up going on the run, hiding wherever they could, oftentimes just one step ahead of Nazi soldiers looking for Jews to relocate to rumored camps. When the family ran out of

money, Clara's father dared to leave their hiding place to get money to continue paying people to allow them to live in attics and rodent-filled, filthy basements.

Clara's survival is thanks to the many Belgian heroes and sheroes she encountered during her secret life in the shadows. Her mother's vigilance saved the family countless times. One of the constant threats was that their "landlords" would take their money to let them hide, only to turn them in to the Gestapo for a reward. Clara's mother had a sixth sense and seemed to know exactly when betrayal was about to strike, and they would flee again.

A cherished memory of Clara's concerns her brother Heshie, who was taken by the Germans and put to work on a Jewish prison crew. When Heshie refused to act as a "kapo," a prisoner who got extra food and better treatment in return for doing anything the Nazis demanded, including helping kill other Jews, he was executed. Heshie's courage in the face of such cruelty and degradation made him a hero to the other prisoners, one of whom searched out Clara's family to make sure they knew of Heshie's heroism and honor in the face of death.

Like many survivors of the Holocaust, Clara suffered from enormous guilt about being one of the Jews who was spared while six million others, including her beloved brother, died. For many years after the war, she was silent about her experience out of shame for living. Clara decided to break her silence after hearing Nobel Prize winner Elie Weisel speak about being Jewish and practicing the faith in the post-pogrom era. Clara realized that she needed to share her story and help the healing process. Clara Isaacman lectured around the world about the Holocaust, especially to young people. An Anne Frank who lived to tell her story, she has written a book for young adults entitled *Clara's Story* about her years of hiding. In dedicating her life to telling her story to help create peace, healing, and remembrance, Clara's sheroic survival is a testament to the human spirit.

SELMA LAGERLOF & NELLY SACHS: NOBEL NOBILITY

In 1909, Selma became the first woman and the first Swedish writer to receive the Nobel Prize in Literature. The Prize was awarded for her body of work, including the 1891 novel, *To the Story of Gosta Berling, a*nd the 1902 two-volume work of fiction *Jerusalem*, the chronicle of Swedish peasants who migrate to Jerusalem. Selma became the preeminent Swedish writer of her day and produced an impressive body of work—33 novels and four biographical narratives. Shero Selma wasn't content to merely be the most brilliant novelist of her age, however; she also worked extremely hard at obtaining the release of Jewish writer Nelly Sachs from a Nazi concentration camp. Sachs, inspired by her savior, won the Nobel Prize for Literature herself in 1966.

ANNE FRANK: BEHIND THE ATTIC WALL

If Anne Frank had lived, what would she think of the fact that her diary of the two years her family spent in hiding from the Nazis would go on to become not only a classic of war literature, but one of the best-read and most loved books of all time? *The Diary of Anne Frank* is now handed down from one generation to the next, and reading the records of Anne's emotions has become a rite of passage for the teens of today. It has been translated into more than fifty languages and made into a play and a movie; a new English version, published in 1995, restored one-third more material that was cut out of the original by her father.

Why such popularity? Anne Frank's diary shows the human face of an inhuman war while it records Anne's emotional growth with great insight. When she passed through the walls behind the bookcases into the secret rooms of the attic in Amsterdam, she left her real life behind. At thirteen, Anne became a prisoner and fugitive at once. Torn from her friends at the onset of her teens, she poured her heart into the diary she called "Kitty," her imaginary friend and confessor. It's an intense experience for the reader who knows what Anne couldn't know—that she wouldn't survive. Anne believed she would make it and shared her hopes and wishes for the children she would one day have. But at sixteen, she died at the Bergen-Belsen concentration camp.

There is heartbreak also in the realization of what a gift for writing Anne had—it is almost unfathomable that some of the passages were written by an adolescent! Her honesty about her feelings, not all of them noble, is the quality that makes Anne's diary eternal. Caged in a hidden world, Anne showed us that a life of the mind could be full, no matter what the circumstances. For her courage and optimism, Anne Frank will always be a shero.

"The best remedy for those who are afraid, lonely, or unhappy is to go outside, somewhere where they can be quite alone with the heavens, nature, and God...I firmly believe that nature brings solace in all troubles."

— **Anne Frank**

MORE INSPIRING AUTHORS

The stories of Clara Isaacman and Anne Frank may inspire you to search for more of these precious documents of sheroic spirit from the Holocaust. I suggest **Etty**

Hillesum's *An Interrupted Life*, the diary of a young Jewish girl hiding from the Nazis in the Netherlands, **Eva Figes's** *Little Eden: A Child at War*, about a girl who escaped to London, and **Hanna Szenes**: *A Song of Life*.

AUDRE LORDE: A BURST OF LIFE

Poet activist Audre Lorde is finally receiving the recognition she has so long deserved. A black lesbian poet who never hid her truth, Audre started writing poetry seriously in grade school. Born in the winter of 1934, her parents were West Indian immigrants who escaped to New York City from Grenada in 1924, just in time for The Great Depression. Audre grew up feeling different from her two older sisters, feeling like she was really an only child or "an only planet, or some isolated world in a hostile, or at best, unfriendly firmament."

Dazzlingly bright, Audre read voraciously. After a stint at the University of Mexico where the atmosphere of racial tolerance really opened her eyes to the racism in the United States, she began attending Hunter College and earned a degree in library science from Columbia. Married and with two small children, she worked for several New York libraries for eight years. Divorcing, she again moved toward her true passion—creative writing, both prose and poetry. In 1968, she started teaching creative writing at City University of New York. She also spent a year as poet in residence at Tougaloo College in Jackson, Mississippi, and went on to teach at many prestigious schools throughout America, where her reputation as an extraordinarily gifted poet grew.

The rare combination of gifted writer *and* teacher, Audre Lorde challenged her students. According to biographer Joanne S. Richmond in *Handbook of American Women's History*, Lorde urged her writing students to "Claim every aspect of themselves and encourage(d) them

to discover the power of a spirited wholeness, knowing that in silence there is no growth, in suppression there is no personal satisfaction."

Her prose includes *The Cancer Journals,* disclosing her battle with breast cancer, from which she ultimately died. Audre encountered a feminist's nightmare in her treatment, refusing to wear the prosthetic breast her doctor tried to force upon her. In 1982, *Ami: a New Spelling of My Name* was Lorde's foray into creating a new genre, what she called "biomythology" and her literary outing of her own lesbianism. In *Ami*, she digs deep into archetype, myth, and women's mysteries through the story of her mother's birthplace, the West Indian island of Carriacou. Lorde reveled in the lore of African goddesses and matriarchal tales, her lusty lovemaking with other black women, and the intrinsic egalitarianism of nature. A staunch feminist and political activist, in her work she also pointed to the patriarchal "I" centeredness of Judeo-Christian traditions and confronted the hypocrisy of her times, angrily decrying sexism and bigotry in such poems as "Cables to Rage" and "The Black Unicorn."

On many occasions, Lorde read her poetry with fellow black poets Amiri Baraka, Nikki Giovanni, and Jayne Cortez. She began, as many poets do, in coffeehouses and humble church basements. But soon she was filling theaters and winning awards, including the American Book Award for *A Burst of Light*, a nomination in poetry for the 1974 National Book Award, and the Walt Whitman Citation of Merit, for which she became New York's Poet Laureate shortly before losing her life to cancer in 1992.

Audre Lorde is a poet's poet. Scratch the surface of many of today's best writers' influences and her name will come up repeatedly. Jewelle Gomez cites Audre Lorde as a major influence on her writing life and on the lives of many others in the African American creative community.

In an article for *Essence* magazine, Gomez recognizes Lorde's work as "a mandate to move through... victimization and create independent standards that will help us live full and righteous lives...She was a figure all women could use as a grounding when they fought for recognition of their worth."

"Poetry is the conflict in the lives we lead. It is the most subversive because it is in the business of encouraging change."

— Audre Lorde

MAYA ANGELOU: HOW THE CAGED BIRD SINGS

Marguerite Johnson's childhood was marked by the hardship of the Depression years in which she grew up. Her parents divorced and packed her off to live with her granny, "Momma" Henderson, who eked out a living in Stamps, Arkansas, running a little general store. Marguerite, known as Maya, attended church devotedly with Momma, who gave her stability and taught her the importance of values and a strong work ethic. The young girl found love and roots with her grandmother and the congregation at their church.

But tragedy struck when she visited her mother in St. Louis for eight months. Her mother had a boyfriend who spent a lot of time at her mother's house and often touched and hugged the seven-year-old overly much, but, in her innocence, she mistook it for a father's love. Later, he raped her, and Maya felt guilty and responsible for his jailing and subsequent death at the hands of other inmates who exacted their own brand of justice on a child molester. She became catatonic as a result of this onslaught of catastrophic violence. With the support of her family and an adult friend, Bertha Flowers, who introduced her to literature, Maya gradually reentered the world, speaking after five years and graduating first in her eighth grade class.

Maya and her mother then moved to San Francisco, where her mother ran a boardinghouse and worked as a professional gambler. Maya met many colorful characters among the boarders and threw herself into school where she flourished. She got pregnant at sixteen and took on the full responsibilities of motherhood with the birth of her son, Guy. For a few years, Maya walked on the wild side: working at a Creole restaurant, waitressing at a bar in San Diego, even an accidental and brief stint as a madam for two lesbian prostitutes. After a two-year marriage to a white man, Maya started dancing at the Purple Onion and got into show biz in the road show for "Porgy and Bess," which toured Africa and Europe. After cowriting "Cabaret for Freedom" with Godfrey Cambridge for the Southern Christian Leadership Conference, Maya drew Martin Luther King, Jr.'s attention for her talent and contribution to the civil rights movement, and he invited her to serve as an SCLC coordinator.

Maya's career was absolutely astonishing after this point, living in Egypt with Guy and her lover, a South African freedom fighter, and working in Ghana writing for *The African Review*. She remained involved with the theater, writing and performing in plays, acting in *Roots*, and writing several volumes of poetry as well as the script and music for the movie of her autobiography. But it is for the six best-selling volumes of her autobiography, starting with *I Know Why the Caged Bird Sings*, that she will go down in literary history. (The *New York Times* called her "one of the geniuses of Afro-American serial autobiography.") Written with captivating honesty, color, and verve, they are read by youth and adults alike for their inspirational message. Listen to this powerful passage from *I Know Why the Caged Bird Sings*: "If growing up is painful for the

Southern Black girl, being aware of her displacement is the rust on the razor that threatens the throat. It is an unnecessary insult." When she was criticized for not being completely factual as a writer, Maya responded, "There's a world of difference between truth and facts. Facts can obscure truth."

Maya Angelou, a name combined from a nickname her brother called her and a variation on her first husband's name, truly reinvented herself. No moment in her wonderfully colorful life illustrates this as much as her reading of her beautiful poem, "On the Pulse of Morning," at President Bill Clinton's first inauguration. She had come a long way from the scared and silent little seven-year-old to a woman come fully into her power, unafraid to share that with the world.

"The ability to control one's own destiny...comes from constant hard work and courage."

— Maya Angelou

MAXINE HONG KINGSTON: LITERARY WARRIOR

Maxine Hong Kingston's appropriately titled magic realism autobiography, *The Woman Warrior: Memoirs of a Girlhood Among Ghosts,* came out in the bicentennial year, 1976. It was perfect timing because Kingston's story is an American story and a rebellion as well. Her tale of a Chinese American girl coming of age in California won the National Book Critic's Circle Award and set off a wave of writing by women of color; suddenly Maxine was a literary shero at thirty-six years old. Her subsequent book *China Men* won the same award in 1980, while her 1989 debut novel *Tripmaster Monkey: His Fake Book* thrilled both readers and critics.

Born in 1940 to Chinese immigrants who ran a Stockton, California, gambling house, Maxine got her name from a very successful blonde patron of their establishment. When some shady fair-weather friends swindled the Hongs out of the gambling business, they operated a laundry that employed the whole family, including Maxine and her five sisters and brothers. It was a life with a lot of drudgery, but Maxine was able to attend the University of California on eleven scholarships. Intending to study engineering, she quickly switched to English literature. Upon graduation, she married a white man, Earl Kingston.

Throughout her childhood, Maxine Hong Kingston struggled with being left out of the books she read. There were no stories of Chinese Americans in the Stockton library, and very few that featured girls. "In a way it's not so terrible to be left out," she said years later in the *Los Angeles Times*, "because then you could see at a very early age that there's an entire motherlode of stories that belong to you and nobody else."

The girl in *Woman's Warrior* had her tongue snipped by her mother in accordance with the superstition that it would allow her to speak many languages. (In *Ami*, Audre Lorde relates having undergone the same frenum cutting) Juxtaposed with the mundane school and laundry work of Maxine's childhood in *The Woman Warrior* are fantastic imaginings of a girl unfettered by chores and mere reality. Kingston cycles through her mother's women ancestors and speaks frankly of Chinese folk antifemale expressions such as "When fishing for treasures in the flood, be careful not to pull in girls" and "There's no profit in raising girls. Better to raise geese than girls."

Perhaps, then, it is little wonder that Kingston has come under the strongest attacks from those within her own culture. Several Chinese men have gone after Maxine, criticizing her for everything from her creative license with Chinese legends to her marriage to a white man. Playwright and activist Frank Chin, on behalf of Chinese American male pride, has issued the most vicious and vitriolic assault on Kingston's *Woman Warrior*, derogating it as "kowtow" and "persona writing." Chin also lays siege to her persona as an example of "Ornamental Orientalia," calling her "a false goddess" created by "the worship of liars."

Clearly, Kingston stuck a nerve with the power of her writing, touching on the critical issues of race and gender in a way that has caused it to become "the book by a living author most widely taught in American universities and colleges," notes former Poet Laureate Robert Hass. In *Warrior Woman*, Kingston's protagonist's inner battle rages silently within the confines of her mind—race, gender, spirit, identity, straddling the duality of a culture that devalues girls at the same time the legends say "that we failed if we grew up to be but wives or slaves. We could be heroines, swordswomen."

A WARRIOR WOMAN'S LITERARY INFLUENCE

Kingston credits Virginia Woolf as being a major influence on her work. "Virginia Woolf broke through constraints of time, of gender, of culture. Orlando can be a man. Orlando can be a woman." Inspired by Woolf to experiment with point of view along gender and race lines, Kingston has crossed over, she says, to where she "can now write as a man, I can write as a black person, as a white person; I don't have to be restricted by time and physicality."

JUDY CHICAGO: GUESS WHO CAME TO DINNER?

Judy Chicago set the art world on its ear with "The Dinner Party," her mixed media installation made from traditional women's crafts—needlework, weaving, ceramics, china-painting, and plastics. Born Judy Cohen in Chicago in 1939, she soon left for the burgeoning art scene in Los Angeles in the early 1960s. After her husband Jerry Gerowitz died in an automobile accident, Judy changed her name to Judy Chicago at the prompting of gallery owner Rolf Nelson. Nelson called her that partially because of her heavy Midwest accent and partially because of her strong sense of purpose. At a show at Cal State Fullerton in 1969, a sign with the following hung at the front door: Judy Gerowitz hereby divests herself of all names imposed upon her through male social dominance and freely chooses her own name, Judy Chicago. Starting in 1973, Chicago began work on "The Dinner Party," but soon realized her ambitious art project was going to require some help and ended up with an army of huge banners spelling out the names featured on the forty-eight foot triangular table set with uniquely designed vulvic plates and sumptuously handmade and embroidered placemats. Every plate is in honor of a woman who made a significant contribution to herstory. The incredibly detailed work of "The Dinner Party" table shows the research, thoughtfulness, and thoroughness of the project. The Amazons' placemat is replete with labyris, the sacred double-axe, and breastplates, a crescent moon, and many other minutiae. A total of 999 women are named in Chicago's opus, with engravings on triangular (Triple Goddess Power!) ceramic tiles on the Heritage Floor.

"The Dinner Party" was probably the climax of artistic expression of the feminism of the 1970s. Despite this splendid achievement, most museums were unwilling to show "The Dinner Party." However, San Francisco feted Chicago and her masterwork with the largest crowd ever gathered to see the opening of a show—more than 100,000 people. Although the uptight suits that run the art world keep spinning out excuses, "The Dinner Party" has had a life of its own. It has been celebrated in photographs, books, and performance art, and is indelibly imprinted in art history. Judy Chicago, whose latest undertaking is "The Birth Project," certainly achieved what she set out to do in "symbolizing the long history of female achievement," underscoring the realization that "the history of Western Civilization, as we have understood it, has failed to represent the experience of half the human race."

Guest List at Judy Chicago's Dinner Party:

Primordial Goddess
Fertile Goddess
Kali
Snake Goddess
Sophia
Amazon
Hatshepsut
Judith
Sappho
Apasia
Boadicea
Hypatia
Marcella
Saint Brigid
Theodora
Hrosvitha
Trotula
Eleanor of Aquitaine
Hildegarde of Bingen
Petronilla de Meath
Christine de Pisan
Isabella d'Este

Elizabeth R
Artemisia Gentileschi
Anna Van Schurman
Anne Hutchinson
Sacajawea
Caroline Herschel
Mary Wollstonecraft
Sojourner Truth
Susan B. Anthony
Elizabeth Blackwell
Emily Dickinson
Ethel Smyth
Margaret Sanger
Natalie Barney
Virginia Woolf
Georgia O'Keeffe

bell hooks: AN UNTAMED TONGUE

Born Gloria Jean Watkins in the small town of Hopkinville, Kentucky, in 1952, poet, feminist theorist, and professor bell hooks grew up as one of six kids watching her father work as a janitor and her mother clean houses for white people. Gloria was in the first round of desegregated classes and grieved for the loss of community and safety that desegregation caused: "It hurt to leave behind memories, schools that were 'ours,' places that honored us." She was raised to be polite and mind her manners, but she "had a mouth." For talking back and saying what she really thought, she was chided by a neighbor as being "kin to bell hooks [her maternal grandmother]—a sharp-tongued woman...Gloria was to have been a sweet southern girl, quiet, obedient, pleasing. She was not to have that wild streak that characterized women on her mother's side. With that, Gloria changed her name and continued finding her own voice and speaking out.

She found her calling at a young age—by the time she was ten, she was composing poems. Then, while working as a telephone operator to pay for classes at Stanford, nineteen-year-old bell shared her writing with her coworkers, working class black women who nurtured her talent and encouraged her to tell the world about the truth of being black and a woman. Since then, while she has continued to write poetry, her fame as a writer has come from critical essays on race, gender, and class.

Obtaining a PhD in English literature, she has taught English and African American studies at various institutions around the country, including Yale, Oberlin, San Francisco State, and City College of New York. She first published her work in 1981 in the book *Ain't I a Woman*, a title quoting and honoring the great shero Sojourner Truth. Bell's book had an immediate impact, named as one of the top twenty most important women's books. More importantly to bell, she received hundreds of letters from black women, including many poor and working class readers all over America who told them *Ain't I a Woman* changed their lives. For bell, the goal of a fully inclusive feminism rather than an "old girl's school" of Ivy League white women was on the way to being realized, a pursuit she continues to this day. "Moving from silence into speech is for the oppressed, the colonized, the exploited, and those who stand and struggle side by side a gesture of defiance that makes new life and new growth possible. It is that act of speech, of 'talking back,' that is no mere gesture of empty words, that is the expression of our movement from object to subject—the liberated voice." She continues to write, including a book with Cornel West, *Breaking Bread: Insurgent Black Intellectual Life*, and to ask us to wake up to the various isms that are socially created and personally painful.

"I was always saying the wrong thing, asking the wrong questions. I could not confine my speech to the necessary corners and concerns of my life."

— bell hooks

GUERRILLA GIRLS: FEMINIST ACTIVIST ARTISTS

The Guerrilla Girls are a group of women artists and art professionals who make posters about sexism and racism in the art world and the culture at large. These self-styled feminist do-gooders see themselves as counterparts to Robin Hood, Batman, and the Lone Ranger, using humor to provoke discussion and wearing gorilla masks to focus on the issues, not their personalities. In ten years, they have produced seventy posters that have been passed around the globe by kindred spirits. Their slogan? "We could be anyone; we are everywhere."

BIBLIOGRAPHY

A&E Television Networks. "Biography." 1997. *http://www.biography.com*.

Willis J. Abbot. *Notable Women in History*. London, England: Greening & Co., 1913.

African Americans: Voices of Triumph-Creative Fire. Alexandria, VA: Time-Life Books, 1994.

African Americans: Voices of Triumph-Leadership. Alexandria, VA: Time-Life Books, 1993.

African Americans: Voices of Triumph-Perseverance. Alexandria, VA: Time-Life Books, 1993.

Helen Ashton and Katherine Davies. *I Had a Sister*. London: Lovart Dickson Limited, 1937.

Seale Ballenger. *Hell's Belles*. Berkeley, CA: Conari Press, 1997.

Daniel B. Baker, ed. *Explorers and Discoverers of the World*. Detroit, MI: Gale Research, 1993.

Olive Banks. *The Biographical Dictionary of British Feminists*, Vol 1. NY: New York University Press, 1985.

Jane DuPree Begos, ed. *A Women's Diaries Miscellany*. Weston, CT: MagiCircle Press, 1989.

Robert E. Bell. *Women of Classical Mythology*. Santa Barbara, CA: ABC-CLIO, Inc., 1991.

Ginia Bellafante."Kudos for a Crusader." *Time*, October 20, 1997, p. 65.

K.A. Berney, ed. *Contemporary Women Dramatists.* Detroit, MI: St. James Press, 1994.

Iris Biblowitz et al. *Women and Literature.* Cambridge, MA: Women and Literature Collective, 1976.

Hans Biedermann. *Dictionary of Symbolism: Cultural Icons and the Meanings Behind Them.* New York, NY: Facts on File, Inc., 1992.

Barbara Carlisle Bigelow, ed. *Contemporary Black Biography,* Vol 5. Detroit, MI: Gale Research, Inc., 1994.

Barbara Carlisle Bigelow, ed. *Contemporary Black Biography,* Vol 6. Detroit, MI: Gale Research, Inc., 1994.

Barbara Carlisle Bigelow, ed. *Contemporary Black Biography,* Vol 7. Detroit, MI: Gale Research, Inc., 1995.

Jean F. Blashfield. *Hellraisers, Heroines, and Holy Women.* New York, NY: St. Martin's Press, 1994.

Danuta Bois. "Distinguished Women of Past and Present." 1997. *http://www.netsrq.com/~dbois.*

Martha Bremser, ed. *International Dictionary of Ballet,* 2 Vols. Detroit, MI: A Bruccoli Clark Layman Book, 1997.

Ivor Brown. *Dark Ladies.* London, England: Collins Press, 1957.

Karlyn Kohrs Campbell, ed. *Women Public Speakers in the United States, 1800–1925.* Westport, CT: Greenwood Press, 1993.

Karlyn Kohrs Campbell, ed. *Women Public Speakers in the United States, 1925–1993.* Westport, CT: Greenwood Press, 1994.

Margaret Carlson. "Back in the Saddle." *Time*, October 27, 1997. p. 27.

Humphrey Carpenter and Mari Prichard. *The Oxford Companion to Children's Literature.* New York, NY: Oxford University Press, 1984.

John Cech, ed. *American Writers for Children, 1900–1960.* Detroit, MI: Gale Research Inc., 1983.

Hsiao-hung Chang. "Gender Crossing in Maxine Hong Kingston's *Tripmaster Monkey*" @ Society for the Study of the Multi-Ethnic Literature of the U.S., 1997.

Neva Chonin. "The Women of Rock Interviews: Joan Baez." *Rolling Stone*, n773, November 13, 1997. p. 155.

Anatole Chujoy and P.W. Manchester, eds. *The Dance Encyclopedia.* NY: Simon and Schuster, 1967.

Ella Clark and Margot Edmonds. *Sacagawea of the Lewis and Clark Expedition*. Berkley and Los Angeles, CA: University of California Press, 1979.

John Coulson, ed. *The Saints*. NY: Hawthorn Books, 1958.

Nadine Crenshaw. *Scully X-posed.* Rocklin, CA: Prima Publishing, 1997.

Nadine Crenshaw. Xena *X-posed.* Rocklin, CA: Prima Publishing, 1997.

Kathryn Cullen-DuPont. *The Encyclopedia of Women's History in America.* NY: Facts on File, Inc., 1996.

David DeLeon, ed. *Leaders from the 1960s.* Westport, CT: Greenwood Press, 1994.

Katherine Dunn. "The Women of Rock Interviews: Courtney Love." *Rolling Stone*, n773, November 13, 1997. pp. 164–166.
Electronic Nobel Museum. "The Nobel Prizes." [Online] Available *http://www.nobel.se/prize*. 1997.

Wolfgang D. Elfe and James Hardin, eds. *Dictionary of Literary Biography*, Vol 75, *Contemporary German Fiction Writers.* Detroit, MI: A Bruccoli Clark Layman Book, 1988.

Elizabeth Ellet. *The Women of the American Revolution.* Vol II. NY: Haskell House Publishers Ltd., 1969.

Encyclopedia Britannica. [Online] Available *http://www.eb.com:180*.

Glenn E. Estes, ed. *American Writers for Children Since 1960: Fiction.* Detroit, MI: Gale Research Inc., 1986.

John Mark Faragher, ed. *The Encyclopedia of Colonial and Revolutionary America.* NY: Facts on File, 1990.

Deborah G. Felder. *The 100 Most Influential Women of All Time.* NY: A Citadel Press Book, 1996.

Malcolm Forbes. *Women Who Made a Difference.* NY: Simon and Schuster, 1990.

FOX News Network. "India's Bandit Queen Threatens Suicide." [Online] Available *http://www.pennyarcade.com/phoolan.html*, November 21, 1997.

John Hope Franklin and August Meier, eds. *Black Leaders of the Twentieth Century.* Urbana, IL: University of Illinois Press, 1982.

Antonia Fraser. *The Warrior Queens.* NY: Alfred A. Knopf, Inc., 1989.

Frontline. "The Karen Silkwood Story." [Online] Available *http://www.pbs.org/wgbh/pages/frontline/shows/reaction/interact/silkwood.html*. November 13, 1997.

Gillian Gaar. *She's a Rebel*. Seattle, WA: Seal Press, 1992.
Ute Gacs. *Women Anthropologists: Selected Biographies.* Illini Books ed. Urbana: University of Illinois Press, 1989, c 1988.

Gale Research, Inc. "Celebrating Women's History Month Biographies." [Online] Available *http://www.thomson.com/gale/whmbios.html*. 1997.

Elysa Gardner. "The Women of Rock Interviews: Bonnie Raitt." *Rolling Stone,* n773. November 13, 1997. p. 157.

Janeane Garofalo. "The Women of Rock Interviews: Jewel." *Rolling Stone,* n773. November 13, 1997. p. 162.

GeoCities. [Online] Available *http://www.geocities.com*, 1997.

Carol Gerten-Jackson. "Georgia O'Keeffe (1887-1986)." [Online] Available *http://www.yawp.com/cjackson/okeefe/ookeefe_bio.htm*, October 31, 1997.

Ronnie Gilbert, *Ronnie Gilbert on Mother Jones.* Berkeley, CA: Conari Press, 1993.

Jim Gillogly. "Modesty Blaise Chronology." [Online] Available *http://www.cs.umu.se/~kenth/modesty.html*, November 20, 1997.

Beverly E. Golemba, *Lesser-Known Women.* Boulder, CO: Lynne Rienner Publishers, 1992.

Mike Gonos. Batgirl On-line. [Online] Available *http://www.netvista.net/~mpg/batgirl/batgirl.html*, December 18, 1997.

Jill Hamilton. "The Women of Rock Interviews: Ani DiFranco." *Rolling Stone,* n773. November 13, 1997. p. 150.

James Hardin and Donald Daviau, eds. *Dictionary of Literary Biography,* Vol. 85. *Austrian Fiction Writers After 1914.* Detroit, MI: A Bruccoli Clark Lyman Book, 1989.

Walter L. Hawkins. *African American Biographies.* Jefferson, NC: MacFarland and Company, 1992.

James D. Henderson and Linda Roddy Henderson. *Ten Notable Women of Latin America.* Chicago: Nelson-Hall, 1978.

Hayden Herrera. "Portrait of Frida Khalo as a Tehuana." *Heresies* #4, Winter, 1978. p. 245.

Mark Hertsgaard. "Who Killed Petra Kelly?" *Mother Jones,* 18(1), Jan-Feb, 1993. p. 13.

Ralph Hickok. *The Encyclopedia of North American Sports History.* NY: Facts On File, Inc., 1992.

Darlene Clark Hine, ed. *Black Women in America: An Historical Encyclopedia,* 2 Vols. Brooklyn, NY: Carlson Publishing, 1993.

Gerri Hirshey. "The Women of Rock Interviews: Madonna." *Rolling Stone,* n773. November 13, 1997. p. 98-100.

Gerri Hirshey. "Jodi Foster." *Rolling Stone,* n600. March 21, 1991. p. 34-41, 88-89.

Fred Ho, ed. *Sheroes Womyn Warrior Calendar.* Brooklyn, NY: Autonomedia, 1998.
Margaret Hooks. *Tina Modotti: Photographer and Revolutionary.* San Francisco, CA: Pandora, 1993.

The International Who's Who of Women. London: Europa Publications, Limited, 1992.

Edward T. James and Janet Wilson James, eds. *Notable American Women 1607-1950.* 3 Vols. Cambridge, MA: The Belknap Press of Harvard University Press, 1971.

Anne Janette Johnson. *Great Women in Sports.* Detroit, MI: Visible Ink, 1996.

Pauline Kael. *5001 Nights at the Movies.* NY: Henry Holt and Company, 1991.

Christina Kelly. "The Women of Rock Interviews: Melissa Etheridge." *Rolling Stone,* n773. November 13, 1997. p. 159.

Ethel M. Kersey. *Women Philosophers.* Westport, CT: Greenwood Press, 1989.

Jamaica Kincaid. "Pam Grier: The Mocha Mogul of Hollywood." *Ms.* August 1975, 1997.

Nancy Kline. *Elizabeth Blackwell: A Doctor's Triumph.* Berkeley, CA: Conari Press, 1997.

Gretchen Kopmanis. "Modesty Blaise." [Online] Available *http://www.cs.umu.se/~kenth/modesty.html*, November 20, 1997.

Howard Kohn. "Malignant Giant." *Rolling Stone*, June 11, 1992. pp. 92–97.

Mary Norbert Korte. "Judi Bari: Hero of the Forest Movement." Original unpublished article, 1997.

Cheris Kramarae and Paula A. Treichler. *Amazons, Bluestockings, and Crones.* London, England: Pandora Press, 1992.

Annette Kuhn and Susannah Radstone, eds. *Women in Film, An International Guide.* NY: Ballantine Books, 1990.

Annette Kuhn and Susannah Radstone, eds. *The Women's Companion to International Film.* Berkley, CA: University of California Press, 1994.

Michael L. LaBlanc, ed. *Contemporary Black Biography,* Vol. 1. Detroit, MI: Gale Research, 1992.

Vicki Leon. *Uppity Women of Ancient Times.* Berkeley, CA: Conari Press, 1995.

Rayford Logan and Michael Winston, eds. *Dictionary of American Negro Biography.* NY: W.W. Norton & Company, 1982.

Christine Lunardini, Ph.D. *What Every American Should Know About Women's History.* Holbrook, MA: Bob Adams, Inc., 1994.

L. Mpho Mabunda, ed. *Contemporary Black Biography*, Vol. 8. Detroit, MI: Gale Research Inc., 1995.

L. Mpho Mabunda and Shirelle Phelps, eds. *Contemporary Black Biography*, Vol. 11. Detroit, MI: Gale Research Inc., 1996.

Frank N. Magill. *Magill's Cinema Annual 1987.* Pasadena, CA: Salem Press, 1987.

Frank N. Magill. *Magill's Cinema Annual 1990.* Pasadena, CA: Salem Press, 1990.

Frank N. Magill. *Magill's Cinema Annual 1992.* Pasadena, CA: Salem Press, 1992.

Frank N. Magill. *Magill's Cinema Annual 1993.* Pasadena, CA: Salem Press, 1993.

Frank N. Magill. *Magill's Cinema Annual 1994.* Pasadena, CA: Salem Press, 1994.

Frank N. Magill. *Great Lives From History: American Series*, Vols. 1&4. Pasadena, CA: Salem Press, 1987.

Frank N. Magill. *Magill's Survey of Cinema: English Language Films*, First Series, Vol 4. Englewood Cliffs, NJ: Salem Press, 1980.

Frank N. Magill. *Magill's Survey of Cinema: English Language Films*, Second Series, Vol 1. Englewood Cliffs, NJ: Salem Press, 1981.

Sharon Malinowski, ed. *Notable Native Americans,* Detroit, MI: Gale Research, Inc., 1995.

Rick Martin and Veronica Chambers. "High Heels, Low Esteem." *Newsweek,* October 13, 1997. p. 71.

Evelyn McDonnell. "The Women of Rock Interviews: Queen Latifah." *Rolling Stone,* n773. November 13, 1997. p. 122.

Susan McElrath. "Mary McLeod Bethune Council House." [Online] Available *http://www.nps.gov/mamc*, 1997.

Robert McHenry, ed. *Famous American Women*. New York, NY: Dover Publications Inc., 1981.

Joyce Millman. "Personal Best: Silence of the Lambs." *Salon.* [Online] Available *http://www.salonmagazine.com/weekly/lambs960930.html*, 1997.

Kay Mills. "Literature by Lode and by Lore." *Los Angeles Times,* August 25, 1985.

Isaac Mizrahi. *The Adventures of Sandee the Supermodel.* 3 Vols. NY: Simon & Schuster Editions, 1997.

Chantal Mompoullan. *Interviews with Eight American Women of Achievement.* Voice of America, 1985.

Burleigh Muten, ed. *Return of the Great Goddess.* Boston, MA: Shambhala Publications, 1994.

Peter O'Donnell. "How It Could Have Been..." [Online] Available *http://www.cs.umu.se/~kenth/modesty.html*, November 20, 1997.

Olga S. Opfell. *Women Prime Ministers and Presidents.* Jefferson, NC: McFarland & Company, Inc., 1993.

Diane K. Osbon, ed. *Reflections on the Art of living: A Joseph Campbell Companion.* NY: HarperCollins Publishers, 1991.

Mary Rosetta Parkman. *Heroines of Service.* Freeport, NY: Books for Libraries Press, 1969.

Shirelle Phelps. *Contemporary Black Biography,* Vol 12. Detroit, MI: Gale Research Inc., 1996.

Shirelle Phelps. *Contemporary Black Biography,* Vol 15. Detroit, MI: Gale Research Inc., 1997.
Steve Pond. "Wild Things Run Fast: Joni Mitchell." *Rolling Stone,* November 25, 1982. pp. 27–29, 87.

Arthur Prager. "The Secret of Nancy Drew: Pushing Forty and Going Strong." *Saturday Review,* January 25, 1969. pp. 18–19, 34–35.

Bruce A. Ragsdale and Joel D. Treese. *Black Americans in Congress, 1870–1989.* U.S. Government Printing Office, 1990.

Susan Raven and Allison Weir. *Women of Achievement.* New York, NY: Harmony Books, 1994.

Phyllis J. Read and Bernard L. Witlieb. *The Book of Women's Firsts.* NY: Random House, 1992.

Don Reisman, ed. *Portraits of American Women,* Vol II. NY: St. Martin's Press, 1991.

Phyllis Rose, ed. *The Norton Book of Women's Lives.* NY: W.W. Norton & Company, 1993.

Bob Rosenberg. "Frequently Asked Questions About Tank Girl." [Online] Available *http://www.cs.ucl.ac.uk/staff/b.rosenberg/tg/FAQ.html*. December 15, 1997.

C. Salem, ed. *African American Women: A Biographical Dictionary.* NY: Garland Publishing, 1993.

Jessica Amanda Salmonson. *The Encyclopedia of Amazons.* NY: Paragon House, 1991.

Jonathan Sanders. "Why Batgirl?" [Online] Available *http://www.geocities.com/EnchantedForest/2635/why.htm*, December 18, 1997.

Virgilia Sapieha (Peterson), Ruth Neely, and Mary Collins. *Eminent Women: Recipients of the National Achievement Award.* Menasha, WI: George Banta Publishing Company, 1948.

Kathleen Scalise. "The Hunmanities Medal for Kingston." *Berkleyan,* October 1-7, 1997.

Paul Schlueter and June Schlueter, eds. *An Encyclopedia of British Women Writers.* NY: Garland Publishing, Inc. 1988.

Bent Schonberg, ed. *World Ballet and Dance 1992-1993. An International Yearbook.* London: Dance Books Ltd., 1993.

Arvind Sharma and Katherine K. Young, eds. *The Annual Review of Women in World Religions.* Vol II, *Heroic Women.* Albany, NY: State University of New York Press, 1992.

Joanne Shattock. *The Oxford Guide to British Women Writers.* NY: Oxford University Press, 1993.

Jessie Carney Smith. *Epic Lives: One Hundred Black Women Who Made a Difference.* Detroit, MI: Visible Ink, 1993.

Jessie Carney Smith. *Notable Black American Women.* Detroit, MI: Gale Research, Inc., 1992.

Jessie Carney Smith, ed. *Notable Black American Women,* Book II. Detroit, MI: Gale Research, Inc., 1994.

Autumn Stephens. *Wild Women.* Berkeley, CA: Conari Press, 1992.

Esther Stineman. *American Political Women.* Littleton, CO: Libraries Unlimited, Inc., 1980.

Willow Ann Sirch. *EcoWomen: Protectors of the Earth.* Golden, CO: Fulcrum Publishing, 1996.

Joseph C. Tardiff and L. Mpho Mabunda, eds. *Dictionary of Hispanic Biography.* Detroit, MI: Gale Research Inc., 1996.

Vincent Terrace. *Television Character and Story Facts.* Jefferson, NC: McFarland and Company Inc. 1993.

Herbert Thurston, S.J. and Donald Attwater, eds. *Butler's Lives of the Saints.* London, England: Burns and Oates, 1956.

Marion Tinling. *Women Remembered.* Westport, CT: Greenwood Press, 1986.

Marion Tinling. *Women into the Unknown.* Westport, CT: Greenwood Press, 1989.

Peter Travers. "A Woman on the Verge: Thelma and Louise." @ *Rolling Stone,* April 18, 1991. pp. 97–98.

Jennifer S. Uglow. *The Continuum Dictionary of Women's Biography.* NY: Continuum, 1984.

Jennifer Uglow and Frances Hinton, eds. *The International Dictionary of Women's Biography.* NY: Continuum; Macmillan, 1982.

Jennifer Uglow and Frances Hinton, eds. *The Continuum Dictionary of Women's Biography.* NY: Continuum, 1989.

Vietnam Veterans of America Foundation. "The Nobel Peace Prize for 1997: International Campaign to Ban Landmines (ICBL) and Jody Williams." [Online] Available *http://www.vvaf.org/landmine.html*, December 30, 1997.

Marina Warner. *From the Beast to the Blonde: On Fairy Tales and Their Tellers.* NY: Farrar, Straus and Giroux, 1994.

Marjorie Weiser and Jean Arbeiter. *Womanlist.* Canada: McClelland and Stewart Ltd., 1981.

Alden Whitman, ed. *American Reformers.* NY: The H.W. Wilson Company, 1985.

Ora Williams. *American Black Women in the Arts and Social Sciences.* Metuchen, NJ: The Scarecrow Press, 1994.

Justin Wintle, ed. *Makers of Modern Culture.* NY: Facts On File, Inc., 1981.

Justin Wintle, ed. *Makers of 19th Century Culture 1800–1914.* Boston, MA: Routledge & Kegan Paul, Ltd., 1982.

Women's International Center Biographies. [Online] Available *http://www.wic.org/bio*, 1997.

Marion Woodman. *Leaving My Father's House: A Journey to Conscious Femininity.* Boston, MA: Shambhala Publications, 1992.

Elizabeth Wright, ed. *Feminism and Psychoanalysis.* Cambridge, MA: Blackwell Reference, 1992.

Yahoo's Web CelebSite Biographies [Online] Available *http://la.yahoo.com/external/webceleb.*

Zbigniew Zwolinski. "Maria Sklodowska-Curie, 1867–1934." [Online] Available *http://hum.amu.edu.pl/~zbzw/ph/sci/msc.htm*, November 21, 1997.

Helen Zia and Susan B. Gall, eds., *Notable Asian Americans.* Detroit, MI: Gale Research, 1995.

Angela Howard Zophy and Frances M. Kavenik, eds. *Handbook of American Women's History.* Garland Reference Library, 1990.

WHO ARE YOUR AWESOME WOMEN?

Dear Reader,

This book almost never made it to the printer because we kept finding more and more fascinating females deserving to be honored in the annals of history. We would love to have a follow-up volume detailing the lives and times of more role models. We invite you to email, tweet, or send a note with your nomination of your Awesome Women. We would love to hear from you about this and continue the celebration of these "great unknowns" who didn't make it into the history books UNTIL NOW!

Below is a simple nomination form, and we would love to credit you, so please include your contact information. Thanks for your participation - you are pretty awesome, yourself!

xoxo
Becca

I Nominate the Following Awesome Woman:

____

____

____

____

____

Mango Publishing 2850 Douglas Road
Suite #301 Coral Gables, Florida 33134

Twitter: @MangoPublishing email info@Mango.bz

CPSIA information can be obtained
at www.ICGtesting.com
Printed in the USA
BVOW10s1140161217
502948BV00001B/1/P